C000132149

THE FALKLANDS-MAL

A READER

edited by Macdonald Daly

London
SPANISH, PORTUGUESE AND LATIN AMERICAN STUDIES IN THE HUMANITIES

The Falklands-Malvinas Conflict: A Reader
edited by Macdonald Daly

This anthology first published in Great Britain by SPLASH Editions, 2022. SPLASH Editions is an imprint of Jetstone Publishers Ltd.

ISBN 9781912399321

Cover image: The Falkland Islands from the International Space Station, image courtesy of the Earth Science and Remote Sensing Unit, NASA Johnson Space Center.

Historic maps reproduced in this book are public domain images available from Wikimedia Commons (**https://commons.wikimedia. org/wiki/Category:Old_maps_of_the_Falkland_Islands**).

Cover design by Hannibal.

CONTENTS

Introduction: Fighting a War and Writing a Conflict   7
Macdonald Daly

Chronology of the Falklands-Malvinas War (1982)   19

History

Statement to the Special Committee on the Situation with   25
    regard to the Implementation of the Declaration on the
    Granting of Independence to Colonial Countries and
    Peoples, 9 September 1964
José María Ruda

Resolution of the United Nations General Assembly   43

1965-1982: The Negotiations   44
Uriel Erlich

The War

First In, First Out: A Casualty of War and Life after   65
    the Conflict
Diego F. García Quiroga

First In, First Out   78
Mike Seear

2nd Battalion, the Scots Guards: The Tumbledown Legacy   104
Alan Warsap

Who Cares About the Enemy?   110
Jeremy McTeague

The Life, Passion and Death of a Rumour   120
Lucrecia Escudero Chauvel

Malvinas-Falklands Revisited: Prelude, War and Aftermath   142
María Cristina Fra Amador

Retrospect

The Anglo-Argentine Post-Conflict Common Ground: 153
    the Combat Veterans' Aftermath
Eduardo C. Gerding

Seeking "The Other" in the Post-Conflict, 1982-2006   164
Mike Seear

"Saving the Nation": Post-Conflict from the Point of View of   173
    the "Guilty"
Sophie Thonon-Wesfreid

On the Making of the film An Ungentlemanly Act   179
Stuart Urban

More Than 30 Years after the Malvinas: 201
    War in Film and on Television
Sandra Savoini

Traumas, Memories and Identity Processes   212
María Teresa Dalmasso

Returning: The Journey to the Islands in Contemporary   227
    Narratives about the Malvinas
Alicia Vaggione

Dancing with Death: Lyric Poetry in and out of Conflict   238
Bernard McGuirk

Notes on Contributors and Sources   279

Index   284

INTRODUCTION

Les Iles Malouines ou Falkland, detail from a map of South America published in Charles Hubert Alexis Jaillot *et al.*, *L'Amérique divisée en septentrionale et méridionale subdivisée en ses principales parties dressée sur les rélationsles plus récentes: Revue, corrigée et augmenté* (Paris: Chez le Sr. Desnos, 1783).

Fighting a War and Writing a Conflict

Macdonald Daly

In 2017, two Argentine legal academics published a book in English, an abridged translation of a volume which had appeared shortly before in Spanish, the back-cover blurb of which read as follows:

> In 2008, Graham Pascoe and Peter Pepper, two British authors who are not academics, published both in English and in Spanish a pamphlet entitled "Getting it Right: the Real History of the Falklands/Malvinas". Since then, a variety of versions of this pamphlet have been published, some abridged, and some not; the most recent version, officially distributed by the British government in the United Nations Decolonization Committee in June 2015, was pompously entitled: "False Falklands History at the United Nations: How Argentina misled the UN in 1964 – and still does". This simply constitutes an attempt to rewrite history. British pamphlet (*sic*) tries in vain to distort the solid historical-legal arguments which prove Argentine sovereignty and to convince the reader that the islands are inhabited by a multinational population entitled to the right of self-determination. The work of Marcelo Kohen and Facundo Rodríguez refutes each of the new British arguments, both from the historical and legal point of view. It gives the reader first-hand information, much of it hitherto not exploited in the abundant bibliography. It is an indispensable source for understanding the positions of the parties to the dispute whose solution is still pending. [1]

[1] Marcelo G. Kohen and Facundo D. Rodríguez, *The Malvinas/Falklands Between History and Law: Refutation of the British Pamphlet "Getting it Right: The Real History of the Falklands/Malvinas"* (2017). Kohen is a Professor of International law at the University of Geneva; Rodríguez was apparently a Ph.D. candidate. The seemingly self-published translation is currently available in its entirety at **https://www.academia.edu/33555946/Malvinas_Falklands_Kohen_Rodriguez.** The original book in Spanish was *Las Malvinas entre el derecho y la historia. Refutación del folleto británico "Más allá de la historia oficial. La verdadera historia de las Falklands/Malvinas"* (Buenos Aires: Editorial Universitaria de Buenos Aires, 2017). The second (allegedly "officially distributed" version) of the two Pascoe and Pepper papers can still be found online at **https://falklandstimeline.files.wordpress.com/2012/02/2012-false-falklands-history-at-the-un-2nd-ed.pdf**.

The blurb's snooty emphasis on Pascoe and Pepper not being academics is rather nugatory if their pamphlet is considered in need of such ponderous scholarly rebuttal. The book's decidedly elongated title and its distended contents (it takes 234 pages, even in its abridged English version, to criticise a fairly concise Pascoe and Pepper essay of just over 8,000 words) suggest in its two authors a parallel pomposity. Not to be outdone, however, Pascoe proceeded to self-publish a refutation of their refutation with a tome whose title and innards, at 359 A4 pages, extend to yet more fantastic lengths. [2]

Like the authors of many words expended on the Falklands-Malvinas conflict, both sides in this ill-mannered spat seem to be preaching to their own converted, reinforcing familiar, mutually incompatible narratives for established audiences respectively in Argentina and the UK. Each is more concerned with what they call "the truth" (perhaps, though they would not admit it, the "truth" that they feel patriotically compelled to construct), principally about a "primal scene" concerning territorial sovereignty which took place almost two hundred years ago. They are not entirely ill-disposed to potential compromises that may help negotiate a course around the fundamentalism which irreconcilable avowals as to sovereignty seem to imply, or at least Kohen is not: he has since proposed a solution, though not one any UK government is likely to embrace. [3] Yet they do not appear to entertain the more delicate possibility that the changes which have taken place in the world in those two centuries, and which apply no less in both countries in the forty years since the War of 1982, may have rendered arguably atavistic approaches to the political impasse superannuated, perhaps even absurd. Their texts do not talk to each other, converse, interactively reflect or constructively engage: rather they berate, condemn, catcall and ridicule; they take pot shots, snipe, strafe and rake. The aim of each is to inflict injury or hopefully fatal blows upon the enemy. The authors quickly abandon

---

[2] Graham Pascoe, *Falklands Facts and Fallacies: The Falkland Islands in History and International Law: A Refutation of Marcelo Kohen and Facundo Rodríguez*, Las Malvinas entre el Derecho y la Historia (n.p.: Pascoe and Pepper Publishing, 2020). As to authorship, however, the annual *Falkand Islands Journal* for 2020 bears an article entitled "Why we Wrote *Falkland* (sic) *Facts and Fallacies*" by "G. Pascoe & P. Pepper" (**https://www.falklandislands journal.org/2020-contents/**).

[3] See "Proposal made by Professor Marcelo Kohen on March 12, 2018 in the Falkland Islands and on March 20, 2018 in Buenos Aires", available at **http://www.malvinas-falklands.net/proposal-to-settle-the-dispute/**.

small arms altogether and take to blasting with book-length howitzers from entrenched positions across the undisturbed no-man's-land between them. If one wants to feel how hostile and intransigent views can be when rival proprietorial claims are still made to a globally negligible archipelago in the South Atlantic – which in the 2012 census numbered fewer than 3,000 residents, but in the same year hosted a comparatively astonishing contingent of 1,300 UK military personnel – one has only to dip into the pages of their miniature, inkhorn war. They went on conducting it, via the internet, in 2021.

The present anthology on the Falklands-Malvinas controversy has its origin in a quite contrary impulse to promote constructive dialogue rather than to deepen adversarial disputation between two parties who, in 1982, became literally embattled. In November 2006, Bernard McGuirk – who was not a specialist in International Studies, or Politics, or Sociology, or Military History, or Legal Studies but, most improbably, a multilingual Professor in Romance Literatures and Literary Theory at the University of Nottingham, UK – convened a colloquium at his university which brought together, as well as others, many ex-combatants from both sides. For the first time, that is, he put many men in the same room who, two-and-a-half decades before, had been officially commissioned to kill one another. Not just that, however: the colloquium also re-united (or led to the re-uniting) of men who had not seen each other since the War, and sometimes one man with another who had saved his life during it.

Discourse on the extremity that is war has always existed in various, often mutually exclusive channels: there is the historical discourse which accounts for it in retrospect, the political discourse which attempts to direct it in the present, the propagandistic discourse which seeks to maintain justification and morale for it, likewise, the military-operational discourse necessitated by its instigation, the media-orientated discourse which arises from its reporting, and so on. Most of these are impersonal, or objective, in a variety of senses of that word: they have certain *objects* (or strategic aims) in mind, and they pay little heed to the *subjective* (or personal) experiences of the human combatants whose every action constitutes the war itself. But if, after a period of time, one puts those human combatants in the same place together over several days, an entirely different, quite unofficially regulated discourse is, and was, bound to emerge. McGuirk's colloquium did involve the standard routines one would expect of university gatherings: there were spoken presentations, formal questions and answers, round-table discussions, agreements and disagreements expressed within the normal bounds of public exchange.[4] The formal talks had been prepared beforehand, with considerable notice given, and were of course gripping in themselves. In many ways, however, it was the unrecorded discussions that took place aside from its formalities which came to constitute the most valuable experience, for many of those present, of the colloquium itself. Indeed, it would not be too much to say, for most attendees, that in these moments the objective or "expected" discourses were replaced by much more "free" and profound personal interactions, more communally shared and more immune to external or self-imposed regulation. From that particular meeting formal and informal initiatives and relationships were developed, some of them becoming integral to later seminal publications, such as Mike Seear's remarkable epic, *Return to Tumbledown*, a voluminous 250,000-word (almost 600 pages long) retrospective in which an ex-British army officer attempted to come to terms with his own role in the War, the personal suffering it caused him afterwards, and his belatedly acquired knowledge of and friendship with those on the "enemy" side.[5]

That particular Nottingham event, although apparently minor in the scheme of things, was therefore a signal breakthrough for many of its participants. It promoted novel and unusually reciprocative discussion about something very "real" to those involved (the War was not merely an historical matter in which they happened to have a shared intellectual interest, but one which had seriously marked many of their lives). The gathering allowed for a genuinely reconciliatory, dogma-free comparison of experience among those who had been at the sharpest end of the Falklands-Malvinas War. Such an initiative of academic origin is unlikely to affect the foreign policy of any government, though one may argue that Argentine officialdom has more warmly welcomed the results of the various publications that indirectly arose from the colloquium because they may give the superficial impression of buttressing the historic

---

[4] The presentations were gathered in a volume felicitously entitled *Hors de Combat: The Falklands-Malvinas Conflict Twenty-Five Years On*, ed. Diego F. García Quiroga and Mike Seear (Nottingham: CCC Press, 2008), later expanded and revised as *Hors de Combat: The Falklands-Malvinas Conflict in Retrospect* (Nottingham: CCC Press, 2009). The present anthology similarly represents the variety of discourses to be found in the existing archive of writing about the War: it encompasses diplomatic communication, historical perspectives, personal memoir, impassioned polemic and academic analysis from various disciplines.
[5] Mike Seear, *Return to Tumbledown: The Falklands-Malvinas War Revisited* (revised ed., Nottingham: CCC Press, 2014).

Argentine "sovereignty" case. In fact, ongoing Argentine examination of and retrospect on the War, its causes and conduct (for example, in the the criminal trials of members of the once-ruling Junta which followed it), and its consequences, have simply kept the issue much more discursively "alive" in Argentina over the years in a way that has not been mirrored in the UK. There it tends to be treated as a closed episode susceptible to no further debate. The publications referred to were in reality various and diverse, and none was particularly partisan. Their being published in English, however, may have conveyed to anglophone readers perspectives of which they had hitherto simply been unaware. In truth, far from being interested in making strong claims as to the legitimacy of one side or the other, they were more concerned to explore the considerable ambiguities and complexities, in event and experience, of the 1982 conflict and the period since.[6] Many of the essays in this anthology are excerpted from texts written by participants in the Nottingham colloquium, because it marked the beginning of a quite different way of talking about and looking at the War.

This reader is divided into three sections ("History", "The War" and "Retrospect"), but these separations are not hard and fast and in individual essays these artificial categories can merge into one another. One can see this most acutely, for example, in Jeremy McTeague's "Who Cares About the Enemy?" in which are presented actual reproductions from his notebook of handwritten battle orders as they were relayed to him on days of military engagement (in a context of radical uncertainty and unsettling fear to which he gives due account) coupled with analytic reflections on his extreme (but not, as he stresses, unusual in the situation of battle) experience. Likewise, as its title suggests, María Fra Amador's "Malvinas-Falklands Revisited: Prelude, War and Aftermath"

---

[6] Indeed all, regardless of the nationality of their authors, used in their titles the compound "Falklands-Malvinas" to denote the Islands, despite the fact that this portmanteau term appears on no map: what it signifies is acknowledgment of the dispute. For example, Bernard McGuirk's *Falklands-Malvinas: An Unfinished Business* (Seattle: New Ventures, 2007), was a comprehensive survey and analysis of the fiction, drama, poetry, film and music (mostly in Spanish and English) which arose from the War. Lucrecia Escudero Chauvel's *Media Stories in The Falklands-Malvinas Conflict* (Nottingham: CCC Press, 2014) examined critically the contemporaneous Argentine media coverage of the War. Diego F. García Quiroga's *Letting Go: Stories of The Falklands-Malvinas War* (London: Jetstone, 2016) explored by means of a sequence of short fictions the author's experience of having fought in the War and of living through its aftermath.

synoptically deals with the three successive phases in a single survey.

The anthology opens with José María Ruda's "Statement to the Special Committee on the Situation with regard to the Implementation of the Declaration on the Granting of Independence to Colonial Countries and Peoples, 9 September 1964". This presentation was instrumental in securing resolution 2065 of the United Nations General Assembly (December 1965, reproduced as the volume's second item), which formally recognised a sovereignty dispute between the UK and Argentina concerning the Falklands-Malvinas. Ruda's "Statement" has therefore since become a foundational text of modern Argentine diplomacy and negotiation with respect to the Islands. Resolution 1514 (XV) of the UN General Assembly (14 December 1960) had earlier proclaimed (among other things) "that all peoples have an inalienable right to complete freedom, the exercise of their sovereignty and the integrity of their national territory" and called for an end to the "subjection of peoples to alien subjugation, domination and exploitation". One can see in its generalised wording the seeds of future disagreement between Argentina and the UK, which Ruda in part anticipates: the former took "the people" to mean the Argentines, that is the national successors of the long-dead inhabitants who had been historically ousted from the territory by the British; the British would increasingly maintain that the later still living settlers (i.e. the modern inhabitants who were descended from those settlers or had since migrated to the Islands) were "the people" who should be self-determining. In many ways, such an Argentine insistence on the historical rights, which arguably issued from the national origins of the dead, in contrast with the British emphasis on the primacy of the wishes of the living, was the understandable difference on which a diplomatic compromise might eventually have been forged, the "peaceful solution to the problem" which resolution 2065 would urge. Such a prospect is not to be found in the Ruda submission; therein, the national origins of the dead seem to be everything and the wishes of the living almost ignorable. Ruda's historical narrative, it should be added, has hardly gone uncontested: indeed, it is the document which the initial Pascoe and Pepper essay (cited above) sets out to refute in considerable detail almost four and a half decades later. It is, however, key to understanding the established Argentine position and its recognition in the official international discussion and efforts undertaken to reach a resolution in the subsequent eighteen years preceding the War. This sometimes neglected interregnum in the Falklands-Malvinas story is summarised, from an Argentine perspective, in the Uriel Erlich essay which follows it.

In this initial period in the UK there was a see-sawing of elected parties in government, two of them Labour administrations (1964-70 and 1974-79), mostly under Harold Wilson (subsequently James Callaghan – who had previously been Foreign Secretary with significant involvement in the ongoing diplomacy – upon Wilson's resignation in 1976), two of them Conservative under Edward Heath (1970-74) and, from 1979, Margaret Thatcher. As various essays in this anthology make clear, there were signs of willingness on the part of the British to amend the *status quo* in the islands during this time, though not in the way the Argentines ideally wished. In Argentina itself, there was general societal collapse during the two years (1974-76) in which Isabel Perón succeeded her late husband as President, culminating in the military coup of 1976 and the ensuing so-called "Dirty War" within the country, during which state terrorism accounted for the murders of between 15,000 and 30,000 Argentine citizens (estimates vary) deemed politically undesirable by the military Junta. This phase is concisely evoked here by Diego F. García Quiroga, whose "First In, First Out: A Casualty of War and Life after the Conflict" also goes on to explain in dramatic detail how this state of affairs catapulted him into being part of the first Argentine landing party shortly before midnight on 1 April 1982, and finding himself hit by three British bullets the next morning, miraculously surviving, and being immediately flown back to the mainland. It is juxtaposed with Mike Seear's identically entitled "First In, First Out", in which an English veteran – who ironically describes himself as "last in, last out" – elicits the fuller and more horrifying story from his Argentine counterpart, a dogged talent which has made Seear a major contributor to the detailed history of the War, and which merits a second essay from him in this collection, "Seeking 'The Other' in the Post-Conflict, 1982-2006".

While the temporary supersession in Argentina of a brutally genocidal right-wing regime does not in itself affect the status of its claims to historic sovereignty over the Islands, nor was it the particular reason for British foot-dragging with respect to Argentine demands (bilateral negotiations resumed, for example, in 1977, and the Thatcher government came closer than any other to signing a "leaseback" deal with Argentina in 1980, withdrawing the initiative only when faced with strong domestic Parliamentary opposition), it is an historic reality which can drastically affect the entire way in which we now view the War which the Junta later precipitated. Successive Juntas murdered many more Argentines in the "Dirty War" than died on both sides (under 1,000) in the much shorter 1982 War on the Islands. Argentina's defeat in that War intensified the conditions which led to the downfall of the Junta and the restoration of democracy to the country. One might reasonably argue (despite any evident imperfections in the "democratic" Argentine polity since, which are well delineated here in Sophie Thonon-Wesfreid's "'Saving the Nation': Post-Conflict from the Point of View of the 'Guilty'") that this was a significantly greater "success" for Argentine society than would have been a triumphant seizure and permanent re-acquisition of the Islands and the likely continuance of terroristic dictatorship on the mainland. It is the one arguable good which renders the bloodshed of 1982 in some ways "meaningful", which is to say not entirely negative. It would be disingenuous to claim that any objective view of the War (and perhaps of the dispute in general, which some modern Argentine commentators still like to discuss as if the War has made no difference to it) can now be artificially separated from these later developments.

The UK, by contrast, has so far benefited meagrely from a conflict which, apart from the loss of life and casualties among its military at the time, has entailed it in appreciable long-term defence expenditure to protect the archipelago which is out of all proportion to the size of the population which lives there (currently about £300 million annually, approximately 0.5% of the entire UK defence budget),[7] unless one dubiously considers the mere display of confident military and political power itself to be a positive. As to the material advantages which might have accrued from its continued possession of the Islands, these appear to have been relatively negligible: the oft-touted promise of hydrocarbon extraction in the waters around the Islands has, for example, even forty years later, amounted to precious little, not least because international oil companies are understandably wary of prospecting in disputed territory.[8] It is reasonable to speculate that, had the 1982 War not taken

[7] These are unofficially sourced figures given by Grace Livingstone, "Oil and British Policy towards the Falkland/Malvinas Islands", *Revista de la Sociedad Argentina de Análisis Político* 14, 1 (May 2020), 147, and pertain solely to defence costs, not Falklands-related expenditure that comes from other budgets. It should be pointed out that differing estimates are somewhat more conservative than this one, but all agree that the defence costs are relatively astronomical, given that the current population of the Islands equates to less than 0.005% of the UK population.

[8] Repeated British claims that the potential for oil discovery had absolutely nothing to do with the UK's response to the sovereignty dispute which led to the Argentine occupation of the Islands have been convincingly undermined by Livingstone, *ibid.*, 131-55. However, Livingstone also concludes that Argentine commentators tend to exaggerate to a similar degree the importance of this factor.

place and not decisively rigidified successive British administrations' position on the sovereignty dispute (for how can any government give up a cause for which its country's still living ex-combatants fought and their comrades died?), the subsequent history of sovereignty may have played out rather more constructively for Argentina.

There is, of course, no obligation now to view the Falklands-Malvinas War in the very specific terms in which politicians of the time defined it or those in which contemporary British foreign-policy analysts are obliged to couch it, or indeed to adjudicate on its moral rights and wrongs at all. Some military historians prefer to see it, dispassionately, as the last, now somewhat curiously "conventional" limited war of the Cold War period; others to view it as an aberration in the history of modern warfare, because it involved a very peculiar time-lag in which the "defending" forces had to sail for numerous weeks towards the territory they were "defending" because they were never really "defending" it at all but only responding to a wholly unexpected "attack" from an enemy with much closer mainland military support; still others (although they are in the minority) to look upon it, without much nuance, as a justified war against an unambiguously wanton, fascistic aggressor.

The present anthology unequivocally tends, by contrast but without partisanship, towards evaluating the war of 1982 more in moral and political, humane and socially consequential terms, of the kind with which military historians and short-term-perspective politicians tend not to concern themselves. It also likewise inclines towards remembering the War as an event in which identifiable individuals, or their friends and comrades, suffered and died, rather than simply viewing these many participants as anonymous pawns on a geopolitical chess board. It takes into consideration the ways in which the war has been mediated in news (Lucrecia Escudero Chauvel), literature (Alicia Vaggione and Bernard McGuirk), film and television (Stuart Urban and Sandra Savoini). Above all, while providing general factual commentary and discussion on the causes, events, consequences of and continuing debate about the War (in essays by María Cristina Fra Amador, Eduardo C. Gerding, Sophie Thonon-Wesfreid and María Teresa Dalmasso), it also gives considerable space to accounts of what it was like, experientially, to have been a combatant on either side in the conflict (Diego F. García Quiroga, Alan Warsap, Jeremy McTeague and Mike Seear).

The War ended hundreds of lives on the Islands in 1982, many of them very young, and definitively contributed to the deaths of many ex-combatants later. It ruined or adversely affected the lives of many thousands more survivors and military relatives. It put a stop to patient diplomacy, which has never again regained the momentum it had in the period of potential for "leaseback" briefly entertained by the UK Thatcher government. Its result resoundingly consolidated the popular appeal of that government (which had domestically been rather beleaguered in its first term) and thus the War helped ensure the dominance of right-wing conservative administrations in the UK for another fifteen years. In Argentina, it contributed to the downfall of a terroristic dictatorship and gave the country a chance to follow a less frightening social path. It galvanized more serious and concerted efforts to address the problems of Post-Traumatic Stress Disorder, and led to the creation of new model networks for veteran peer support. Neither side really won anything concrete by means of it, although the residents of the Islands themselves undoubtedly gained in military security, financial subsidy and political attention. One other advantage they acquired was British citizenship, thanks to the British Nationality (Falkland Islands) Act 1983.

The 1982 South Atlantic conflict is largely a sad tale of loss, grief, suffering and waste. Contained and short as it was as it was compared to many other wars, it does have something to teach us about the dangers of reaching into the distant past as a ground for pursuing violent political or nationalistic purposes in the present. That is a game that sometimes might not be worth the candle, and if one is going to play it, one ought seriously to ponder the truths that history is not easily predicted and that war especially tends to have multi-dimensional outcomes that few can readily determine in advance. Forty years on, when we are now further in time from the conflict than its participants were from the end of the Second World War, the UK and Argentina are both very different societies and cultures than they then were, and the War is partly why that is so in both cases. It is difficult to imagine any solution to the sovereignty dispute in the foreseeable future, and the reason for that is also that something as terrible as the War took place. The young in both countries have inherited the changes it brought, as well as a generally transformed and globalised world which makes the realities of 1982 look now like vanishing history: one can forgive them for asking, as many of them must, if it was a fight for which the justifications offered and aims pursued were defensible when weighed against the heavy damage it caused.

CHRONOLOGY OF THE FALKLANDS-MALVINAS WAR (1982)

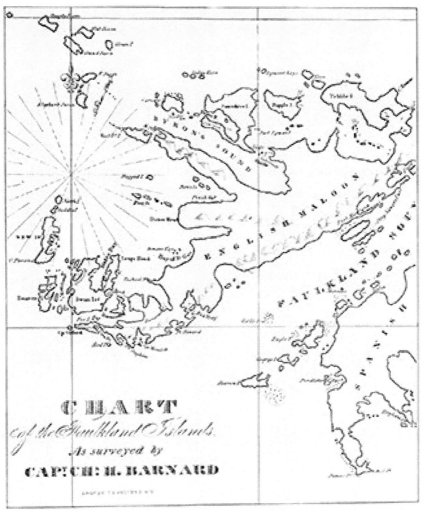

Pre-1829 map of a part of the Falkland Islands, first published in Charles Barnard, *A narrative of the sufferings and adventures of Capt. Charles H. Barnard: in a voyage round the world, during the years 1812, 1813, 1814, 1815, & 1816: embracing an account of the seizure of his vessel at the Falkland Islands, by an English crew whom he had rescued from the horrors of a shipwreck; and of their abandoning him on an uninhabited island, where he resided nearly two years: Embellished with six copperplate engravings; also a chart, drawn by himself* (1829).

18-19 March Argentine scrap-metal merchants land at Leith Harbour, South Georgia, and raise the Argentine flag.

1-2 April Operación Rosario: Argentine troops land and occupy the Falkland-Malvinas Islands.

3 April Argentine Marines land at Grytviken, South Georgia. United Nations (UN) Security Council adopts Resolution 502. Operation Corporate: the British Prime Minister, Margaret Thatcher, announces the dispatch of the British Task Force to re-capture the Islands.

5 April Lord Carrington resigns as the UK Foreign Secretary and is replaced by Francis Pym.

6 April Argentine 9th Infantry Brigade (comprising the 8th Infantry Regiment and 25th Infantry Regiment) starts deploying to the Islands.

7 April Fleet replenishment ship RFA *Stromness* departs Portsmouth with most of the Royal Marines' 45 Commando on board. The British Government declares a Maritime Exclusion Zone of 200 miles centred on the Islands to come into effect at 04.00Z hours on 12 April. Brigadier-General Mario Benjamín Menéndez assumes his appointment as Argentine Military Governor of the Islands.

8 April Argentine 5th Marine Infantry Battalion is deployed from Río Grande to the Islands and Sector Bronce (Bronze) of Tumbledown and Mount William. This unit's O Company is also initially deployed onto Mount Longdon. US Secretary of State for Foreign Affairs Alexander Haig begins his diplomatic shuttle between Washington DC, London and Buenos Aires.

9 April P&O cruise ship SS *Canberra* departs Southampton with the Royal Marines' 40 and 42 Commando, and 3rd Battalion, Parachute Regiment on board.

11 April Argentine 10th Infantry Brigade (comprising the 3rd Infantry Regiment, 6th Infantry Regiment and 7th Infantry Regiment) starts deploying by civil Boeing 707 aircraft from El Palomar, Buenos Aires to Comodoro Rivadavia. These Brigade units are then flown from there by military aircraft to the Islands. They are in position by 16 April, the 7th Infantry Regiment replacing the 5th Marine Infantry Battalion's O Company on Mount Longdon.

24 April Argentine 3rd Infantry Brigade starts deploying to the Islands with the 5th Infantry Regiment and 12th Infantry Regiment flying from Comodoro Rivadavia. The latter Regiment deploys onto Mount Challenger and later moves to Goose Green, whilst the 5th Infantry Regiment is based at Port Howard.

25 April Operation Paraquet: Royal Marine Commando forces land at Grytviken, South Georgia and the Argentine garrison surrenders. The Roll-on/Roll-off Ferry MV *Norland* departs Portsmouth with 2nd Battalion, the Parachute Regiment on board.

26 April After initially being deployed to Patagonia from their Monte Caseros base in the northern Corrientes province to protect the Argentine border with Chile, the other infantry unit of 3rd Infantry Brigade, the 4th Infantry Regiment, flies from Río Gallegos to the Islands in aircraft of Austral airline. The following day, this Regiment's B and C Companies deploy to Wall Mountain and start preparing defensive positions.

29 April Argentine 3rd Infantry Brigade is in position.

30 April British Total Exclusion Zone of 200 nautical miles around the Islands comes into effect. US President Reagan announces support for the UK.

1 May Operation Black Buck 1: pre-dawn raid carried out by a single Vulcan bomber on the airfield north of Stanley. Afterwards Harrier aircraft carry out first air strikes on the airfield and elsewhere in the Islands.

2 May Peru offers a new peace plan for resolving the crisis. UN offers similar services. The Royal Navy submarine HMS *Conqueror* torpedoes and sinks the Argentine cruiser ARA *General Belgrano* outside the Total Exclusion Zone.

4 May Royal Navy destroyer HMS *Sheffield* is hit by an air-launched Exocet missile within the Total Exclusion Zone and eventually sinks. Operation Black Buck 2: second pre-dawn raid carried out by a single Vulcan bomber on the Stanley airfield.

6 May British Government formally accepts offer of UN mediation.

7 May The British Total Exclusion Zone is extended to within twelve miles of Argentina's coastline. The UN Secretary General Javier Pérez de Cuéllar announces a new peace initiative.

12 May UK decision made to land troops at San Carlos Water. The Cunard cruise liner RMS *Queen Elizabeth 2* departs from Southampton with the 5th Infantry Brigade aboard.

21 May Operation Sutton, Phase I: the reinforced British 3 Commando Brigade of 4,000 men carry out an amphibious landing virtually unopposed at San Carlos, East Falkland. Heavy attacks by the Argentine Air Force and Navy aircraft are launched against British shipping in this first day of the overall five-day Battle of San Carlos Water. The frigate HMS *Ardent* is bombed, set on fire and abandoned. Other British vessels are also damaged.

24 May The frigate HMS *Antelope* sinks after an unexploded bomb on board detonates as it is being defused.

25 May The destroyer HMS *Coventry* is sunk by bombs from an Argentine air attack, and aircraft transport containership SS *Atlantic Conveyor* is hit by two air-launched Exocet missiles. The latter vessel is set on fire and eventually sinks. The Battle of San Carlos Water ends. Argentine Air Force Commander Brigadier-General Lami Dozo sends a peace envoy to New York.

26 May UN Security Council adopts Resolution 505. 2 Para advances towards Darwin and Goose Green.

27 May RMS *Queen Elizabeth 2* and other vessels carrying the 5th Infantry Brigade rendezvous at South Georgia. Transfer of troops commences. 2nd Battalion, Scots Guards and 1st Battalion, Welsh Guards cross-deck to SS *Canberra*, whilst 1st Battalion, 7th Duke of Edinburgh's Own Gurkha Rifles cross-deck to MV *Norland*.

28 May 2 Para commences its attack on Darwin and Goose Green. Cross-decking of the 5th Infantry Brigade is completed at South Georgia by late afternoon of 28 May. The Brigade sails for San Carlos, East Falkland.

29 May Argentine garrison at Goose Green surrender to 2 Para. Approximately 1,000 prisoners are taken. 3 Para reaches Teal Inlet and 45 Commando begins its advance on Douglas.

30 May Major-General Jeremy Moore arrives at San Carlos and assumes command of British land forces in the Islands. 45 Commando and 3 Para secure Douglas and Teal respectively.

31 May UN Secretary-General proposes a new peace plan.

1 June Operation Sutton, Phase V: 1st Battalion, 7th DEO Gurkha Rifles land at San Carlos and are flown by Chinook helicopter Bravo November to Darwin. 3 Commando Brigade forward base established at Teal Inlet. Argentine 4th Infantry Regiment re-assigned new positions at Two Sisters (C Company) and Mount Harriet (Battalion Headquarters and B Company).

2 June Remainder of the 5th Infantry Brigade land at San Carlos. Surrender leaflets are dropped over Stanley. 2 Para elements are airlifted by Chinook Bravo November to Bluff Cove.

3 June 1st Battalion, 7th DEO Gurkha Rifles garrison Goose Green. Versailles Summit opens. President Reagan presents a five-point plan to the British.

5 June 2nd Battalion, Scots Guards embark on RFA *Sir Tristram* for transport to the Fitzroy-Bluff Cove area.

6 June 2nd Battalion, Scots Guards land at Fitzroy, East Falkland and establish a 5th Infantry Brigade forward base. 1st Battalion, Welsh Guards start moving up to Fitzroy by sea. Landings at San Carlos completed with about 8,000 British troops on the Islands.

7 June 1st Battalion, 7th DEO Gurkha Rifles start moving up to Fitzroy, initially by sea, and later by helicopter. The UN Secretary General announces another peace plan.

8 June RFAs *Sir Galahad* and *Sir Tristram* attacked by Argentine aircraft whilst anchored at Port Pleasant, near Fitzroy. Fifty men are killed and one hundred and thirty-two wounded. *Sir Galahad* is crippled and, after the war, is towed out to sea and torpedoed.

10 June By midnight, 1st Battalion, 7th DEO Gurkha Rifles are in position at Wether Ground.

11-12 June On the night of 11-12 June, 3 Para attacks Mount Longdon defended by elements of the Argentine 7th Infantry Regiment, 45 Commando attacks Two Sisters, which is defended by elements of the Argentine 4th Infantry Regiment, and 42 Commando attacks Mount Harriet and Goat Ridge also defended by 4th Infantry Regiment elements. All objectives are captured by first light on 12 June.

13-14 June On the night of 13-14 June, 2 Para attack Wireless Ridge which is defended by elements of the Argentine 7th Infantry Regiment, whilst 2nd Battalion, Scots Guards attack the Tumbledown and 1st Battalion, 7th DEO Gurkha Rifles attack the north-east spur of Tumbledown and Mount William. These latter objectives are defended by elements of the Argentine 5th Marine Infantry Battalion, and are captured by 16.00Z hours on 14 June. The Gurkhas seize their two objectives unopposed.

14 June After negotiations, Brigadier-General Mario Benjamín Menéndez surrenders all Argentine forces on East and West Falklands.

12 July UK announces that active hostilities over the Falkland Islands are regarded as ended. Argentina does not make a similar Malvinas Islands statement.

22 July The British Total Exclusion Zone around the Islands is lifted.

HISTORY

A French map of the Falkland Islands from 1827 (cartographer anonymous). It uses mostly French and English, frequently giving alternate names in the two languages.

Statement to the Special Committee on the Situation with regard to the Implementation of the Declaration on the Granting of Independence to Colonial Countries and Peoples, 9 September 1964

José María Ruda

Mr President:

The Malvinas are a part of the Territory of Argentina, illegally occupied by Great Britain since 1833, following upon an act of force which deprived our country of the possession of the Archipelago. Thereupon, Great Britain then imposed a colonial regime on the area.

Since that time, since 1833, the Argentine republic has required redress for this outrage suffered, from Great Britain. In the course of these 131 years, we have never consented – and will never consent – to have part of our national territory wrested from us by an illegal and untenable act.

We come to this Sub-Committee to restate our rights to the Malvinas to the International Community, strengthened as we are by the will and the unanimous feelings of the Argentine people, and by a sound and unbroken position of protest at the outrage maintained by all Argentine Governments that have succeeded one another since 1833.

Our intention is to persuade the International Community that the islands in question are an integral part of Argentine territory and that Great Britain's moral and legal duty is to restore them to their true owner, thereby setting the principle of the sovereignty and territorial integrity of states on a sure footing of peaceful international relations. This will fulfil the generous purpose implicit in Resolution 1514 (XV), and thus a long-awaited act of justice will have been rendered.

England is today the possessor of the Malvinas Islands, solely thanks to an arbitrary and unilateral act of force. The Argentine authorities settled in the Island were expelled by the British fleet. Legally speaking, this act of force cannot generate nor create any right, and, politically speaking, the events of 1833 were only another aspect of the imperialist policies that the European powers developed for America, Africa and Asia during the nineteenth century. The Malvinas may, perhaps, be considered one of the most outstanding symbols of this fortunately outmoded policy. Under the threat of its guns, the British fleet evicted a peaceful and active Argentine population that was exercising the legitimate rights that the Argentine Republic possessed as the Heir of Spain.

Prior to 1833, the English had never effectively possessed *the totality of the Malvinas Archipelago*. In 1766, they merely founded a fort of Port Egmont on one islet called Saunders Isle. In 1774, they voluntarily abandoned it and only 59 years later they appeared, in order to oust violently the Argentine population and thus set up their sole claim.

But the history of the Malvinas does not begin in 1833 – nor even in 1765. Quite the contrary, these islands were the concern of the Chancelleries of Europe many years earlier, and a number of diplomatic incidents had taken place in the eighteenth century that touched upon them.

In order to gauge the illegality of the British act of 1833, the previous events have to be examined – events that are not recounted in document A/AC.109/L.98/Add.2, which this Sub-Committee had before it, but which surely prove the wantonness of the act committed in 1833.

We shall not go into a study of the question of the discoverer of the Malvinas Islands. Documentation published as the time shows conclusively that the Islands were discovered by Spanish navigators. In Spanish maps and charts of the beginning of the sixteenth century, the Islands already appeared. The first map is that of Pedro Reinel (1522-23) which shows an archipelago situated on the parallel 53°55' latitude South. Then there is the work of Diego Rivero, Principal Cartographer to Charles V, who inserted the islands in the Castiglione (1526-27), Salviati (1526-27) and Rivero (1527) maps and also in two charts of 1529. Then come the Maps of Yslario de Santa Cruz of 1541, the Planisphere of Sebastián Gaboto of 1544, the map of Diego Gutiérrez of 1561 and that of Bartolomé Olives of 1562, among others. It is to Esteban Gómez, of the Expedition of Magallanes in 1520, that the discovery of the archipelago must be attributed. The area was also sailed by Simón de Alcazaba in 1534 and Alonso de Camargo in 1540. All these were pilots of Spanish ships, sailing towards the Straits of Magellan, also discovered by Spain and one of the bases for its claims over the islands as being adjacent to the said Straits. Sarmiento de Gambón, in 1580, took symbolic possession of the Straits in keeping with the usage of the times, and in 1854, founded a settlement.

The Dutch navigator, Sebald de Weert, in his log book for 24 January 1600, stated that he had sighted the Islands. The British contend that in 1592 John Davis, and in 1594 Richard Hawkins, had discovered the Archipelago, but the truth of the matter is that the English cartography of the period does not show the islands, nor does there exist any proof that will substantiate the hypothetical discoveries.

Basically, until the middle of the eighteenth century, knowledge of the existence of the Islands was not certain in London, and at times they were confused with some imaginary Islands called The Pepys, which shows the degree of ignorance of the period. It was then, in 1748, that on the suggestion of Admiral Anson, England decided to send an expedition to "discover" and settle the Malvinas and Pepys Islands. Great Britain consulted Spain and, in view of the latter's objections, desisted from the plan. I should like to quote here the instructions received by the British Representative regarding the communication to be made to the Spanish Court in Madrid: "Since there is no intention of making settlement in any of the aforementioned islands and since His Majesty's corvettes wish neither to make nor touch any part of the Spanish coast, His Majesty fails to understand how this project can in any way cause objection from Madrid." The first matter that was aired in this original diplomatic skirmish over the islands was whether the British had any right to enter the regions.

The acts of consultation of 1749, addressed to the Spanish Court, are a clear proof of England's recognition of the rights of Spain over the islands and the coasts of South America, in areas where British ships could neither sail nor trade, much less give themselves to occupation.

We shall not mention the rights granted to Spain by virtue of the Papal Bulls *Inter Coetera* and *Dudum si Quidem* or of their validity *erga omnes*, nor of the Treaty of Tordesillas between Spain and Portugal, in our defence of the position that we have stated, but we shall speak of the treaties between England and Spain.

The Peace Treaty of 1604 between Spain and England returned matters and rights to the *status quo ante bellum*, nullifying anything that might have been obtained prior to the signature, including the so-called English discovery. Later, in the Treaty of Madrid of 1670, it was agreed that Great Britain would retain all the lands, islands, colonies and dominions she possessed in America; but this recognition of British sovereignty in North America was accompanied by a counter-recognition, whereby in another clause it was stated that "the subjects of Great Britain would not direct their trade to, nor sail in, ports or places which His Catholic Majesty possesses in the above-mentioned Indies, nor will they trade with them." Furthermore, the Treaty of Madrid of 1713 established that "His Britannic Majesty has agreed to issue the most stringent prohibitions and threatened with the most strict penalties, so that no subject or ship of the English Nation shall dare to sail to the Southern Sea nor traffic in any other part of the Spanish Indies". This provision, which prohibited sailing and trading by Great Britain in areas not open to traffic at the end of the seventeenth century, was again ratified in 1713 in the Treaty of Utrecht.

Therefore, in 1749, when Great Britain tried to send the first expedition, she could not have considered the Malvinas Islands *res nullius*, and therefore open to appropriation.

In February 1764 there occurred the first essay at colonization and then it was by a French sailor, Louis Antoine de Bougainville, who founded Port Louis in the Eastern Malvinas in the name of the King of France.

Spain considered this settlement an encroachment of her rights and started negotiations with Paris to obtain handing-over of the French settlement. England then dispatched a clandestine expedition which in 1766 founded Port Egmont on Saunders Island, which is near Western Malvina, close to a place that Bougainville had christened Port de la Croisade.

In the meantime, Spain formally protested to the French Government and her rights of dominion were recognised. King Louis XV ordered Bougainville to hand over Port Louis on the compensatory payment of all expenses incurred. The transfer was solemnly performed in a ceremony held on 1 April 1767 in Port Louis itself, thus recognising the legal rights of the Spanish Crown to these Islands. Previously the Government had issued a Royal Bill dated 4 October 1766 which declared the Islands to be dependencies of the Captaincy General of Buenos Aires, and Don Felipe Ruíz Puente was designated Governor. The Spanish were thus left in possession of the Port, whose name was changed to Port Soledad with Spanish settlers about and a military establishment located.

On Saunders Isle, however, there was still the small British garrison of Port Egmont, which had been set up in 1766. At the time of the transfer of Port Louis by France to Spain, the British had been silent and made no reservations regarding their presumed sovereignty. Once her difficulties with France were solved, Spain turned her attention to Port Egmont, and the British garrison was evicted from Saunders Isle by the Spanish forces of the Río de la Plata Fleet under the command of the Governor of Buenos Aires, Buccarelli, on 10 June 1770. Spain had thus reacted clearly and categorically in the face of both intruders and ensured respect for her sovereign rights, since the French had withdrawn after diplomatic pressure and the British after force had been exercised.

Britain, however, felt that her honour had been impugned by the use of force against Port Egmont and presented a claim at the Court of Madrid.

The diplomatic negotiations – in which France also participated – were long and involved, and a solution was finally arrived at on 22 January 1771. Spain's ambassador to London, Prince de Masserano, declared that his Sovereign "disapproves the aforementioned violent enterprise and binds himself to reestablish matters as they were prior to the episode", adding that "the restoration to His Britannic Majesty of the Port and Fort called Egmont, cannot and must not in any way affect the question of prior sovereign rights over the Malvina Islands." This declaration was accepted by the Government of His Britannic Majesty on the same day and, under Lord Rochford's signature, it was stated that His Britannic Majesty would consider the declaration of the Prince of Masserano, with the entire fulfilment of the agreement by His Catholic Majesty as adequate redress for the affront done to the Crown of Great Britain. From this diplomatic act, there stands out, first and foremost, the *acceptance* of the Spanish declaration, an acceptance which does not contain any rejection of the express reservation on the part of Spain regarding sovereignty over the Islands. Great Britain's silence in the light of such an express, and written, reservation, can only be interpreted in its true form, namely, as an acceptance which, furthermore, is borne out by the original title of the British document, which is not called a "Counter-Declaration", as Lord Palmerston called it in 1834, but "Acceptance", according to the Official Edition of the State Papers of 1771.

We must also point out that in all the documentation covering these diplomatic negotiations, and in all the final papers, mention is made only of the restoration of Port Egmont to the *status quo ante*, but not of the Malvina Islands in general, which latter area, however, was clearly included in the express declaration regarding Spanish sovereignty. Furthermore, while the negotiations were taking place, and unin-terruptedly after it was restored by France, Port Soledad was occupied by the Spanish without Great Britain's making the slightest move or reservation. What is more, as can be seen in the papers covering the restoration of Port Egmont, it is specified that the United Kingdom receives it from the hands of the "Commissioner General of His Catholic Majesty in Port Soledad". Both owners found themselves face to face and respected one another for three years, but those whose rights were more legitimate had to prevail.

On 22 May 1774, the English voluntarily abandoned Saunders Isle, which at the time the British called Falkland Island (in the singular). The

English, on leaving the Island, left behind a metal plate reading: "BE IT KNOWN TO ALL NATIONS THAT FALKLAND'S ISLAND WITH THIS PORT ...". And we must point out that Falkland's Island is mentioned in the possessive singular, which, linked to the British acceptance of the fact of the Spanish possession of Puerto Soledad, proves that the English claims were limited – during their stay in Port Egmont – exclusively to this settlement and not to the entire archipelago.

59 years were to elapse before the English returned to the Malvinas and the only title they were able to show in 1833 was this metal plate which had been removed by the Spanish and taken to Buenos Aires. Great Britain's astounding claim in 1833 was based on a presumed possession in the form of a metal plate, which was contrary to international law of the period, which required, as proof and condition of dominion, effective possession.

We do not wish to go into the discussion that has lured so many scholars, namely the existence of a secret pact between the British and the Spanish Crowns regarding the honourable redress in the form of a restoration of Port Egmont, and its subsequent abandonment by the British, but the English silence on the Spanish reservation regarding the Malvinas Islands is significant, as is also the fact that the British quitted these Islands almost immediately on the Spanish transfer. The truth of the matter, Mr Chairman, what we can be sure of, is that the British only stayed on the island for three years after the return of Port Egmont, and that they did not go back until 1833. 59 years elapsed, during which, with no protest whatever from Great Britain, the islands remained in the possession of Spain first, and then of Argentina, which Governments exercised all prerogatives not only in Port Soledad, but in the entire Archipelago and the neighbouring seas, with the consent of the British Crown.

Spain exercised all sorts of acts of dominion over the Malvina Islands until the Revolution of May 1810, which was the beginning of Argentine independence.

In 1776 she created the Vice-royalty of the Río de la Plata, including the above-mentioned islands, which belonged to the Governorship of Buenos Aires – and England said nothing.

In 1777, all buildings and installations of Port Egmont were razed in order to avoid awakening the cupidity of ships flying other flags – and England still said nothing.

The Spanish Government named numerous and successive Governors of the Islands between 1774 and 1811 who exercised uninterrupted authority over them and their neighbouring seas – and still England said nothing.

England's silence over the Malvinas between 1774 and 1829 confirms her recognition of Spanish rights and her desire not to return to the Archipelago.

Not only did Spain exercise effective possession between 1774 and 1811, but Great Britain did not bring to bear any rights over Port Egmont in the different instruments dated around the end of the eighteenth century and dealing with territorial questions, although she had complete and public knowledge of the sovereign occupation of the Archipelago by Spain. Thus, in the 1783 Peace Treaty of Versailles, at the end of the North American War of Independence, there was a ratification of the previous stipulations of 1670, 1713 and others that prohibited the English from sailing in the Southern Seas. Even further, the conflict that was motivated by England's trying to found a settlement on Nootka Sound, on the West Coast of Canada, led to the signing of the Saint Lawrence Convention of 1790. This agreement granted freedom of navigation to the British in the Pacific on three conditions: the first, that this navigation would not be a pretext for illegal trading with Spanish dominions, it being prohibited within "ten maritime leagues from any coasts already occupied by Spain"; the second, that there be free trade between the settlements founded in the North Pacific since 1789 and those subsequently to be set up; and finally, article 7 of the convention established that "It has also been agreed, regarding both the Eastern and Western coasts of South America, and its adjacent Islands, that the respective subjects shall in the future make no settlements in those parts of the coasts situated South of the said coasts and of the adjacent islands already occupied by Spain".

This agreement did away with the contention that there were closed seas on the East or West coasts of America. But the British right to establish colonies was only recognised regarding the coasts of North America; with regard to other areas, the Spanish Crown only acknowledged mere fishing rights, and the parties bound themselves not to establish new colonies in the South Atlantic or Pacific, and what existed would remain the *status quo*. This was precisely the interpretation given by Great Britain to the Nootka Sound Convention signed after the incident on the Canadian frontier in 1826 between Great Britain and the United States.

When, in the 1790 Convention, Great Britain recognised the *status quo* existing in the South of America, she was thereby giving the definitive legal proof of her lack of grounds upon which to base her claims to set up settlements of any permanence in the Malvinas. It is, by the same token, one of the grounds for the Argentine claims over the Islands of the South. The English had no right to people the South of the coasts or Islands already occupied by Spain, that is to say, including the South of the Malvinas and of Puerto Deseado in Patagonia.

Regarding the Malvinas themselves, there had been a renunciation of any rights England might have contended, for the commitment was not to settle any place already occupied by Spain, aside from not sailing within 10 leagues of the coast.

In one word, gentlemen, after Great Britain's voluntary abandonment of Port Egmont in 1774, Spain was left as unchallenged and unchallengeable Mistress of the Malvina Islands, and as such, she exercised absolute authority over them, she occupied them, she designated authorities for them, without the slightest protest on the part of Great Britain. International instruments of the nature of those I have just cited were signed, which even reaffirmed Spain's rights, and these were the rights that the Argentina Republic inherited in 1810.

The process of Argentine independence was a long and painful one. Its armies travelled half of America, helping in the independence of the sister countries; and this struggle was carried on without outside help and at the cost of great sacrifices. Yet, in 1820, the Government of the Argentine Republic sent the frigate "Heroina" to the Malvinas. Don David Jewett, commanding the ship, notified vessels in Malvinas waters of the Argentine laws regulating sealing and fishing in the area and informed them that trespassers would be sent to Buenos Aires to stand trial. Furthermore, in a solemn ceremony, he took formal possession of the islands that belonged to Argentina as the Heir of Spain. There was no opposition to the statement of Argentine rights over the archipelago, nor was any claim raised against it, despite the fact that the communication was published in newspapers in the United States and elsewhere.

In 1823 the Government of Buenos Aires designated Don Pablo Areguati Governor of the Malvinas Islands.

That same year, the government granted lands and also the rights of exploitation of wild cattle on the islands and of fishing on the Western Malvina, to Don Jorge Pacheco and Don Luis Vernet. An expedition took out the supplies needed for the new settlement, but it only prospered partially, due to climatic conditions which were unfavourable. In January 1826, the concessionaries again sent groups of families, and these managed to remain.

The colonizing enterprise in the archipelago gained ground in the course of subsequent expeditions which took men, supplies and animals to Port Soledad.

In 1828, a decree was signed granting Vernet concessions in Eastern Malvinas and, in its desires to encourage the economic development of the archipelago, the Government of Buenos Aires declared the settlement exempt from all taxes excepting those required to ensure the upkeep of the local authorities.

At no time did England object to the Argentine settlement of the Malvinas, despite the fact that extremely important legal acts had taken place between the two countries, such as the signing of the Treaty of Friendship, Trade and Navigation of February 1825. This instrument does not contain any British reservation whatever on the Malvinas Islands, and despite the action of the Commander of the "Heroina" in 1820 and other acts that the Government had carried out and authorised touching the Islands.

The settlement established under the protection of laws of the Government of Buenos Aires had prospered and was in good condition in 1829.

This being the case, on 10 June of that same year, 1829, the Government of Buenos Aires created the Political and Military Commandancy of the Malvinas Islands, located in Port Soledad, whose competence included all the islands adjacent to Cape Horn on the Atlantic side. The same Mr Luis Vernet was named Commandant.

It was then, in the heyday of the expansionist eagerness of Great Britain, that the English interest in the Archipelago was awakened, an interest that was nothing but the renewal of its old aspirations of possessing land in the South Atlantic. That had been the intention that had led Great Britain to invade Buenos Aires in both 1806 and 1807, being violently repulsed by the population both times. She had also occupied the Cape of Good Hope on the southernmost tip of Africa in 1806, which served as a spearhead for later expansion. In 1815 she took Saint Helena and in 1816 the Isle of Tristan da Cunha.

The expansionist ambitions in the South Atlantic were again resumed by the British Admiralty, which hungered for a naval station on the strategic route, via Cape Horn, to Australia and the South Pacific, where Britain's aspirations had to compete with another European power.

Commercial interests linked with the fishing wealth also moved her, and these were all tied in with her strategic desires to own a base in the South Atlantic.

Impelled by these interests, Great Britain decided to protest against the establishment of the Political and Military Command. On 10 November 1829 she made her claim, stating that the Argentine Government had assumed "an authority that is incompatible with the Sovereign Rights of His Britannic Majesty over the Islands".

Here a brief parenthesis should be made in order to recall some of the salient facts. In 1766, England had clandestinely founded a fort and a port of Egmont on the Isle of Saunders. In 1770, the English were forced out by the Spanish fleet. In 1771, they again occupied Port Egmont, following upon reparation offered by Spain, with the corresponding reservation of sovereignty. In 1774, three years after the transfer, the British voluntarily abandoned Port Egmont and from then on, from 1772 until 1829, for over half a century, they made neither protest nor claims on the Spanish and later Argentine occupations. The truth of the matter is that during all that time, Great Britain was not interested in the Malvinas, and she only became so and turned eyes to them when they played a part in her plans of imperial expansion. The archipelago assumed great importance for colonial navigation.

There are, in point of fact, two situations, that are independent of one another, namely (a) the eighteenth century incident that ended for Great Britain with her withdrawal from the Islands, and (b) a totally new situation, in 1829, determined by strategic factors connected with her access to her possessions in the Pacific, which were threatened at the time, and her fishing and sealing interests.

But it was not only the British ambitions and interests that came into play. The United States also showed an interest in protecting the sealing activities of her nationals, off the Malvinas coasts. When Vernet endeavoured to implement Argentine legislation relating to fishing, and held up three North American vessels, another powerful country came into the picture.

On 31 May 1831 the North American corvette Lexington appeared before Port Soledad; she flew the French flag and carried signals asking for pilots, and headed for the wharf. Thus the American sailors managed to land, destroyed the settlement and committed other acts of violence. The reason for this act was the rejection by the Argentine Government of a claim by the North American Consul whereby he sought the immediate return of one of the still detained fishing vessels. He also wanted the Politico-Military Commandant of the Malvinas to stop any intervention in the activities of the United States citizens in the area. The Lexington incident provoked a diplomatic clash between Argentina and the United

States, which wound up with the virtual breaking-off of diplomatic relations between the two countries.

During his stay in Buenos Aires, the representative of the United States established a close relationship with the Chargé d'Affaires of Great Britain and their talks, which are documented in the correspondence published by their respective countries, shows that, at a given moment, the interests of these two powerful states united in order to oust a young and weak country from the Malvinas islands.

In 1832, for the third time, Argentina returned to settle in Puerto Soledad, and a new Civil and Military Governor was designated.

But the British die was cast: the British Admiralty instructed captain Onslow to set sail for the Malvinas, and on 3 January 1833 the corvette Clio appeared off Puerto Soledad. A small Argentine vessel, the Sarandi, was riding at anchor. The English captain insisted that the Argentine detachment withdraw. The difference in numbers allowed of no possible fight, and added to that was the element of surprise.

The Argentine leader replied to the order by saying that "he held Great Britain responsible for the outrage and the violation of the respect due to the Republic, and its rights that were being assaulted by force – as blind as it was irresponsible", and added that "he was withdrawing, but that he refused to lower his flag".

The British thereupon lowered the Argentine flag and, by force, occupied Port Soledad. Thus, by plunder, another chapter of colonial history was written. Almost all the Argentine inhabitants of the Islands were then evicted.

On 3 January 1833, almost 60 years after the voluntary withdrawal of 1774, the British committed the act of force in Port Soledad on the Island of Eastern Malvina, in a place where they had never been. And by the next year, they had occupied the entire archipelago.

What I have just described is an act that is simple and easy to understand. In 1833, Great Britain, having no right on her side, could only resort to force in order to occupy the Islands. And the situation has not changed since that time: force is still the cornerstone of Britain's presence in the archipelago.

At the beginning of this statement we said that this act of force, this arbitrary and unilateral act, was never and shall never be consented to by the Argentine Republic; and we added that it cannot generate nor create any rights for Great Britain.

But the Argentine reaction was not long in coming. The population of Buenos Aires gave vent to its indignation at the incident and, in the Islands themselves, the rest of the settlers who resisted the invaders were taken and sent to London for trial under different pretexts and never returned. On 15 January, the government protested to the British Chargé d'Affaires, who replied that he lacked instructions. On 22 January the protest was reiterated and the English Minister renewed his passive stand. In the meantime, the Minister, Manuel V. Maza, notified the American Foreign Offices of the events in a circular. The reply of Brazil is worthy of mention, for that country instructed its Minister in Great Britain to offer to his Argentine colleague in London "the most frank and diligent cooperation to ensure success to his endeavours". Bolivia also replied that she would be among the first countries "to seek reparations for such dire *outrage*".

On 24 April 1833, the Argentine representative in London, Don Manuel Moreno, on instructions from Buenos Aires, presented a note of protest to His Britannic Majesty's Government, which he reiterated on 17 June, in a lengthy and documented protest memorandum. Viscount Palmerston replied on 8 January 1834, contending that the rights of Great Britain "were based on the original discovery and subsequent occupation of the said Islands", arguments which Moreno rejected on 29 December 1834.

Since then, whenever possible, the Argentine Republic has repeated its protests at the act of force and illegal occupation.

Gentlemen, the Argentine Republic was a recently independent country, lacking in the material means of the great powers of the period, yet it reacted with determination at the outrage suffered. Protests were raised a few days after the plunder of Port Soledad. Taking into account the distances, and the difficulties through which the country was going, more speed could not have been expected. The outrage caused a wave of indignation all over the country, and that feeling of protest still imbues the Argentines today.

Mr Chairman, in the course of the last 131 years, we have never ceased to clamour to the deaf ears of Great Britain for the restoration of the Islands, which are ours. Today, a new hope is offered the Argentine Republic, a hope that we may find the understanding and the support of the United Nations, one of whose noblest purposes is to end the colonial era all over the world.

The colonialist policies of that period have an outstanding example in the case of the Malvinas Islands.

At that time, advantage was taken of a country that was in the throes of organization and struggling, as are many new countries in Africa and Asia today, to achieve political and economic progress.

We defended ourselves on the strength of our dignity and of law, but we had no means to offer resistance. Our friends, the new nations of Latin America, also in the midst of their own formation, could only tender us their moral support, for they shared our material weakness. Nor was there, then, an international forum to which we might carry our complaint, and the European Concert was apportioning the world and its spheres of influence according to its own interests. It was not the age of justice – it was the age when the Great Powers used force and Great Britain acted in the Malvinas in keeping with the habits of the day.

According to Lord Palmerston's note, Great Britain contended that in 1834 that "the discovery and subsequent occupation" constituted the source of her rights, and added that these rights were given an extra sanction by the fact that Spain had restored the Port of Egmont to Great Britain in 1771.

As far as the discovery is concerned, we have seen that, if anyone first sighted the Malvinas, it was the Spanish navigators. Apart from the historical facts, the legal problem must be examined in the light of the moment when the problem was born, and we must bear in mind the fact that since the end of the sixteenth century, international law provided that, for the acquisition of *res nullius* territories, occupation was necessary, and it prevailed over discovery, which only offers preliminary and precarious rights and titles. This title – called inchoate title – had to be affirmed by means of effective occupation; in the eighteenth century neither discovery nor fictitious or symbolic occupation sufficed.

Regarding occupation, it can in no way be termed, firstly, "subsequent" to discovery, since the first English sailor who is supposed to have sighted the Islands, according to the British themselves, was Davis in 1592, and it was only 174 years later, that is in 1766, that the English settled in Port Egmont. The presence of the English, challenged by the Spanish, was only in a location called Port Egmont, and lasted between 1766 and 1774, with the protests of Spain and the resulting events and voluntary abandonment. The first effective occupation was that of France in 1764, which recognised the rights of Spain, restoring the settlement to her, whereby the effective Spanish occupation antedates the British presence. The latter continued during the eight years when the English were in Port Egmont and afterwards. It has been correctly stated that the English occupation only showed negative facets: it was illegal, since it violated existing treaties; it was clandestine, that is, it was kept secret until the Spanish found out about it; it was challenged, because Spain resisted it and made an express reservation in its regard; it was partial, because it only applied to Port Egmont, whilst Spain possessed Port Soledad and the whole of the Archipelago; it was fleeting, for it only lasted eight years; it was precarious, for after 1774 it was no more. On the other hand, while the Spanish occupation preceded the English, it coexisted with it without disturbance and outlasted the abandonment by England. The 1833 British arguments only serve to cloak a clear fact: the use of arms against a new nation that possessed the Islands by virtue of its right as Heir to Spain, rights which were unchallengeable.

Gentlemen, in 131 years we have been unable to evict Great Britain from the position into which she entrenched herself by force. But times have changed and today we are witnessing the twilight of colonialism, which is why the British presence in the Islands is an anachronism and must be eliminated. The days are gone forever when a young nation lacks voice and decision in international affairs. In the course of its entire history, my country has opposed this way of handling international relations, and we have constantly given proof of our sense of responsibility and our willingness to settle our international disputes peacefully. Almost the entire length of the Argentine frontiers were established by arbitration, without our ever having resorted to violence to settle territorial problems.

Furthermore, in 1933, at the Seventh American International Conference in Montevideo, the American States set forth a fundamental doctrine of American law when they stated that "The Contracting States set forth as a definitive norm of conduct their specific obligation not to recognise territorial acquisitions or special advantages obtained by force, whether this be by the use of arms, by threatening diplomatic representations or by other coercive measures. The territory of States is inviolable and cannot be the object of military occupation or of other measures of force imposed by another State, whether it be directly or indirectly, for any reason or even of a temporary nature."

Convinced of this, we signed the Charter of the United Nations in 1945 not only as a peace-keeping machinery and to ensure international peace and security, but also as a system whereby to find just solutions to international problems, and especially those that emanated from the colonial system. Even at the San Francisco Conference, the Argentine made an express reservation regarding our country's rights over the Malvinas Islands.

From the inception of this Organization, Argentina was well aware of the importance of Art. 73e of the Charter. As soon as Great Britain began to supply information on the Malvinas, the Argentine Republic informed the United Nations – as it had so often in the past – of its rights of sovereignty over the territory. And thus, through the General Assembly, Argentina yearly reminded the Organization of its rights, and stated that the information supplied by the United Kingdom on the Malvinas Islands, the Georgias and the South Sandwich in no way affected Argentine sovereignty over these territories, that the occupation of Britain was due to an act of force, never accepted by the Argentine Government, and that it reaffirms its imprescriptible and inalienable rights. At the same time, in the Organization of American States, my country has advocated an end to colonial situations in America.

The Tenth Inter-American Conference of Caracas in 1954 adopted Resolution 96 on Colonies and Territories occupied in America, and declared "that it is the will of the peoples of America that an end be put to colonialism maintained against the will of the peoples and also the occupation of territories". It proclaimed also "the solidarity of the American Republics with the just claims of the Peoples of America regarding territories occupied by extra-continental countries", and, finally, it repudiated "the use of force in the perpetuation of colonial systems and the occupation of territories in America".

After 1955, the United Nations was renewed by the admission of new members, especially of those that emerged from the process of decolonization imposed on the European powers by the new political structure of the world. Thus, a new perspective was created in our over one-hundred-year-old claim for the Islands.

When in 1960, with our support, there was adopted the now historic Resolution 1514 (XV), "Declaration on the Granting of Independence to Colonial Countries and Peoples", the process of decolonization all over the world took on a new impetus.

Clearly, calmly and constructively, our country supported and will support this process of decolonization which is taking place today with the help of the United Nations. We ourselves being a product of a similar process of independence – which we achieved by our own means – we are consistent with our historical tradition and determined supporters of the elimination of the colonial system. Thus, we wholeheartedly voted in favour of the additional resolutions to 1514 (XV), that is, Resolutions 1654 (XVI), 1810 (XVII) and 1956 (XVIII).

Today, this Sub-Committee III of the Committee of 24 is to take up the question of the Malvinas Islands.

The Malvinas Islands are in a different situation from that of the classical colonial case. *De facto* and *de jure*, they belonged to the Argentine

Republic in 1833 and were governed by Argentine authorities and occupied by Argentine settlers. These authorities and these settlers were evicted by violence and not allowed to remain in the territory. On the contrary, they were replaced, during those 131 years of usurpation, by a colonial administration and a population of British origin. Today the population amounts to 2,172 souls, and it is periodically renewed to a large extent by means of a constant turnover: thus in 1962, 411 persons left and 268 arrived; in 1961, 326 left and 244 arrived; in 1960, it was 292 that left and 224 who arrived. This shows that it is basically a temporary population that occupies the land and one that cannot be used by the colonial power in order to claim the right to apply the principle of self-determination.

Our government holds, and has thus stated it to successive General Assemblies, that this principle of self-determination of peoples, as set forth in Article 1, paragraph 2 of the Charter, must, in these exceptional cases, be taken in light of the circumstances which condition its exercise.

Therefore, we consider that the principle of self-determination would be ill-applied in cases where part of the territory on an independent state has been wrested – against the will of its inhabitants – by an act of force, by a third State, as is the case in the Malvinas Islands, without there being any subsequent international agreement to validate the *de facto* situation and where, on the contrary, the aggrieved state has constantly protested the situation. These facts are specifically aggravated when the existing population has been ousted by this act of force and fluctuating groups of nationals of the occupying power supplanted them.

Furthermore, the indiscriminate application of the principle of self-determination to a territory so sparsely populated by nationals of the colonial power would place the fate of this territory in the hands of a power that has settled there by force, thus violating the most elementary rules of international law and morality.

The basic principle of self-determination should not be used in order to transform an illegal possession into full sovereignty under the mantle of protection which would be given by the United Nations.

This strict interpretation of the principle of self-determination is specifically based upon Resolution 1514 (XV), whose main aim should not be forgotten, namely: to end colonialism in all its forms.

After recognising the principle of self-determination, the Preamble of that Resolution states that the peoples of the world "ardently desire the end of colonialism in all its manifestations". It also adds that "all peoples have an inalienable right to complete freedom, the exercise of their sovereignty and the integrity of their national territory".

Article 2 of the Declaration reaffirms the principle whereby "All peoples have the right to self-determination: by virtue of that right they freely determine their political status and freely pursue their economic, social and cultural development."

But this Article is conditioned by Article 6, for it clearly states that "Any attempt aimed at the partial or total disruption of the national unity and the territorial integrity of a country is incompatible with the purposes and principles of the Charter of the United Nations." In its Article 7, while reaffirming the above, it goes on to state that "All States shall observe faithfully and strictly the provisions of the Charter of the United Nations, the Universal Declaration of Human Rights and the present Declaration on the basis of equality, non-interference in the internal affairs of all States, and respect for the sovereign rights of all peoples and their territorial integrity."

The purposes of the Resolution – as its wording makes manifest – is quite in keeping with the true interpretation of the principle of self-determination insofar as the Malvinas Islands are concerned. Colonialism in all its manifestations must be brought to an end; national unity and territorial integrity must be respected in the implementation of the Declaration. It shall not be used to justify the outrages perpetrated in the past against newly independent countries.

Resolution 1654 (XVI), pursuant to which this Special Committee was established, stresses this fact when in its Preamble it states the deep concern on the part of the Assembly that "contrary to the provisions of paragraph 6 of the Declaration, acts aimed at the partial ot total disruption of national unity and territorial integrity are still being carried out in certain countries in the process of decolonization".

The American regional Organization adopted a resolution at its Tenth Foreign Ministers' Conference setting forth "the need for extra-continental countries having colonies in the territories of America, speedily to conclude the measures defined according to the terms of the Charter of the United Nations in order to allow the respective peoples fully to exercise their right to self-determination, in order once and for all to eliminate colonialism from America". But, bearing particularly in mind the situation of states whose territorial unity and integrity are affected by foreign occupation, this same resolution went on to state that it "does not refer to territories under litigation or the subject of claims between extra-continental countries and some countries of the hemisphere". The resolution was also transmitted to the United Nations.

The future of these islands, separated from the Argentine Republic, would be both illogical and unreal. Geographically they are close to our Patagonian coasts, and enjoy the same climate and have a similar economy to our own south-lands. They are part of our own continental shelf, which, by International Law and since the Geneva Convention of 1958, belongs in all rights to the coastal state.

Their economic development on a stable basis is linked to that of the Argentine Republic, with which they at present have neither communication nor direct maritime trade because of the prevailing situation.

Furthermore, if we carefully analyze the same document submitted by the Secretariat of the United Nations on the strength exclusively of the information supplied by the British, we note how the colonial system manifests itself in the economic side of the life of the Islands. Ownership of the land is virtually in the hands of the Falkland Islands Company Limited, among whose Board of Directors – located in London – figure members of the British Parliament. This Company – which we have no compunction in labelling monopolistic – owns 1,230,000 acres of the best land, in outright freehold, and on them 300,000 sheep graze. The next largest landowner is the British Crown, with 56,500 acres. The company, and its subsidiaries, control all the export and import trade. It also holds the wool monopoly which is the main source of wealth of the Islands.

British domination of the Malvinas Islands is not only contrary to the Charter of the United Nations, but it also creates a sterile situation in a territory which could enjoy a greater economic boom if linked to its natural and legal owners. Proof positive of this is the fact that the statistics for 1912 show that there were 2,295 inhabitants in the Malvinas Islands and that since that time the population has remained stagnant. According to a census taken on 18 March 1962, 2,172 souls live in the Islands. It is the only human family in America that instead of increasing, shrinks.

Gentlemen, the United Kingdom has no right to continue in the Islands, nor does the spirit of the day allow it.

Resolution of the United Nations General Assembly

2065 (XX). Question of the Falkland Islands (Malvinas)

The General Assembly,

Having examined the question of the Falkland Islands (Malvinas),

Taking into account the chapters of the reports of the Special Committee on the Situation with regard to the Implementation of the Declaration on the Granting of Independence to Colonial Countries and Peoples relating to the Falkland Islands (Malvinas),[1] and in particular the conclusions and recommendations adopted by the Committee with reference to that Territory,

Considering that its resolution 1514 (XV) of 14 December 1960 was prompted by the cherished aim of bringing to an end everywhere colonialism in all its forms, one of which covers the case of the Falkland Islands (Malvinas),

Noting the existence of a dispute between the Governments of Argentina and the United Kingdom of Great Britain and Northern Ireland concerning sovereignty over the said Islands,

1. *Invites* the Governments of Argentina and the United Kingdom of Great Britain and Northern Ireland to proceed without delay with the negotiations recommended by the Special Committee on the Situation with regard to the Implementation of the Declaration on the Granting of Independence to Colonial Countries and Peoples with a view to finding a peaceful solution to the problem, bearing in mind the provisions and objectives of the Charter of the United Nations and of General Assembly resolution 1514 (XV) and the interests of the population of the Falkland Islands (Malvinas):

2. *Requests* the two Governments to report to the Special Committee and to the General Assembly at its twenty-first session on the results of the negotiations.

1398th plenary meeting,
16 December 1965.

---

[1] *Ibid., Nineteenth Session, Annexes,* annex No. 8 (part I) (A/5800/Rev.1), chapter XXIII; *ibid., Twentieth Session, Annexes,* addendum to agenda item 23 (A/6000/Rev.1), chapter XXII.

1965-1982: The Negotiations

Uriel Erlich

For 132 years, Britain was reluctant to negotiate sovereignty rights over the Islands. It was in 1965, a year after Ambassador Ruda's statement, that the United Nations General Assembly passed Resolution 2065 (XX), which recognized the sovereignty dispute over the Islands between Argentina and Britain, and urged both parties to reach a resolution. The United Kingdom agreed for the first time to enter into negotiations.

Political instability and the process of decolonization

Foreign policy must be understood in relation to its contexts, both internationally and domestically. The Malvinas Question was framed, in this period, within the decolonization process undertaken by the "big five" countries which had won the Second World War and dominated the United Nations Security Council. Mainly, it was the movement of non-aligned countries[1] that gave greater impetus to this process, as they began to exert pressure on the United Nations in the context of an increasingly bipolar world.

Argentina had supported the United Nations from its creation in 1945. The foreign policy of President Arturo Illia, in 1965, was one of *rapprochement* with the region, including the United States. It also opened up new international markets, which allowed its external debt to be reduced and its economy to become more dynamic. The UK, on the other hand, faced a different situation. In the United Nations, for example, it suffered harassment from the socialists and non-aligned countries for its colonialist history and what remained of it in the present. The question of the "Falkland Islands" was part of a long list of problems facing the Labour administration of Harold Wilson, including "the British predicament in Rhodesia, and the increasing Spanish pressure on Gibraltar, which particularly concerned policy-makers in Whitehall" (González, 2009). For the United Kingdom, Argentina was:

---

[1] The Non-Aligned Movement (NAM) is a forum for political consultation, established in 1961, that has as its foundation principles agreed at the Bandung Conference of 1955. Its main objective during the Cold War consisted in achieving the neutrality of countries in the confrontation between the antagonistic blocs of the United States and the Soviet Union.

An important regional player that could affect the votes of other Latin American countries [...] Anglo-Argentine relations were cordial and had a rich history, despite the islands, and Buenos Aires was perceived as a more reasonable claimant than Spain, Guatemala (with respect to British Honduras) or even Venezuela (which coveted a third of the territory of British Guyana). (González, 2009)

The Islands themselves were experiencing a severe economic crisis which called into question their future self-sufficiency:

The drop in the world price of wool threatened their only source of income [...] Solutions were difficult to find because most of the land and sheep were owned by the London-based Falkland Islands Company, whose profits went mainly to its shareholders in England. (González, 2009)

In the context of the Cold War, the United States began to develop a new policy towards the region, mainly on account of concern about the advance of communism after the Cuban Revolution of 1959. Thus, the 1966 military coup in Argentina, carried out by General Onganía, marked an important break, both in internal and foreign policy. The *de facto* government of Onganía proposed to discipline society, "adhering to the National Security Doctrine, promoted by the United States throughout Latin America [...] whose main objective was to combat the 'internal ideological enemy'" (Rapoport, 2007). This continued until the last years of the military regime, when foreign policy abandoned the idea of "ideological borders", established relations with China and Cuba, and signed a trade agreement with the Soviet Union.

Towards 1973, the external context was dominated by the oil crisis, the fall in the international trade and European protectionism. In Argentina, democracy was returning, in a brief period overseen first by Héctor Cámpora and later by Juan Domingo Perón. An attempt was made to diversify economic and diplomatic relations "especially with the bloc of Eastern countries. Important sales were made to Cuba, granting generous credits and trying to help it against the North American blockade. Relations with the Soviet Union also deepened" (Rapoport, 2007). These policies began to be abandoned after the death of Perón in 1974, "in the government of his wife Isabel, with the rising influence of López Rega and the Perónist right and the sharpening of dissent within the ruling party" (Rapoport, 2007).

South America endured various military regimes during the period. Repressive governments had been installed in Paraguay (1954-1989), Brazil (1964-1985), Bolivia (1971-1978), Chile (1973-1980), and Uruguay (1973-1985), as well as Argentina (1976-1983). From October 1975, based on the so-called Operation Condor, a "coordination and security office" was created which functioned throughout the remainder of the 1970s and into the 1980s, and was made up of the intelligence services and security agencies of several South American countries with the shared objective of "confronting the action of guerrillas". Its method was illegal repression.

The civic-military dictatorship in Argentina, which began on 24 March 1976, created a profound transformation in society. It modified the operating rules of the financial system, generated trade openness and an accelerated de-industrialization process, along with a State terrorism policy. It was the bloodiest dictatorship in Argentine history, and it aimed to "dismantle the political, union and social resistance of the population" (Rapoport, 2007). The military government proposed, on the one hand, to:

> tilt the "political pendulum" in favour of the agrarian elites and large local economic groups and external capital intermediaries, cutting off national industry and the internal market, headquarters of the strength of the labour movement and of the business sectors that support economic nationalism and the main support base of the "populist alliances" that had contributed, according to the ideological mentors of the new scheme, to the radicalization of vast sectors of the population. On the other hand, Minister Martínez de Hoz sought to readapt the economy within the framework of a type of international division of labour that was presented as a return to the sources: to Argentina "open to the world" of the agro-export era that had built the generation of 1880. (Rapoport, 2007)

Regarding foreign policy, a new type of triangular relationship emerged, with the United States on the financial and technological level, and with the Soviet Union on the commercial level.

> The latter became evident after the Soviet invasion of Afghanistan and the refusal of the Videla government to join the grain embargo against the USSR promoted by Washington, since that country was the main client of Argentina with 30% of the total exports [...] the apparent contradiction of a government that defined itself as

"Western and Christian" and the deepening of economic relations with the main "enemy" power is explained by the duality of the dominant economic interests, financially and ideologically linked to the US but in which the agro-export sector had influence, needing to expand its markets to the East in the face of North American protectionism and the European Community. (Rapoport, 2009)

If the political period between 1965 and 1982 in Argentina was characterized by the political instability of democratic governments that were interrupted by military coups,[2] foreign policy on the Malvinas Question was marked at this stage by the negotiations between Argentina and the UK. This was favoured by the ongoing global decolonization process and, in particular, driven by the general recognition of the validity of United Nations Resolution 2065 (XX).

Diplomatic achievements

The United Nations was entrusted with promoting the decolonization process, which was successful in many cases in transforming colonial territories into independent states. In the 1960s, among other countries, Algeria (1962), Rwanda (1962), Jamaica (1962), Trinidad and Tobago (1962), Kenya (1963), Zambia (1964) and Barbados (1966) all became independent. The decolonization formula had two main mechanisms: the return of the territories to their original inhabitants, based on the right to self-determination of peoples; and the right to territorial integrity.

Self-determination is the "capacity that sufficiently defined populations from the ethnic or cultural point of view have to dispose of themselves and the right that a people has in a State to choose the form of government" (Bobbio *et al.*, 1991). However, the right to self-determination comes into tension, in some cases, with territorial integrity.

If by virtue of the principle of self-determination a people has the power to determine its political status and the exercise of that political status necessarily supposes the existence of a territory as a

---

[2] The government of Arturo Illia, which commenced in 1963, was interrupted by the military coup of 1966. The government of Héctor Cámpora and that of Juan Domingo Perón in 1973-1974, succeeded by María E. Martínez de Perón after the latter's death, was deposed by the civic-military dictatorship on 24 March 1976.

framework within which public power is exercised, the effective control of the territory of a State as an attribute of that quality is necessarily linked to the exercise of the right of self-determination. In this same sense, secession as the partition of a non-autonomous territory or an independent State to become another Nation-State is the antithesis of territorial integrity. (Pastorino, 2013)

Thus, the application of the principle of self-determination was not seen as appropriate in two cases:

This mechanism worked efficiently in all those territories in which the inhabitants – or their vast majority – were native, sometimes with the addition of a small number of citizens of the colonial power. But it got stuck in two cases: Gibraltar, where a good part of the inhabitants were British (or aspired to be) and the Malvinas, where the Hispanic and Argentine inhabitants, historically original (there were never natives in the islands), were expelled by force in 1833 and replaced by British and temporary workers. (Cisneros and Escudé, 2000)

The UK wanted the right to self-determination to apply to the Islands as well, but this was not recognized by the United Nations. "Consulting citizens from the colonial power was a contradiction in itself: self-determination corresponds to the wishes of the natives, not to those of implanted populations" (Cisneros and Escudé, 2000).

From 1833, and until 1965:

There was a dialogue of the deaf between Argentina, which demanded the return of the islands, and the United Kingdom, which replied that it did not doubt its rights over them. In this way London managed to keep the dispute frozen and ignored by international opinion. (García del Solar, 2000)

This "dialogue of the deaf" lasted until the Argentine diplomatic achievement that marked a milestone in the debate over the Malvinas Question, namely Resolution 2065 (XX) of the United Nations General Assembly. Following it, the UK agreed for the first time to enter into negotiations to find a peaceful solution to the dispute.

Article 1 of the resolution:

Invites the Governments of Argentina and the United Kingdom of Great Britain and Northern Ireland to proceed without delay with the negotiations recommended by the Special Committee on the Situation with regard to the Implementation of the Declaration on the Granting of Independence to Colonial Countries and Peoples with a view to finding a peaceful solution to the problem, bearing in mind the provisions and objectives of the Charter of the United Nations and of General Assembly resolution 1514 (XV) and the interests of the population of the Falkland Islands (Malvinas).

Resolution 2065 (XX) granted Argentina international recognition of its historic claim and categorized the Islands as a case of British colonialism. The resolution expresses the central issues of the the Malvinas Question: the existing situation is one of the forms of colonialism that must be put to an end. It is a sovereignty dispute between two states that should be addressed without delay through negotiation in order to find a peaceful resolution. To do this, the objectives and provisions of the United Nations Charter must be taken into account (including Article 33, which contains the obligation of the parties to a dispute to seek a solution first of all through negotiation; and Resolution 1514 [XV], which enshrines the principle of territorial integrity and the interests of the population of the Islands, leaving aside the principle of self-determination).

Likewise, the name Islas Malvinas, in Spanish, was henceforth incorporated into all UN documents. Until then, only the Falkland Islands were listed. The solution to the dispute required considering the *interests* of the islanders, and not their *wishes*, since they were not a native people but rather an implanted population. "It is the territory that has a colonial character and not the population that occupies it, which is simply the tool of occupation" (Pastorino, 2013).

In turn, Resolution 2065 (XX) was based on Resolution 1514 (XV) of 1960, the Declaration on the granting of independence to colonial countries and peoples, which established the General Assembly's backing of the global process of decolonization. It was approved by eighty-nine votes for and none against. There were nine abstentions, one of them being the United Kingdom.

Among the grounds for this resolution, the UN belief is explained in that "the process of liberation is irresistible and irreversible and that, in order to avoid serious crises, an end must be put to colonialism and all practices of segregation and discrimination associated therewith". The ruling contains conceptual elements of great importance for Argentina and the Malvinas Question. One of them is the principle of territorial integrity that limits the principle of self-determination: "Any attempt aimed at the partial or total disruption of the national unity and the territorial integrity of a country is incompatible with the purposes and principles of the Charter of the United Nations". This principle is related to the origin of the Malvinas Question: the forceful occupation of the Islands Argentina suffered in 1833 has not conferred the right to acquire the territory through the passing of time.

Another relevant pronouncement is that on the subjects of the decolonization process: "The subjection of peoples to alien subjugation, domination and exploitation constitutes a denial of fundamental human rights, is contrary to the Charter of the United Nations and is an impediment to the promotion of world peace and co-operation". Those who began to inhabit the Malvinas Islands in 1833 were not a people subject to "alien subjugation, domination and exploitation", but residents of an illegally occupying power.

In 1961 the General Assembly had created the Special Committee on Decolonization, also known as the C-24,[3] to monitor decolonization processes. This committee was where Argentine diplomacy focused its work on the search for resolutions that would promote a subsequent negotiation with the UK. It was within this body, in Subcommittee III, that the Argentine delegate, José María Ruda, had presented the fundamentals of the Argentine position. The said Subcommittee unanimously approved the following conclusions and recommendations: it confirmed that the provisions of Resolution 1514 (XV) were applicable to the territory of the Malvinas Islands; it noted the existence of a dispute between the British and Argentine governments; it recommended that the Special Committee invite both governments to enter into negotiations in order to find a peaceful solution to this problem, taking due account of the provisions and objectives of the Charter and Resolution 1514 (XV), the interests of the population and also the opinions expressed in the course of the general debate; and it recommended that the Special Committee invite the two aforementioned governments to inform the said Committee or the General Assembly of the results of their negotiations. In September 1964, the majority of the members of the

[3] Its full name is The Special Committee on the Situation with regard to the implementation of the Declaration on the Granting of Independence of Colonial Countries and Peoples.

organization favoured the Argentine position. As a consequence, the existence of a dispute over the sovereignty of the Islands was accepted, Resolution 1514 (XV) was seen as applicable to the territory of the Islands, and not to the population.

The year following the Ruda statement, and the recognition obtained, United Nations Resolution 2065 (XX) was agreed, during the government of President Arturo Illia, whose chancellor was Miguel Ángel Zavala Ortiz. It was approved first by the Decolonization Committee and then by the United Nations General Assembly. The then Argentine representative at the United Nations was Ambassador Lucio García del Solar.

Resolution 2065 (XX) enabled Argentina to point to the existing colonial situation in the Malvinas Islands and was a recognition of the legitimacy of its claim. Likewise, it enabled a period of negotiations, on two levels. On the one hand, there were official and informal conversations on different formulae that might resolve the underlying dispute, the sovereignty rights over the Islands. On the other, understandings and cooperation in various practical aspects derived from the dispute.

> The case of Malvinas suddenly became known, like that of Gibraltar, in all the Foreign Ministries and specialized media in international relations and, second, the United Kingdom was forced to accept a process of negotiations since then. (García del Solar, 2000)

The Illia government set out to build contacts with the inhabitants of the Islands, whose isolation was then considered significant.

> These contacts made it possible, on the one hand, for the islanders to see how the descendants of Anglo-Saxon immigrants had integrated and prospered in Argentina and, on the other, to guarantee respect for their cultural and political habits and the recognition of their material assets in the case that the islands were restored [...] It is the interests and not the wishes of a non-indigenous population that must be taken into account to settle a dispute originated in the violation of the territorial integrity of a country, as a consequence of a colonial situation. (García del Solar, 2000)

The first meeting to address the question of the Malvinas Islands, between the Foreign Ministers of Argentina and the United Kingdom was

51

held in 1966. It was understood to be the beginning of negotiations. The joint communiqué of 14 January 1966, signed by Miguel Ángel Zavala Ortiz and Michael Stewart, established the commitment to find a peaceful solution to the dispute, as suggested by Resolution 2065 (XX).

The negotiations that arose from the United Nations pronouncement represented, in themselves, an important change in the European power that, since 1833, had argued that there was "nothing to discuss". They also showed the legitimacy of the Argentine position. The talks were not without difficulties. The records of the meeting between the Ministers show that "the British Secretary tried to emphasize to his counterpart that the wishes of the islanders were paramount to the United Kingdom, despite the fact that the General Assembly had not mentioned them in its Resolution, and that consequently 'It was not him who Ortiz had to persuade, but the islanders themselves'" (González, 2009).

For part of the British administration, in particular, there were vexatious problems:

> The Gibraltar and South Atlantic Department would find it complicated – domestically but also internationally – if the way in which they compromised with respect to the *wishes of the Gibraltarians* was at the same time ignored in the case of the Falkland Islands [...] This could establish a dangerous precedent, which threatened the legal position of London in the Rock (in which Great Britain did have a real strategic interest) and would have greater negative repercussions for its policies regarding Rhodesia, British Honduras and Hong Kong. (González, 2009)

The period of negotiations between 1966 and 1968 was marked by this tension between the British position, which required – because of the possible consequences in its remaining colonial territories – upholding the "wishes" of the islanders and therefore the principle of self-determination, and the Argentine position, which focused on the guarantees offered to the islanders, respecting their "interests", in the event of a restitution of sovereignty. Argentina, as stated in Resolution 2065 (XX), did not accept the islanders as a third party to the dispute, nor did it want to facilitate their veto power over the restitution of the Islands (González, 2009).

Under the *de facto* government of General Onganía, both governments reached a Memorandum of Understanding of 1968. It stated:

The Government of the United Kingdom, as part of such final settlement, will recognize Argentina's sovereignty over the Islands from a date to be agreed. This date will be agreed as soon as possible, after: i) the two governments have resolved the presented divergence between them as to the criteria according to which the UK government shall consider whether the interests of the islanders would be secured by the safeguards and guarantees to be offered by the Argentine Government and; ii) the Government of the United Kingdom is then satisfied that those interests are so secured. (Oliveri, 1992)

Ultimately, the Memorandum was unsuccessful.

Among the hypotheses, some authors blame Argentina for being unable to seize the moment. The inflexibility and slow pace of its diplomacy (on which see Cisneros and Escudé, 2000 and Franks, 1983), the undemocratic nature of the regime that came to power in June 1966 (Zavala Ortiz, 1977 and Calvert, 1982), and the timidity of its leadership in putting enough pressure on the British (Moreno, 1982) have been offered as explanations. But most of the work is focused on the British government. Some say that the Foreign Office was trying to sustain the reverse of the Argentine claim at the United Nations to delay negotiations (Holmberg, 1977). In his memoirs, then Foreign Minister Costa Méndez (who would be in the same post in 1982) claims that he trusted the good faith of British career diplomats but doubted the sincerity of the administration as a whole, accusing it of being responsible for the failure of the talks (Costa Méndez, 1993). Others point to persistent British interests in the Islands, either in terms of access to Antarctica or as a reservoir of marine resources (Hoffmann and Hoffmann, 1984), and to individual officials and the way in which the agreement was presented to the British public (Beck, 1988). Finally, some analysts argue that the islanders themselves were largely responsible for the collapse of the negotiations, on account of the effectiveness and impact of the lobby they formed in the UK Parliament in 1968 (Ellerby, 1982). Others point to the poor negotiation margins of the British government, which had to consider the possible consequences in the rest of its colonial possessions, when it came to resolving the dispute in the Malvinas Islands (González, 2009).

Specifically, the possibility of reaching a solution became "a controversial question of British domestic politics" (Airaldi, n.d.), which led to the memorandum of agreement being abandoned. In the statement

Minister Stewart made to the UK House of Commons on 11 December 1968, he said that there would be no transfer of sovereignty against the wishes of the islanders.

> Although he admitted that both governments had reached "a certain measure of understanding", he dismissed this and his words of March 1968 in the same room, saying "there is a basic divergence with respect to the insistence of the Government of HM in which there can be no transfer of sovereignty against the wishes (no longer the "interests") of the inhabitants of the Islands. (Airaldi, n.d.)

Contrary to Resolution 2065 (XX), the United Kingdom discontinued negotiations.

The following week, on 17 December 1968, the Argentine delegate to the United Nations General Assembly rejected the reasons the British government had given for not being prepared to formalize the understanding achieved. He declared that the sovereignty dispute was between Argentina and the United Kingdom and that while the interests of the population of the Islands should be taken into account, their wishes should not. He recalled the principle of territorial integrity and the origin of the current population. But the negotiations had suffered a first setback.

Practical agreements
Resolution 2065 (XX), the diminishing interest the UK seemed to show in the Islands and the decision of the Falkland Islands Company to withdraw from service the ship that carried supplies between Montevideo and Puerto Argentino, enabled a period of negotiations between the UK and Argentina on practical issues, which resulted in the 1971 Communications Agreement. This agreement was produced under a formula taken from the Antarctic Treaty of 1961, called the "sovereignty umbrella", which allowed that the various understandings established between the two parties, as well as the actions of third countries related to them, did not imply a modification in the respective sovereign positions.

As of the 1971 agreement, the two nations began to cooperate in the matter of regular air and maritime services, in postal, telegraphic and telephone communications, and in the fields of health, education, agriculture and technology. The agreement established a weekly air transport service for passengers, cargo and correspondence between the Islands and the Argentine mainland under the responsibility of

Argentina, and a regular maritime service under the responsibility of the UK, as well as the *carte blanche*, a document without nationality identification which permitted islanders and continentals to come and go freely between the Islands and the mainland without a passport stamp.

The following year, in 1972, the agreement was extended. An aerodrome was built on the Islands and regular flights were commenced by the State Air Lines (LADE), which opened an office in Malvinas. Medical assistance and evacuation services were operated, a YPF fuels storage plant was installed, scholarships were awarded to islanders to study in bilingual schools on the mainland, and Spanish-language teachers came to the Islands.

The Communications Agreement created an important link between the Islands and the Argentine mainland. It contributed to the building of links between the islanders and the continentals on a multiplicity of subjects – education, health, work, travel and communications – and it promoted a favourable climate for a possible negotiation over sovereignty. Argentina complied with the commitments assumed, which required significant expenditure by the State. However, the UK continued to show reluctance to address the dispute.

In 1973 and 1976 the UN General Assembly approved two resolutions favourable to Argentina that complemented the principles of the 1965 pronouncement. Resolution 3160 (XXVIII) of 1973, with 116 votes in favour, none against and 14 abstentions – one of them from the UK – established that the sovereignty dispute had to be resolved in order to settle the colonial situation. Resolution 31/49 of 1976 enunciated the principle of not innovating in the matter of non-renewable natural resources while the dispute went unresolved. It was passed with 102 votes in favour, one against – the United Kingdom – and 32 abstentions.

This latter pronouncement arose in response to the first investigation into the resources of the Malvinas and their potential, carried out unilaterally by the UK on the continental shelf of the Islands in 1975, within the framework of the Shackleton Mission, which was looking for hydrocarbon sediments. The 1973 oil crisis had led to the exploration for oil in spaces not controlled by the Organization of the Petroleum Exporting Countries (OPEC). One result of the Shackleton Mission was that the British began to include a new factor in bilateral negotiations: the exploration and exploitation of hydrocarbon, mining and fishing resources, which "had a direct impact on the 'wishes' and 'interests' of the islanders, at the same time that it violated what was expressed by the United Nations and what was agreed with Argentina" (Bernal, 2009).

The Shackleton Report (vol. II):

Reviews the history and geography of the archipelago and its demographic, labour and economic structure; then the different current and potential economic activities are analyzed in detail: agriculture (focused on sheep farming), fishing, mining (mainly underwater hydrocarbons), industry and crafts, transport and communications, trade and services, tourism; lastly, the social infrastructure and public services (government, housing, education, medical assistance, social security, etc.). Chapter 16 is devoted to an analysis of the Falkland Islands Company and its dominant position within the economic activity of the Islands. The second volume [...] proposes what it calls "a strategy for development" and modifications, even, in the government of the Islands. (Shackleton, 1976)

The results of the prospecting were positive and the areas with the highest probability of finding oil were identified. The work was carried out by two geologists from the University of Birmingham, hired by the British Crown through Parliament, and their results were published in 1976: the areas identified are exactly the areas that are currently under exploration, except for one, the most important and probably the most economically profitable, an elliptical basin that practically connects Cabo Belgrano of Gran Malvina with the city of Río Grande.

The sovereignty dispute
During Perón's government the United Kingdom was open to a dialogue on the underlying question.

The United Kingdom was perceived as a "colonialist" stronghold because of its position in Rhodesia, Namibia and South Africa and its support for the Portuguese Overseas Territories, Guinea, Angola and Mozambique. Furthermore, the West was in crisis due to rising oil prices, the United States' withdrawal from Vietnam, the appearance of the Palestine Liberation Organization, the presence of Cuba in Africa and the radicalization of the Third World. (Petrella, 2010)

In 1974, almost a decade after Resolution 2065 (XX) and three years after the practical agreements of 1971, the UK offered a solution to the sovereignty conflict. The British embassy proposed to the Argentine Foreign Minister Alberto Vignes that the official languages henceforth would be Spanish and English, the islanders would have dual citizenship, and that passports would be abolished. Governors of the Islands would be appointed, alternately, by the Queen and by the Argentine President, and the two national flags would fly on the Islands.

Again, the UK decided not to proceed with this alternative and, after Perón died, the British government formally withdrew the proposal. The new UK strategy, according to official British documents, was to "buy time" by delaying negotiations. To a negative external context (the oil crisis, downturns in trade, European protectionism), there was added an acute internal political conflict "marked by the existence of left-wing guerrilla movements and right-wing paramilitary forces protected by another minister, José López Rega, with a history of armed actions, kidnappings and assassinations [...] The following months saw the erosion of the government and the preparation of a 'declared' coup" (Rapoport, 2007). Along with this, the results of the Shackleton Mission of 1975, which had shown the existence of hydrocarbon resources in the disputed area, diminished the British will to work for a solution.

The next instance of negotiations for sovereignty took place during the last civic-military dictatorship, in 1980. The dominant political-diplomatic context by this time could be described as a "credible threat" situation whereby "if the negative attitude of the United Kingdom leads to a dead end, the Argentine government will be forced thoroughly to review the policy followed up to now". In other words, sooner or later Argentina would be "forced to say enough and do justice by its own hand" (Palermo, 2006).

According to the British historian Lawrence Freedman (2005), the British were concerned about the possibility that the dictatorship would decide to initiate military action. Among the elements that gave plausibility to this hypothesis was the direct action of the *de facto* government, in 1977 of initiating a military occupation, disguised as scientific activity, of an island in the South Thule archipelago, as well as "the recurring attitude of wanting to force the hand both in negotiations and through cooperation and integration measures between the islands and the continent" (Palermo, 2006).

On 10 and 11 September 1980, in Switzerland, a new round of negotiations between Argentina and the UK took place. This led to a trip to Buenos Aires and the Islands by the Foreign Secretary, Nicholas Ridley. The focus was a proposal from the UK similar to the one made in respect of Hong Kong: "immediate recognition of our sovereignty and a lease agreed in favour of the Crown, with growing Argentine co-administration" (Cisneros and Escudé, 2000). A session of the British

Parliament on 2 December 1980 ended this alternative, after the strong opposition of Parliamentarians from both sides of the House in conjunction with the lobby of the islanders (established in 1968).

In January 1981 Argentina proposed a new round of negotiations, which was accepted the following month. Most of our knowledge of this exchange comes from the suppressed Rattenbach Report of 1983 (published by the Argentine government only in 2012). In a confidential meeting on 21 February, prior to the formal negotiations, Ridley said that the islanders had a complete lack of information about the Argentine position and Argentina's urgent wish to resolve the issue. He requested the collaboration of Commodore Cavandoli in helping the Islands' representatives fully to understand the Argentine position. Cavandoli's response anticipated that Argentina would reject the proposal to freeze negotiations for ten years, that Argentina had reached the limit of its patience, and that it was determined to remove all existing cooperation and withdraw from the negotiations if the issue of sovereignty was not seriously addressed.

In the round of formal negotiations that took place on 23 and 24 February 1981, Ridley sought agreement for "the freezing of the Argentine sovereignty issue for ten years". Argentina predictably rejected the proposal. A private exchange was then held between the British side and the island representatives, and then they presented the following demands to Argentina:

1) on the basis that the British have a democratic system of government and accepting that self-determination and independence of the Islands was not possible, they should be offered assurances of being able to continue under a democratic regime and freedom from pressure in the future to modify such an agreement;
2) control of fishing and its exploitation in the area, and exclusion of third states, as well as the opening of the trading possibilities of the Islands to investors.

Argentina responded:

a) that time was running out;
b) that the investments and the effort hitherto made by Argentina did not justify their size, largely because they had been met with distrust by the islanders;
c) that Argentina was an exemplar of compliance with its

international obligations;

d) that the United Nations would be an excellent guarantor of the commitments made;

e) that any other questions were subject to agreement on the issue of restitution of sovereignty.

The round of negotiations ended with a joint statement that there had been little progress in the negotiations. The British delegation consisted of two members of the Council of the Islands, so it was assumed that the response from the Argentine side would be transmitted to the islanders. This did not happen.

Upon re-assuming the role of Foreign Minister on 22 December 1981, Nicanor Costa Méndez met with General Leopoldo Galtieri, who required him to "activate to the maximum the diplomatic actions aimed at the recognition of our sovereignty in the Malvinas, adding that he did not rule out that they had to arrive at something more than diplomacy" (Rattenbach Report, 1983). On 26 and 27 February 1982, a new round of negotiations was held in New York. For Argentina, Ambassadors Ross and Ortiz de Rozas participated; on the British side, Ministers Luce and Fearn, Ambassador Williams, and two councillors from the Islands. The negotiations ended with the apparent willingness on the British side to recommend the Argentine proposal to its government. "This present-ation, called the Reactivation Proposal, favoured the establishment of a Permanent Negotiating Commission, which should meet every first week of each month, alternately in each capital, in order to maintain the continuity and momentum of the negotiation" (Rattenbach Report, 1983). On 1 March 1982, a joint communiqué was issued, which described the cordial and positive atmosphere of the meeting since the two "parties reaffirmed their decision to find a solution to the sovereignty dispute and considered in detail an Argentine proposal on procedures to achieve greater progress in this regard" (Rattenbach Report, 1983).

The following day, the military government published an expanded statement:

Argentina has negotiated with Great Britain with patience, loyalty and good faith, for more than 15 years, within the framework indicated by the pertinent UN resolutions, the resolution of the sovereignty dispute over those islands. The new system constitutes an effective step for the prompt resolution of this dispute. Moreover, if that does not happen, Argentina maintains the right to terminate the operation of that mechanism and freely to choose the procedure that best suits its interests. (Rattenbach Report, 1983)

This statement was "effectively an ultimatum and historical explanation of what would happen less than three months later" (Cisneros and Escudé, 2000).

In the last meetings in New York prior to the war, Argentina hardened its position and urged the UK to make a decision. At that time, the island councillors, two representatives of the "hard line", were not willing to negotiate sovereignty. They accepted only practical agreements. In one of the last bilateral meetings between Argentina and the United Kingdom, prior to 2 April 1982, two commitments were agreed: the first, that the councillors would advance toward some kind of definitive agreement on the sovereignty issue if the Argentine government guaranteed certain rights. The councillors did not communicate this proposal to the islanders. The second commitment was from the Argentine government: it would not take further measures, but allow a pause and then resume negotiations the following year.

References

Airaldi, Eduardo. (n.d.). "La cuestión de las Islas Malvinas en la diplomacia multilateral". Available at **https://www.cancilleria. gob.ar/userfiles/ut/07-eduardo_airaldi.pdf**.

Beck, P. (1988). *The Falkland Islands as an International Problem*. London: Routledge.

Bernal, Federico. (2009). "Malvinas: 'La Arabia Más Austral Del Mundo'", *Le Monde Diplomatique*, n°118 (April).

Bobbio, Norberto, Nicola Matteucci and Gianfranco Pasquino. (1991). *Diccionario de política*. México City: Siglo XXI.

Calvert, P. (1982). *The Falklands Crisis: The Rights and Wrongs*. London: Francis Pinter.

Cisneros, Andrés and Carlos Escudé. (2000). *Historia general de las relaciones exteriores de la República Argentina, Vol. XII: La diplomacia de Malvinas, 1945-1989*. Buenos Aires: Grupo Editor Latinoamericano.

Costa Méndez, N. (1993). *Malvinas: Ésta es la historia*, Buenos Aires: Editorial Sudamericana.

Ellerby, C. (1982). "The Role of the Falkland Lobby, 1968-1990", in A. Danchev (ed.), *International Perspectives on the Falklands Conflict*. New York: Palgrave Macmillan.

Franks, O.S. *et al.* (1983). *Falkland Islands Review: Report of a Committee of Privy Counsellors*. London: HMSO.

Freedman, Lawrence. (2005). *The Official History of the Falklands Campaign*. London: Routledge.

García del Solar, Lucio. (2000). "Normalización de las relaciones entre la Argentina y el Reino Unido. Acuerdos de Madrid de 1989/1990. Antecedentes y análisis", in Silvia Ruth Jalabé (comp.), *Década de Encuentro: Argentina y Gran Bretaña 1989-1999*. Buenos Aires: Nuevo Hacer.

González, Martín Abel. (2009). "Missed Opportunity? The Anglo-Argentine Negotiations over the Sovereignty of the Falkland Islands, 1966-1968", Documento de Trabajo n° 241. Buenos Aires: Universidad de Belgrano.

Hoffmann, F. L. and O. M. Hoffmann. (1984). *Sovereignty in Dispute: The Falklands/Malvinas, 1493-1982*. Boulder, CO: Westview Press.

Holmberg, A. M. (1977) *¿Cree Ud que los ingleses nos devolverán las Malvinas? Yo no*. Buenos Aires: Editorial Grandes Temas Argentinos.

Moreno, J. C. (1982). "La visita de Lord Chalfont a Puerto Stanley", in Gambini, H. (ed.), *Crónica documental de las Malvinas*, Vol. I. Buenos Aires: Biblioteca de Redacción.

Oliveri, Ángel M. (1992). *Malvinas: La clave del enigma*. Buenos Aires: Grupo Editor Latinoamericano.

Palermo, Vicente. (2006). "Malvinas: causa, diplomacia y guerra. Una mirada de la historia a la luz de contribuciones recientes", *Clarín*, 10 June.

Pastorino, Ana. (2013). *El derecho de libre determinación de los pueblos y la población de las islas*. Buenos Aires: EUDEBA.

Petrella, Fernando. (2010). "La disputa de las islas Malvinas y su contexto histórico". Available at **www.ancmyp.org.ar/user/files/01%20 Malvinas.pdf**.

Rapoport, Mario. (2007). *Historia económica, política y social de la Argentina (1880-2003)*. Buenos Aires: Ediciones Macchi.

Rapoport, Mario. (2009). "Argentina: Economía y Política Internacional: Los procesos históricos", in *Diplomacia, Estrategia & Política*, n° 10.

Rattenbach Report. (1983) (suppressed until 2012).

Shackleton, Edward. (1976). *Relevamiento económico de las Islas Malvinas: Informe*, vol. II. Buenos Aires: Instituto Argentino de Estudios Estratégicos y de las Relaciones Internacionales.

Zavala Ortiz, M. A. (1977). "Islas Malvinas", *Revista Estrategia*, n° 45.

THE WAR

A detail from J. H. Colton's map of Patagonia, the Falkland Islands, South Georgia Islands and the Powell Group, published in George Woolworth Colton's *Atlas of the world, illustrating physical and political geography* (London: Trübner and Co., 1855), vol. 1, p. 63.

First In, First Out: A Casualty of War and Life after the Conflict

Diego F. García Quiroga

At the time the war broke out Argentina was struggling to find its way back to the democracy it had enjoyed until almost forty years before, when the first of a series of *de facto* regimes took over the rule of the land. Peppered with honest but unsuccessful democratic periods, those years succeeded in widening the already significant social differences and created a distinctive aversion to authority that found its common expression in widespread mistrust towards the government, the military, the police and politicians.

This state of affairs also represented an enormous opportunity for any ideology other than democracy to penetrate and take root, a fact swiftly grasped by the international left. From late 1950s and, almost inaudibly at first but soon increasingly openly, the military and state-dependent intelligence services began to pay increasing attention to the operations and propaganda of left-wing organisations within and around the country's borders, and already in the seventies these activities had led to a dreadful internal war that – in spite of its success – further discredited the military.

This was the background against which Argentina, not finding an echo to its public insistence on the urgency to solve the issue of the islands, decided to make a show of force and help revitalize the national pride of its (by then) deeply divided people.

What followed was in many senses an odd war, the kind we will probably not see again. Argentina and Britain had a long history of collaboration, and to many on both sides of the Atlantic it all came as a big surprise. This effect reached also a large number of the military that were to fight, but a mixture of professional ethos and the swiftness of events minimised the effects of the amazement.

*

In 1816 Argentina declared its independence from Spain, and in 1823 the new republic took possession of the Malvinas islands, which had until then belonged to the Spanish crown, sending a governor and ninety settlers there in 1826. In 1833 Britain invaded the islands, ousted the Argentine governor, and set up a colony in Port Stanley.

Argentina's first Constitution was penned in 1853. A prolonged civil war held the country in unrest until the battle of Pavón in 1861 put an end to the fight. Thereupon the country enjoyed sustained growth and relative political stability under a series of democratic governments until the 1929 Wall Street collapse destroyed the international status quo, fatally wounding the country's economy, which depended heavily on foreign trade.

In September 1930 a military coup removed the elected president, Hipólito Irigoyen. It was the first intromission of the military in government since Pavón, and from then on their participation became increasingly prominent as a series of *de facto* regimes (punctuated by attempts to return to democracy) continued, until 1946. In that year Colonel Perón, with the orchestrated support of unions and mobs, was elected president. A right-wing demagogue admirer of Franco and Mussolini, he was to hold office uninterrupted for almost ten years, characterised by increasing corruption, manipulative rhetoric and state supported jingoism. Though Argentina's claim about its sovereign rights upon the Malvinas had regularly and tenaciously been upheld in international fora, it was Perón who made the issue sink into the minds of the people and established it as a national cause.

Perón was deposed in 1955 through another military coup. The leaders of the revolution held power for three years before delivering it once again to a democratic government. Ten years (three presidencies) went by until the military came back to power in the figure of General Juan Carlos Onganía. This was 1966, the Cold War was at its height, and anti-communism was the call of the day. Many important democratic freedoms were limited, when not denied. Two other military dictators followed Onganía's repressive regime until the military grasp came to a brief pause in 1973 with the return of Perón from his Spanish exile.

Perón was now old, sick and ineffectual. If anything, his return served only to aggravate the confrontations that the last twenty years of repression had tried to silence through totalitarian measures. By 1974 Perón had died, leaving his third wife, María Estela "Isabel" Martínez, in charge. Inflation was mounting, the economy was in chaos, and riots were exploding everywhere. To make things worse, leftist guerilla groups which Perón had initially helped grow with a view to using them as supporters were spreading chaos throughout the land, growing stronger by the day and threatening to "liberate" areas as large as provinces, sequestering them from control of the central government.

These groups had been developing since the early 1960s. They answered to a mix of ideologies and received significant support from abroad, with Cuba, China and the USSR as their most active supporters. Before jumping into the second phase of their mission – spearheaded by Che Guevara's failed attempt at establishing a victorious rural guerrilla war in Bolivia – they were active in major cities, operating through a network of cells whose members scarcely knew each other. While every now and then they staged carefully planned propaganda gatherings, secrecy and deception were prominent among their policies. Several of these organisations included cadres that had received training abroad (mainly in Cuba, Palestine, Libya and Angola) and their intelligence ability and combat capacity posed a very real threat to government forces. They kept substantial cash-flow through threats, extortion and kidnapping of wealthy or otherwise prominent persons; were technically speaking well equipped; and their efforts were mainly directed to weakening the police, the military and every other law enforcement organisation in order to reduce the state's influence and spread chaos, instill fear in the people, and gain power for the Cause. Most prominent among these groups were FAR (Revolutionary Armed Forces), ERP (People's Revolutionary Army) and Montoneros. In 1973, FAR and Montoneros became one organisation under the latter's name.

For most Argentines it was a dangerous and confusing time to live in. Carrying a gun was not unusual, tension was constant and everywhere was the potential danger of a bomb exploding near you or your being caught in the middle of a firefight. People lived in fear and it was never clear where threats would come from nor whom one could trust. While the use of fake IDs was rampant – if not mandatory – among the guerrillas, most members of the military, the police and other law enforcement agencies were seldom seen in uniform. Equally, wearing uniform in public places was discouraged for cadets in military academies.

In October 1975, following a particularly vicious attack of Montoneros on the 29th Mountain Infantry Regiment in Formosa, the government of Isabel Perón issued three decrees ordering the Armed Forces "to carry out all the military and security operations necessary to annihilate the action of subversive elements in all the territory of the Nation". Congress immediately ratified the decrees, none of which was made public until 24 September 1983.

At the beginning of 1976 the country was riddled with 600% annual-rate inflation, riots and crimes were escalating, and terrorist activities were out of control. The administration was paralysed. On 26 March, answering demands from almost every political leader in the opposition and with strong public support, a military Junta took power, beginning the six-year long period named "Process of National Reorganisation".

It proved to be disastrous. To begin with, the Junta was made up of the three most senior officers of each force, the Army, the Navy and the Air Force. These three branches had a history of mutual mistrust and differed fundamentally in their philosophy and background.

While the Navy was – and still is – shaped around Nelsonian values, the Army was modeled on the pattern of the German soldier. While the Navy was traditionally and fiercely anti-Perónist, the Army was split. The Air Force was mistrusted by both the Navy and the Army. A "newcomer" created under Perón, its members were often referred to as "pancakes" by the other two branches, in reference to their ability to "turn upside-down" in the air. The infamous moniker dates back to 16 June 1955, when a group of military and civilians opposing Perón's regime – which was far from democratic – tried to stage a coup and kill the president. During the attack, naval planes bombed and strafed the iconic Plaza de Mayo, facing the Government Palace, killing 380 and wounding around 700. The Air Force planes accompanying them were supposed to do their share, but in a tardy show of loyalty to Perón, they decided not to use their weapons and just flew over the plaza. To their credit, they were to prove their valour beyond everyone's expectations during the Malvinas war.

This lack of trust between services reached to all ranks and was not a good start. Additionally, personalities played a crucial role in the Junta. General Videla, chief of the Army, was a dedicated professional of strong Catholic conviction. He was an honest soldier, and lacked the political abilities the task claimed. Admiral Massera, chief of the Navy, was another animal altogether: smart, charismatic and with an agenda of his own, he was ruthless and ambitious. Unlike Videla, he was popular both with the officers and the ranks, and had craftily and patiently raised the loyalty of a group of senior officers to being almost unconditional. He disliked Videla's cautious ways but was very much aware of the Army's importance as the largest armed force. Historic revisionism has revealed that, aside from several well known efforts to get Perón's blessings while being already chief of the Navy, he also carried out negotiations with the top cats of several terrorist organisations.

To fight the urban guerrillas who were growing stronger by the day, the Junta resorted to unconventional fighting methods that had been learned at officer-level courses in French-occupied Algiers and in CIA training camps in Central America, and had been practised in the 1950s in conflicts that were by then almost forgotten. These were, after all, the seventies.

What started as a dim light at the end of the tunnel of Argentine politics soon turned into a very dark night. While still adhering in principle to the initial aim of returning government to the people as soon as possible, successive Juntas proved their lack of competence to administer the State, while the already fragmented base of the deposed political structure continued to weaken under every possible kind of repressive measure.

By 1981, General Leopoldo Fortunato Galtieri led the Junta as chief of the Army. His Junta co-member, Admiral Isaac Anaya, had been long obsessed with the idea of returning the Malvinas to national sovereignty. Driven by a combination of Anaya's enthusiasm and demands, growing social unrest and the apparent inability of the British government to answer the country's claims for sovereignty over the Malvinas, he ordered the creation of a plan to retake the islands. It was initially to be carried out in late 1982, but complications (widely published since) made Operation Rosario take place earlier.

What followed was the war, brief and brutal.

*

On the early afternoon of 26 March 1982 I was ordered to gather a group of eight men from my Special Forces unit for a special mission. I was then serving as the Operations Officer in the APBT (Agrupación de Buzos Tácticos). Although in the previous few days the Wardroom had been buzzing with rumours about the developments in South Georgia, no hint of the upcoming operation had reached us yet. That night, together with a group of Comandos Anfibios led by Lieutenant (Junior Grade) Bernardo Schweitzer, we travelled down to the Puerto Belgrano Naval Base, some 400 kilometres south of our units' location. On arrival we met Lieutenant-Commander Pedro Giacchino, who was to be our group commander. In total we were sixteen, a mix of BBTT (Buzos Tácticos) and Comandos Anfibios.

The Task Force sailed on 28 March, and the first men to land on the Islands were our group's scouts, Lieutenant Schweitzer and a corporal from the Comandos Anfibios. This happened, contrary to the description of the operation in several books on the war, with the use of rubber boats and shortly before midnight on 1 April. Led by Lieutenant-Commander Pedro Giacchino, we navigated the distance from Mullet Creek to Government House at the Islands' capital in the dark, and reached our target before first light. Thus on the morning of 2 April, as we were trying to overcome the resistance of the Royal Marine Commandos shooting at us from inside the house, Lieutenant-Commander Giacchino was hit in the chest and fell to the ground. I was shadowing his movements, and was also then hit by three different aimed shots: one went through my right elbow, another through my lower torso and the third struck the top of the Swiss Army pocket-knife fastened to my belt over my left groin. All bullets came from different weapons.

I was immediately stunned, but nevertheless remained conscious. More than one and a half hours later we were finally assisted, once the firing had stopped and the area was secured. By then, Corporal Urbina had been seriously wounded while trying to help us, and Lieutenant-Commander Giacchino had lost so much blood that he died before reaching the hospital at Stanley. Once in the hospital, my injuries were inspected by a team of doctors. I clearly remember a female doctor providing me with a confusing diagnosis. "You're through, baby," she said. I wondered for a long time whether this had meant that I was alive or already dead. After this came a ride on a stretcher lashed up to the side of a helicopter that landed on the deck of ARA *Almirante Irizar*, our designated hospital ship, followed by another flight back to the airport, where I was lifted on board an aircraft, still strapped down on the same stretcher, and evacuated to Comodoro Rivadavia on the mainland.

I arrived in the local hospital once again via a helicopter and was already very weak. Everything reached me through a dense fog that was growing increasingly darker. Whilst my wounds were being X-rayed, I heard a nurse ask my name. On hearing my answer, the radiologist asked if I was related to a friend of his, who indeed, happened to be my father. Happy at the unexpected coincidence, he then told me that none of my vital organs seemed to be severely damaged. Those words are the last thing I was to remember from the whole episode before waking up several hours later, after three consecutive surgery operations.

My wife and parents were at my side, having been flown in by the Navy. My Executive Officer was also there, still in combat clothes. Then he told me about Lieutenant-Commander Giacchino's death and the outcome of the mission. It took me months to recover completely, and the conflict was already over when I was declared fit for duty. From an almost perfectly executed military operation engineered to place Argentina in a better bargaining position concerning the Islands, it had evolved into a full-fledged confrontation, killing hundreds of men and plunging their families into grief and filling them with hatred that was not there before the conflict.

I was decorated as a hero before the conflict ended. At the time my feelings were that I did not deserve this. I still think that way. I have been told that a nation needs heroes, but it still feels unfair. Many braver people died on the Islands. I was perfectly prepared for this "first in" as a career officer and member of an elite unit. Indeed this operation met all the expectations I had of the life I had chosen At twenty-eight years of age and married just three months before, I was a member of the prototype "band of brothers". The same elation that William Shakespeare had applied to King Henry V's words just before the Battle of Agincourt was in the air, although there was nothing that one would label "patriotic" in my attitude. I was as sceptical as ever about the soundness of the decision, and cannot recall many of us having intense feelings about the Islands. Speaking only for myself, the whole idea of fighting was a personal challenge.

We were to spearhead an operation directed against an enemy I had learned to admire. As a young man, my concepts of courage and duty were shaped on a mixture of Argentina's own war-waging tradition and many of Rudyard Kipling's characters, probably because I had been educated at an English school in Buenos Aires. Combat was the perfect arena to find out the type of stuff I was made of. And there I was, going in with a group of men who were as brave as, or possibly braver than, myself. We were perfectly honed for the mission, fit as fiddles, and happy as partygoers. I trusted all and everyone, as as I have not trusted anyone since.

Others may discuss whether the cause of this campaign was evil or just, but as a young officer it was not for me to analyse the politics behind the decisions. Today I am convinced that the fog of war as defined by Clausewitz had a significant role in the escalation of events that followed, but such is the danger of waging war and such is the nature of men. The Clausewitzian statement that "war is not only a political issue but more precisely a political instrument, or a continuation of political relations; a way of handling these through other means" applies in my view to both the Argentine and British Governments, who sought not only to put an end to their diplomatic differences, but also overcome their respective internal political situations. In retrospect, I marvel at the inability of our Government to realise at the time that Great Britain had already embarked on a war. Well into the campaign I remember our leaders' political objective was still to induce the international community into voting for a diplomatic solution to regain the sovereignty of the Islands. Mrs Thatcher's objective was only to punish the aggression.

I make this digression in order to introduce an anecdote told to me shortly after the war which, apparently, is true. In the early planning stages of the invasion, probably early December 1981, a highly respected retired Argentine Admiral was called in by the planners of Operation Blue (later renamed Rosario) to express his views on the issue. As soon as he learned about the invasion, he asked to see the plans made to attack London. Aghast, everybody turned to look at him, and one of the most senior officers asked: "London! With all due respect, sir, are you out of your wits?" The retired Admiral looked back at him and said: "If you are planning to make war on the Brits and do not have plans to attack London, then the mad one is not me!"

Nonetheless, the sad result was that from both sides a grand total of 904 lives were lost in the conflict: a ratio of precisely one war fatality for every two inhabitants of the Islands. This is a unique statistic. Thirty warships and support ships were sunk or damaged, and 138 aircraft were either destroyed or captured. As for that morning, all of this was still part of the future. Life was beautiful and everything exciting in a way I have never experienced since. The examples of heroes were in our minds and, with them, the feeling of playing a small, but meaningful, role in the history of our nation. It was a great moment, and I have never felt a similar intensity from life since.

As mentioned before, I was physically powerless after having been hit three times by the enemy's bullets. Lieutenant-Commander Giacchino lay at my side. I recall witnessing what appeared to be his death when he was being lifted onto something that resembled a stretcher. I was somehow confused, and felt weird rushes of pain from my injured back. My right arm hurt terribly. However, by and large, I appeared to be all right even though feeling very light-headed after an injection of morphine given to me by a quick-thinking Royal Marine Commando. Using my blood as makeshift ink, he daubed the letter "M" on my forehead to indicate that morphine had already been injected. Another morphine injection by error could have had fatal consequences.

It was extremely cold. I remember a bundle of funny details and anecdotes from these moments which were probably ones of the utmost gravity and drama. Nevertheless, I retain a feeling of having lived through them all not only from a certain distance, but also through a gauze curtain. There were, of course, flashes of family and personal memories. But most of my thoughts were monopolised by things that were happening there and then, as if I had entered another reality which possessed its own particular separate urgencies.

Questions about life or death were not at all on my mind. I can understand perfectly that these types of thoughts torture the minds of men who are unlucky enough to come under heavy shelling or bombing. This mind-shattering nightmare did not apply to me. I was incredibly lucky by being wounded as fast and clean as it can possibly be.

All memories from the moment I was hit until collapsing at the hospital X-ray room remain vivid. Things seemed to be happening in a strange, quieter rhythm. Lieutenant-Commander Giacchino was speaking to me in an urgent and obviously painful way. The Governor's geese were walking clumsily around us. Oblivious of the bullets, I heard Corporal Urbina's cry of frustration when he was hit. All this was occurring while I gradually slid from that fantastic excitement into a peaceful quietness. I could not move and had lost the grip on my weapon. The sun was quickly coming up and I could still hear the voices and bullets, but was sinking away very fast. I heard the rotating blades of a chopper, but could not see it. The sky was blue and I remember thinking that it was not bad to die on such a beautiful morning, amongst friends, and lying on the grass.

The Royal Marine Commando who gave me the morphine snapped me out of my reverie. I could not speak or move, and my vision was already tunnelling. I nevertheless could interpret he was not one of us and, for one endless moment, was convinced that he had come to finish me off with his combat knife. After being given the morphine, I clearly remember my desperation at feeling unable to draw enough air into my lungs.

While at the hospital ship, I remember the sailors were having difficulties in getting my stretcher through the narrow passages on board. There was blood pouring from it and, as it was tilted at every door entrance, a mess was made on the deck. All the faces I saw were talking to me – but I could not hear them. Once again, one question came to mind. Was I still alive? A classmate recognised my face under the camouflage and grasped my wounded arm passionately. It hurt like hell, but I could not tell him to let go. I could not speak at all. Members of my APBT unit were standing on the tarmac as I was being lifted inside the aircraft. My Commanding Officer was there with them. As the stretcher went by, I saw them looking at me, their faces grey with exhaustion and eyes lowered. Nobody spoke. Nobody reached to touch me. I was certain that death had incurred. It did not feel too bad.

The interior of the aircraft had been stripped bare of all seats and, throughout the flight to Comodoro Rivadavia, a soldier kept slapping me on the face to prevent me from losing consciousness. I would not have survived without him. I was angry with myself for being unable to get back to the front in the Islands. The war was certain to end soon, and I felt the opportunity of experiencing it had been missed by my being shot on its very first day.

However the war did indeed eventually end, but I was still unable to return to military service, my right arm being still useless. On rejoining my unit in November, I made a couple of parachute jumps in order to leave no doubts about my recovery. Life continued. Again, I consider myself very lucky. I had enjoyed the privilege of fighting alongside brave men and surviving almost unscathed. It could be said that I was just a visitor to the front having, through my wounds, escaped the long and dreadful hours of vigil, the bombing, the freezing nights, the darkness, the hunger and the horror of seeing men killed, blown to pieces or gruesomely dismembered at my side.

I cannot speak as a war casualty. I do not know what these extremes do to men's minds but, still, war is part of our nature. It is also a terrible affair. Yet life can be quite hard even in the absence of war, and many veterans of terrifying situations are able to suppress their emotional experiences in order to become functional again. It is widely accepted that the effects of combat on men have a direct relationship with several factors regarding each individual, for example, heredity, upbringing, the way he and his immediate group "feel" about the war, the relationship with his comrades, or the harmony of his private life. Some of these factors can be overshadowed by those instruments of collective influence that are used in the military, such as discipline. I was very well equipped in these areas, and it was this foundation, along with the briefness of my combat experience, that provided no time for me to crack.

No doubt the excitement of that day magnified my impression of everything happening around me. I believe this explains the bright aura that surrounds each of my memories of that morning. The sounds were louder, the light brighter, the deeds worthier. As regards any negative effect I may have suffered as a consequence, then virtually every new experience is dulled in comparison. On the other hand I became over-sensitive to trivialities that before would have not prompted me to react. Another possible effect is that some of my memories have become quite scrambled, while others have disappeared with no trace at all. There are periods of my life of which I can recall hardly anything. Most of these are very short, but some become significant deficiencies, as when meeting people I have met in the past, yet I cannot remember them. Many of those who knew me before that morning in the Malvinas agree on saying that the war affected my personality radically, a fact which I find difficult to either accept or deny. According to these opinions, patterns of thought that I am convinced had always been with me were not there before.

If anything, I feel the experience strengthened me. Along with the pride I felt immediately from having been part of re-taking the Islands on 2 April 1982, I gained the satisfaction of proving my faithfulness to my comrades, profession and country. I cannot imagine a better deal. If I were to pinpoint oddities of my character possibly emerging from some sort of post-war trauma, then the following ought to be highlighted: a tendency to downplay the urgency or graveness of situations, a deeper lack of interest in competition, and an enhanced scepticism about almost everything.

To many others, destiny was not so merciful. I can barely imagine the horror and anguish of a bombardment; the despair of the trenches; the filth; the cold and the misery. Nor can I grasp the gruesome agony of those unlucky ones whose ships and aeroplanes were sunk or destroyed.

Wars are ugly affairs in which people break important patterns of behaviour, and this one also saw a few former enemies joining efforts behind the same cause. It could be said that despite all its misery it briefly offered a grim but effective way to heal a distressed society. In a more general view, sometimes it seems to me that the war happened in another world, under a different code than the one we now live by. This was a war between two countries which share comparable cultural values and love freedom. In spite of a few crude and relatively ineffective propaganda stunts, the contenders were not dehumanised in the minds of their opponents and I still believe that hatred was never a major factor. It was not bitterness that drove either side against the other, as much as plain realism. It was a soldiers' war with no civilian targets. Combat was close, it had a human scale.

*

After attending the Nottingham University conference in November 2006, at which participants on both sides of the war met, and before leaving the UK, I paid a visit to Victoria Cook and Victoria Main from the Research and Information Department at the Imperial War Museum in London. They had approached me earlier at the suggestion of Mike Seear, in order to see whether I could somehow contribute to the exhibition that the museum was staging throughout the summer of 2007 to mark the twenty-fifth anniversary of the conflict. Needless to say, they were extremely kind and interested in my story, so they invited me to the exhibition's opening. Though I was keen to provide them with an item for the exhibition, in the end this was not possible.

This was how I ended showing up at the Imperial War Museum on 14 May 2007. I was greeted there by the Museum Chairman Air Chief-Marshal Sir Peter Squire and was immediately charmed by his warm welcome. To my delight, I was then introduced to other former opponents some of whom I was able to recognise at first sight, having seen their faces in pictures before. There were Rick Jolly, the intense and humane combat medic who made no distinction of sides when it came to help the suffering; Major-General Julian Thompson with his irresistible sincerity and warmth and his subordinate Lieutenant-Colonel Peter Cameron, a man of enormous sympathy and arresting friendliness; Admiral Sir Alan West, whom I recognised from pictures I had seen with mutual friends in Argentina; the brave and silent Sergeant Bill Belcher; Nicci Pugh, the festive nurse; charming Peter Holdgate and Lieutenant-Colonel Ewen Southby-Tailyour. I had wanted to meet Ewen from the first time I heard of him and always found it grim to be on opposing sides, for all I heard about him could tell me that we had many interests in common. Needless to say, my expectations fell short. These were fantastic people and they made me feel extremely welcome. This was the day for interviews, so I had the pleasure to meet Cliff Caswell from *Soldier* magazine as well as to talk to BBC radio, *The Sun* and the *Daily Telegraph*. BBC TV and BBC History also asked me about my story and how I felt twenty-five years after. After these meetings and having toured the Exhibition, most of us gathered at a nearby pub to celebrate with a few pints. It was unforgettable. All I can say is that moments like those are what make all life worth it.

The evening ended at "the Rag" – the Army and Navy Club in St James – where we all sat to dinner under the gaze of impressive-looking portraits of uniformed heroes. After dinner there were spirits and cigars at the bar of this venerable institution. Another dream come true.

The following day we arrived a bit late, blame it on London traffic for beginners. As we were ushered to the hall where the opening ceremony was to take place, I found my friends already involved in conversations. Rick Jolly came forward and introduced me to the late Major-General Sir Jeremy Moore, also informing me that Margaret Thatcher was present. It was only then that the phrase whispered at our arrival by one of the staff girls ("the Baroness has just arrived") made sense to me. I shook the old warrior's hand and he seemed pleased to meet me. This gentleman, many years my senior, had received my commander's surrender. He looked a little frail twenty-five years later as he stabbed the air with his walking stick – alas, he would pass away in a few months – but it was easy to tell I was in front of serious soldiering.

Suddenly and as I was turning to face Julian Thompson, who had appeared at my side, an energetic giant spotted me from the other end of the room and approached with large steps and an immense grin. "I've been looking for you!" he almost shouted, his arms wide as he offered his hand and hugged my shoulder. It was Major Mike Norman, the officer who led the Royal Marines defending Government House in Stanley that distant morning, the guy who ordered his men to open fire on us, the man whose orders resulted in the first Argentine casualties of the war. He merrily led me to meet Sir Rex Hunt, the former Governor of the Islands and his wife Mavis. We all shared a great moment, not the less cheerfully when Lady Mavis scolded me for trampling on her rose bushes during the morning of our attack.

Sir Peter Squire was now up on the stage and the voices quickly died away. As Museum Chairman, he introduced the Exhibition offering a short account of the conflict and its circumstances, the challenges met and the bravery of the British forces. For the first time in the morning I realised that I was the only Argentine on the premises, a discovery that I met with both sorrow and pride. When his words praised Baroness Thatcher's steadfastness and thoroughness I was delighted to hear isolated voices around me shouting Aye! or Yes!, the feet stomping the floor in support of the speaker's statements with apparent disregard of etiquette. This fantastic expression of the British spirit of individuality has always sparked my imagination, for I imagine it comes to us from ancient feudal times when semi-barbaric warriors vowed their support to their sovereign.

Shortly after his words, Sir Peter joined us, tactful and smiling. He then whispered to me: "The Baroness is aware that you are in the room and wishes to know if you would care to approach." Not only the invitation, but the way it was worded, redoubled my impression of reviving an era I thought did not exist anymore.

Soon he was back to guide me towards a sitting group amongst whom Baroness Thatcher was present, her back to the assembly. At a sign from one of her companions she rose and turned towards us, her hand extended. I was a trifle stunned. Slightly taller than me, she was exactly what I expected, elegant, pale and measured. Almost like a Gainsborough I thought, to the Reynolds that would have been a better brush to Sir Jeremy Moore who was sitting beside her. We shook hands and she said she was pleased to meet me and see me there. She added that the conflict had been a sad occasion but "very convenient for the kingdom". I did not comment, but instead replied something along the lines of having regretted Sir Rex's rejection to my invitation for tea that distant morning. The lady is bright. Smiling dangerously, she said "But they told me you hadn't brought the tea! In any case," she added, "I wouldn't repeat it if I were you. Please don't do it again." She then asked me about the veterans in Argentina, how were they received and taken care of after the conflict. Then she inquired on how and why I had come to the Exhibition, about my present life, and what it was like to live in Norway. It was all very polite, quite jolly indeed. As I was about to take my leave she asked how did it feel to have come back alive. I told her it felt great, though sometimes I missed the excitement. She was holding my hand in hers when she replied, "I do too...".

Twenty-six years after the conflict, I was old enough to look back on it as the memories of a world already gone. We had a way then, an understanding of things, of relations between people that has changed dramatically since. It is natural that it happens this way, but it is nevertheless somehow unsettling to behold. Most of the characters of this fantastic adventure that began in Nottingham lived through that world. They remember it, too. It held something which made possible that former opponents share a laugh and be fearlessly human to each other, in a greater sense. Even the Iron Lady felt this, I know. And now that I have looked into her eyes, isn't it grand to think that she knows that I also do?

First in, first out

Mike Seear

And so the method of employing the military –
  When ten to one, surround them.
  When five to one, attack them.
  When two to one, do battle with them.
  When matched, then divide them.
  When fewer, then defend against them.
  Thus a small enemy's tenacity
  Is a large enemy's catch.
                                    – Sun Tzu, 2002, chapter 3

Retired *Capitán de Fregata* Diego F. García Quiroga of the Armada de la República Argentina had a liking for literature, and his English school education in Buenos Aires gave him a strong Anglophile tendency. These two factors and shared military backgrounds undoubtedly enriched our conversations. It was usual that these contained a joke or two which, in turn, triggered characteristic whinnies of laughter from him. The mutually rewarding friendship contributed to a swift delivery, after my bold request, of his version of the Argentine Task Force deployment to recover the Malvinas. Prior to his extraordinary week, which had culminated in that pivotal Friday of 2 April 1982, the dark, powerfully built young officer had enjoyed six years of service. He had sailed in the Antarctic on both a naval cargo ship and small corvette, cruised to the USA and Europe (including a visit to Southampton to pick up the special Sea Dart missile containers mounted on Argentine Navy 42 Type frigates), patrolled in the Beagle and Magellan channels, trained for nine months in 1980 at the Mar del Plata Navy Diving School to qualify as a combat diver, and completed a one-month parachute training course near Buenos Aires.

Finally, twelve months later, he earned his "weapons" orientation by attending the Surface Officers' School before being posted in mid-January 1982 to the *Agrupación de Buzos Tácticos* (Tactical Divers Group) at the Mar del Plata Naval Base 400 kilometres south-east of Buenos Aires. As a twenty-eight-year-old *Teniente de Fregata* (Sub-Lieutenant) recently married to Alejandra, he became this unit's Operations Officer (O3) and also commanded one of its (three) operational Sections, that is Combat Divers, Mini-subs and Amphibious Operations. Initially he was training with the latter, but officers were expected to rotate within the year to perform a minimum of two operations with each Section. The APBT was attached to the Submarine Forces Command and considered themselves the premier Argentine Navy special operations force, with their highly qualified combat divers, underwater demolition technicians and parachutists who operated in extreme environments such as tropical, maritime and Antarctic-equivalent climates. But it was not the only Special Forces unit at Mar del Plata. There was also the *Agrupación de Comandos Anfibios* (Amphibious Commando Group). Diego explained the "in-house" difference:

If one has to draw similarities, you could think of the *Buzos Tácticos* as the US Navy Seals. These guys are Navy blue, all the way. While not in the unit, they serve on ships and carry on with the normal life of a sailor or "deck officer". The *Comandos Anfibios*, on the other hand, is a unit born from within the Marines. In Argentina, the Marines are still a force within the Navy, but both are essentially different (not a difficult thing to grasp if you are a sailor). Chronologically, at least in Argentina, the *Buzos Tácticos* came first by a long way. Most of the stealth tactics the *Comandos* use today are (we like to believe) copied from ours. They do not employ them a lot, though: they are too noisy (after all, they are Marines). Again, trying to compare them to something in the US Armed Forces, you could think of them as the Recon units within the US Marines. Armed Services being what they are, and with Argentina's Armed Services in constant need of budget improvement, spares and supplies, the fight for resources can become nasty between units that, although belonging to different Services, carry out similar operations. The result was an historical animosity between the *Buzos Tácticos* and "our cousins". Yet many of us still regard *Operación Rosario* as the successful event that brought these units closer together in such a fraught time.

Operación Azul (Blue), the planned re-taking of South Georgia on Saturday, 3 April 1982, was already being mounted when, on 26 March, Diego received his briefing to relieve the Duty Officer of the Day at the Mar del Plata Naval Base:

We had been training quite hard and the previous few days had been hectic, with our spirits fuelled by a new tension. This affected all conversations in the base's wardroom, with a focus on analysing the scarce information received from certain operations in the South Georgias. Our CO, Lieutenant-Commander Alfredo Cufré, had been summoned up to the Puerto Belgrano Naval Base, where the Naval

Operational Command was located. Our unit knew that a "star team" of *Buzos Tácticos* had been hastily put together some days before and deployed to a still secret destination. Such a procedure was not uncommon, as not all *Buzos Tácticos* in the Navy are lucky enough to serve in the unit. After receiving the special one-year training that makes them "one of us", they are released to the Naval Detailer and go off to serve on "normal" postings throughout the Fleet, eventually returning to the unit. Some never serve in the unit again, but only join it for special tactical exercises.

As the day's routines were coming to an end, I received a message from our CO to put the teams on standby for immediate deployment. To everybody's joy I cancelled all leave warrants right away, making myself immediately popular. Our CO arrived back soon that evening and, as I had been already relieved from the duties of my watch to attend to "things that mattered", he instructed me to proceed to our neighbours, the *Agrupación de Comandos Anfibios*, and make myself available to their CO, Lieutenant-Commander Sánchez Sabarots. Orders are orders and, despite the historical animosity, I went to them.

When I entered the holy "Action Room" in the *Comandos'* building, their Executive Officer (XO), Lieutenant Bardi, was busily scribbling on a blackboard the list of personal equipment that men should carry for this operation, of which I still knew nothing at all. The CO was there, and he did not hesitate in announcing that, along with seven other *Buzos Tácticos* of my choice, we were to join a mixed assault group made up of *Buzos* and *Comandos* under the command of a *Comando* by the name of *Capitán de Corbeta* (Lieutenant-Commander) Pedro Edgardo Giacchino. I knew Giacchino briefly from before (he was also the XO of the 2nd Marine Infantry Battalion) and liked the guy, but had not seen him in a while. It was then I learned of *Operación Rosario* (although it did not have that name as yet), and that we were destined for the Malvinas. Such news was quite exciting, but what amazes me today was the speed with which one ignored any previous personal notion of the political issues at stake. That is what training does to you. It gets you focused on the mission, but makes you virtually blind to anything else. I still wonder if this is altogether a good thing.

There was also nothing that could be called "patriotic" in my attitude. Indeed I was sceptical, and remain so, about the whole affair, and do not recall many of us feeling very strongly about the Islands either. For me, the whole idea of fighting was a personal affair.

Information at this stage, though, was scarce. More specifics would be made known once we met Giacchino and remainder of the team in Puerto Belgrano the next day. My task was to concentrate now on picking up the men, ensure we had all the required equipment, and make it to the buses which would depart from the base at 23.00 hours.

There was clearly considerable urgency to proceed with their mission as they would be travelling most of the night to Puerto Belgrano, the largest naval base in Argentina, situated some 400 kilometres south of Mar del Plata:

Back at the *Buzos Tácticos* HQ, I was debriefed by my CO. It was clear to us that, while Giacchino's assault group was to carry out a typical commando raid in which he would not need any assistance from us, some internal politics were evident in setting up the combined operation. There was actually more to it, as I learned later. Cufré was for some reason not willing then to make clear what, in retrospect, was a major shortfall in the *Comandos Anfibios'* organisation. It should be noted that, being recruited from the core of Marine infantry battalions, the *Comandos Anfibios* lacked any technical skills. But this mission would need, as I would soon learn, men with navigation, communications and power-plant operating skills. In other words, the mission needed us, as most of our men had undergone that type of training by serving on ships in the Fleet. It also needed somebody who could communicate in English.

The other *Buzos Tácticos* (more than forty men) would be employed in the way our field manual dictates. Operating from a submarine submerged way beyond the surge line, they would paddle and swim ashore to clear the landing beaches of obstacles and set up signals to mark the landing alleys, secure the areas near the beach and its exits to the hinterland, and wait for the main force to land on the Malvinas at first light.

Quickly I made a mental selection of the men who would accompany me. This would be no swimming contest, so I chose those whom, in my opinion, were experienced, mature and calm. These were not only the oldies, but also some of the jocks. All were tough and had been at it far longer than me. They would know how to take care of themselves and, as long as things were done according to regulations and logic, I was not interested in imposing on them my personal views on their choice of weapons. All went for the Para FAL[1] – a very reliable 7.62 mm calibre light Argentine rifle with a folding stock that was the *Buzo*'s "sleeping companion". I was convinced that my choice was better in picking an Argentine- manufactured *Halcón* sub-machine gun commonly used by our police forces. It is easy to carry, has a decent firing rate and an 11.25 mm calibre round that kills what it hits.

I was going over these arrangements when Lieutenant Carlos Robbio, the unit's XO, arrived on deck. Using British terminology, Second-in-Command equates to XO. But in such a specialist and small unit this function was also required to participate in the Section Commander *roulement* along with the other officers. So, far from having just an administrative role, the *Buzo Táctico* XO is also quite operative and works closely with the Operations Officer, his immediate subordinate. Carlos and I go way back. We started our naval life together when we entered the Naval High School as thirteen-year olds. It was 1967. He then entered the Naval Academy without pausing for a doubt, while I entertained my flower-power dreams for a couple of years more before deciding to re-enlist. Since then he was my senior in rank, and we have always been the best of friends.

Carlos was rapidly absorbing the facts, for he had been out minding his own business until called and was not yet fully aware of the details of the deployment. He had driven into the base hoping to have dinner together, and brought both our wives to say goodbye. My wife had with her two books for my trip: an annotated edition of von Clausewitz's *On War* and a pocket volume of American short stories. Little did I know that soon these were to become my contribution to counteracting somebody else's boredom on the battlefield rather than mine. We were quite busy, so dinner plans were ditched, the goodbyes hastily said there and then, and off departed the girls. Neither of them knew, and we did not say, that we were bound for the Malvinas the day afterwards.

Later that evening, the bus departure was postponed until 01.00 hours. We used a couple of hours to drive home, touch base once more with our families, and finally have dinner. At precisely 00.15 hours on 27 March, Sub-Lieutenant Bernardo Schweitzer of the

---

[1] Para FAL – *Fusil Automático Liviano*. Exactly like the Argentine Marine and Army standard-issue FAL rifle but with a hollow collapsible stock, the weapon is so named because it was designed for paratrooper use.

Comando Anfibio rang our doorbell. Still with a light heart, I said my goodbyes to Alejandra and drove to the base in Bernardo's car. He was probably the only *Comando Anfibio* at that time I could refer to as a friend. His father and mine had been classmates in the Military High School before my father entered the Navy. Bernardo is a great chap, and a very capable officer. The magnitude of the mission, though, and its possible outcomes, had started to cross our minds. Although no one showed any gloominess when we met at the bus, it was clear to me that those who did not know yet what we were being sucked into could easily tell that this was no exercise. Memories of 1978 and the Chilean border crisis were still fresh. [2]

We arrived at Puerto Belgrano excruciatingly early in the morning. It was cold. The trip had been uneventful, and the only thing everybody wanted badly was to fall sleep as soon as possible. This was better said than done in an old Navy bus. While we were snoring, the submarine ARA *Santa Fé* was casting off from Mar del Plata with all the other *Buzos Tácticos* on board. She was making for a rendezvous with the Task Force at "El Rincón", a patch of water right out of Bahía Blanca, some 30 nautical miles from Puerto Belgrano.

Once breakfast and transit accommodation were arranged for the men, the officers were summoned to attend a briefing in the Wardroom of the 2nd Marine Infantry Battalion. Giacchino was not there on my arrival, but I met Sub-Lieutenant Lugo (*Comando Anfibio*), who was serving as the Communications Officer in the 1st Marine Infantry Battalion. One year my senior in rank, he would be our Second-in-Command. Shortly afterwards Giacchino entered,

---

[2] In late December 1978 all Argentine military garrisons stationed along the Chilean border went to Alert 1 and the fleet was deployed on *Operación Soberanía* (Sovereignty), awaiting orders to block the Southern passages. This situation (which some consider as being Argentina's own "Cuban missile crisis") was the climax to that year of sabre-rattling between Argentina and Chile regarding the sovereignty dispute over three islands located near the eastern mouth of the Beagle Channel. An imminent war was finally averted by Papal mediation, which favoured the Chilean position. However, for the Argentine military on the ground (including Diego) it meant deployment, excitement, uncertainty and a big brouhaha at higher levels of command, which re-examined a large number of operational procedures. The crisis also became a catalyst that rapidly enabled the military to regain awareness of its real mission after a long decade of focusing on counter-insurgency.

trailing Sub-Lieutenant Alvárez (*Comando Anfibio*) who was the last officer to join us. Alvárez was a classmate of Robbio's, and had been the Officer Cadet in charge of my division while at the Naval Academy. We knew each other and always got along well. He was the Intelligence Officer in the 1st Marine Infantry Battalion. We were told nothing memorable at the briefing, but had now got the entire group together, and Giacchino confirmed Stanley was the target. More information was to be given out as soon as we were underway.

The rest of that day was spent in arranging accommodation for us on board the ARA *Santísima Trinidad,* a British Type 42 destroyer similar to HMS *Sheffield*, which was hit and sunk by one of our air-launched Exocet missiles five weeks later. We were also co-ordinating schedules, chasing misplaced equipment and reviewing checklists. Lugo and I were busy resolving these issues, while Alvárez and Giacchino attended several, endless co-ordination meetings for this first major combined military operation since our Wars of Independence from 1810-18. Somehow expecting our group to be the first out, we stacked all our things inside the helicopter hangar, leaving good space for the chopper's crew to go around in case of an unexpected take-off. It was late when we collapsed on our bunks after reviewing the little information gathered by Giacchino and Alvárez, and managing to set this up – along with some pictures from the Islands and a profile map of the Stanley area – on a makeshift blackboard in the cabin that the four of us were sharing.

Designated Task Force 40.1, the landing force ships consisted of the amphibious landing ship ARA *Cabo San Antonio*, two Type 42 destroyers (one of which was the flagship *Santísima Trinidad*), two frigates, a submarine, a polar vessel and a transport ship. There were 904 men in the amphibious force bound for the Malvinas. The bulk were on board the *Cabo San Antonio*, which would eventually land them at Yorke Bay in the Port William area north-east of Stanley. One key sub-unit was a platoon from the 25th Infantry Regiment commanded by Lieutenant-Colonel Mohamed Ali Seineldin, my dinner table companion at the Military Circle building in Buenos Aires twenty-five years later. Although they were the 25th Infantry Regiment's Advance Party, which would become the permanent garrison, their first vital task was to capture Government House. However, the Special Forces would be the first to land and carry out the preliminary operation of seizing the Royal Marine barracks at Moody Brook and (Giacchino's task) various key points in the town. They would be launched from *Contralmirante* (Rear-Admiral) Gualter Allara's flagship onto their target beach at Mullet Creek three kilometres south of

Stanley. The aircraft carrier ARA *Veinticinco de Mayo* would be the flagship of Task Force 20, comprising all other serviceable naval ships, which would give distant support to the landing force.

Whether by design or coincidence, the Argentines had followed one tenet in Sun Tzu's "strategy of attack" to the letter. Surround the diminutive British garrison of Naval Party 8901, comprising sixty-nine Royal Marines and eleven armed Royal Navy sailors (the local small Falkland Islands Defence Force was a *de facto* non-combatant unit), with such overwhelming force that resistance would be pointless. Success and minimal casualties then would be guaranteed. It worked out like that too, because "a small enemy's tenacity" did indeed become "a large enemy's catch".

Santísima Trinidad cast off from Puerto Belgrano next day on Sunday, 28 March. She carried all the *Agrupación de Comandos Anfibios* (eighty-four men) with their CO and staff and us eight *Buzos Tácticos*. I do not remember anything special about the voyage, but then again, I am used to sailing. Everyone I have met who was there said that the Task Force went through a terrible storm which made most seasick. I do not recall it at all: one of the memories that have slipped from me, along with undoubtedly many others. My only recollection which may have a relation to this elusive storm is of an endless concern for the security outside on deck of the extraordinary amount of stacked inflatable rubber boats and equipment which had been tied down with straps and cables. Several inspection rounds were made daily to check these bundles in spite of the fact that normally, when this type of vessel is underway, circulation through external decks is forbidden.

On 30 March Giacchino issued his mission orders and gave out the assault group's organisation. Altogether we numbered sixteen. This included twenty-two-year-old medical assistant, Sergeant Urbina, who was a late addition and, at the time, undergoing *Comando Anfibio* training. The patrol's code name was *"Técnico"*, soon to be re-named *"Techo"*. Secretly I was already fed up with all this "typical Marine pompous gibberish" from my sailor's point of view. But the power balance was obviously dramatically tilted towards the "greens", as we call Marines, on account of their daily use of combat uniform instead of regular Navy blues. It was my bad luck to be so junior an officer. However, I soon realised nothing could be done about it but behave and do my best.

In the landing operation, twenty-one inflatable boats would be used to carry *"Técnico"* and sixty-eight *Comandos Anfibios*. The organisation of *"Técnico"* was carefully devised to ensure that a cocktail of *Buzos Tácticos* (BT) and *Comandos Anfibios* (CA) flavoured each section. Diego gave me the assault group's detailed composition. It would be divided into four sections with each allocated to a boat. The standard traffic-light colour start sequence was utilised neatly to avoid any confusion in the order of march both at sea and on land. Red Section in Boat 18 was commanded by Lieutenant-Commander Giacchino. One BT, *Cabo Principal* (Sergeant) Alegre, was in this section, the CA members being Sergeants Ortiz and Flores. Sub-Lieutenant Lugo commanded Orange Section in Boat 19. All his men were BTs: *Suboficial Segundo* (Second Petty Officers) Salas and López, and Sergeant Ledesma. In Boat 20 would be Green Section commanded by Diego. Sergeant Urbina was in his section as well as two BTs, Second Petty Officer Cardillo and Sergeant Gómez. Finally, Boat 21 would contain Blue Section. This had the final BT representative in *Suboficial Primero* (First Petty Officer) Mansilla, together with two CAs, Second Petty Officer Gutiérrez and Sergeant Vargas. Their commander was Sub-Lieutenant Alvárez. Moreover, after the Malvinas landing, specific tasks were to be carried out by each section:

Red was to take over the Police Station at Stanley. Orange had to support Green in taking over the Power Station and keeping it running as if nothing had happened. Once this objective was secured, Orange was to support Red in its next task – seizing the Central Telephone Exchange. Blue's task was to detach itself from the assault group on the outskirts of town and set off independently to neutralise a secondary airfield lying further to the east. This was known to us as "antenna range" because of its suspected communications capability with the UK. Intelligence was also utilised. This was contained in a set of 8 x 12cm copies of photographs that Lieutenant-Commander Gaffoglio had managed to snap while working in Stanley as Head of the Argentine Naval Transport Office. Amongst these I remember a sort of family photograph taken in what looked like the living room of Government House.

We spent some hours together with our respective sections planning as much as possible, and reviewing each and every movement to be taken through a built-up area suspected of being very similar to several of our towns in Patagonia. Gómez was to carry the assault group's radio. He was a promising young man, later to be commissioned as a Sub-Lieutenant one year after these events. The radio would let us keep the ships informed of our progress. This would be done by using short English phrases.

On the eve of our 1 April amphibious landing, we were informed of a drastic change in our plans. Naval Central Intelligence suspected that the English on the Islands were already aware of our approach and intentions. Thus it was decided that all of *"Techo"* (now renamed) was to storm Government House so as to take the Governor, Mr Rex Hunt, hostage and then force him to broadcast a radio message to the people of Stanley. This would inform them that the town had been overpowered by Argentine forces and that therefore there was no point in resisting. Every weapon in town had to be surrendered to the detachment waiting in the Town Hall, and daily chores carried out as usual. There was also a minor collateral mission. It consisted of marking a helipad on the soccer field that lay just east of Government House. This was to be the landing place for the helicopter carrying the support echelon sub-unit.

But at the time when all this information reached us, Gaffoglio and his set of photographs had already been flown off to the icebreaker ARA *Almirante Irizar*. This meant that we were left with no other image of the objective than the memory of that living room photograph. Giacchino was not happy. So off he went in search of more useful intelligence, but returned only with a "heavily reliable intelligence report" that the place would be practically undefended. The truth is we were not even sure of where the damn residence was located, not to say of where we might find its front door!

This change of plan had an odd effect on morale because, as we neared the time for landing, there was almost a single thought in everybody's mind: "Please let it happen! Please don't let them abort this operation!"

It was the higher state of British alert that had, in the first instance, led to Seineldin's platoon being redirected from its original Government House objective to another, the seizure of Stanley Airport and clearance of its runway blocked by the Royal Marines.[3] Furthermore the direct action on Government House was key to taking the town with the least possible casualties on either side. But the Royal Marines prime mission on the Islands was to defend the seat of Government. So Giacchino's assault group, at less than half the strength of Sieneldin's well prepared platoon, would discover quickly enough the wildly optimistic nature of

[3] This change of plan, Giacchino's revised mission and other adjustments are contrary to Bicheno (2006, 121) which incorrectly states that the original plan remained as it was because of inflexible Argentine decision-making.

their newly acquired intelligence.

Spirits were still high when the *Santísima Trinidad* sailed at her minimum possible speed into the kelp-thick narrows of Port Harriet. Radar sweeps were now limited to a single sporadic pulse. She would remain at least one nautical mile off Mullet Creek. If one could possibly have checked the depths closer in, the conclusion would have been that no serious sailor with that kind of vessel ought to enter such waters, as these were shallower than two times *Santísima Trinidad*'s draft. Furthermore, manoeuvring space was extremely restricted because of the cove's narrowness. All lights were out. Messages were in whispers, speaker's hands cupped over listener's ear. It was dark and cold.

Supper in the Wardroom had been simple and fast. There was lots of black humour. Giacchino lamented the lack of a camera for photographs. "Some of us might not come back," he prophesied with precision. [...]

The destroyer heaves to. All kitted up and ready, we emerge from the lightless hangar into the freezing night. One by one, the inflatable boats are being lowered into the water. When at deck level, one man jumps into each boat ready to start the outboard engine he had previously covered with a thick dark blanket to prevent the noise being heard from ashore. One, two tugs on the engine's starter cord as soon as the boat touches the sea. If it does not start, ditch it. Another is instantly lowered to replace the valuable asset now hitting the bottom of the icy cove. I see two beautiful outboard engines go down this way.

The heavy nets for allowing the men to scramble down *Santísima Trinidad*'s side are hung out. Everything is happening with incredible swiftness. Not a sound is heard or a question asked. A complex operation is being implemented like a smooth routine. Briefly I sight the scouts setting off in a kayak. They are my good friend Bernardo Schweitzer and a *Comando Anfibio* Second Petty Officer. Using directional "blind" torches, their task is to signal to our boats from the mouth of Mullet Creek.

Camouflaged faces are impossible to identify in the dark. I am hoping not to screw up and land in a boat other than mine. Then somebody grabs my hand, puts a piece of candy in it and whispers in my ear, "Good luck!" It is Lieutenant Vara, the vessel's Ordnance Officer and a caring man. There is no time for thanks. A gentle push tells me it is my turn. As swiftly as possible, I descend into the inky blackness. [...]

Inspirationally as a career officer and member of an élite unit, I was perfectly prepared for this "first-in" operation. It matched all the expectations belonging to my chosen life. We were spearheading an action against an enemy I admired. My concepts of courage and duty were shaped after a mixture of Argentina's own warring tradition and many of Kipling's characters. Combat was the perfect arena to discover and test my true capabilities. The men accompanying me were as brave as or, possibly, braver than me. They were perfectly honed for the mission, fit as fiddles, and happy as party-goers. I trusted them all as I had not trusted anyone before. Life was beautiful, the intensity unique and everything exciting in a way never to be experienced again. It was a great moment.

With the outboard engine fired but idling, each boat was paddled back to its specific position in the row that bobbed one after the other from a length of mooring line towed behind the destroyer-cum-mothership. Once everybody was counted, we cast off from the mooring and started to power up in the wake of the leading boat. The kelp was annoyingly thick. Some of the boats' propellers became entangled in the stuff and one of their occupants had to reach with his arm underwater to remove the seaweed from the screw. Soon all hope of keeping formation vanished and I began to wonder if some of the boats would go astray.

While in this thought-mode, we overtook one of the toiling crews and overheard their conversation, intermingled with their swearing at the kelp. One was asking, "Hey mate! D'you think we'll get some extra dough for this?" He was referring to the "supplementary salary" that the Navy pays to those sailing in latitudes further south than that of Puerto Belgrano. I did not have much to worry about, I thought, as long as our guys were reacting like this to their first war operation.

We arrived at the beach in enough disorder. My Green Section was to provide the security, together with Alvárez's Blue Section, while the others emerged like newborn butterflies from inside their wet suits. Soon afterwards we switched these roles. Swiftly the *Comandos* were swallowed up by the dark in their advance towards Moody Brook. Then we moved off. It was 23.14 (02.14Z) on 1 April. Somehow our assault group had landed more to the east than planned. The error prevented us from rapidly finding the fence marked on the map, so Giacchino decided to drop this reference point. Instead we started to proceed directly towards a dark bulk to the north, guessing that this must be Sapper Hill.

Marching over the soft terrain was difficult. Darkness did not assist our physical efforts although it concealed us well. Giacchino, followed by Ortiz, Alegre and Flores, in the role of navigators, were up front as point section. Behind them were Orange, then Green and, at the rear, Alvárez with Blue. Although trying to focus with all my senses, I missed a step in the darkness and my knee struck a jutting-out rock. It caused formidable pain and this slowed me down. So Giacchino ordered me to change my position in the column to just behind the scouts in order not to delay the march. I felt vexed at my stupidity.

We were wary. About every fifty paces we halted. Then there was a brief wait for our scouts to whistle the all-clear. As we approached Stanley's southern outskirts, the darkness became less intense due to the blazing streetlights. Because of this, the halts became fewer. But the scouts would then take off to check the ground ahead for up to twenty minutes.

Feeling better after my fall, I returned to the head of Green Section. We were extremely close to the lower slopes of Sapper Hill when vehicle lights were spotted. These were approaching from the west on a line that lay between our current location and the hill, but still a good distance away. So Giacchino decided to continue. Running like devils towards the hill, we never stopped to look back until almost at the top. I saw the lights cruising way below my position and made sure everyone in my section had closed on me.

First light was imminent as we rested from the sprint. But to our east the streetlights' brightness seemed to indicate they were celebrating something. They sure know we're here, I thought – and then looked 1,500 metres to the north. There it was! A building we all assumed to be the Governor's residence. Everything was in place. Just to its north was the flag mast. On its eastern side was the soccer field. It had a garden. We were at the correct end of town. That had to be it!

Our instructions indicated that we now had to radio a sitrep (situation report) to the ships and state our readiness to proceed – and thereafter wait (again, the frightful wait!) for the affirmative response order. This also implied, conversely, that even now the whole operation could be aborted. That scenario would have forced us to creep all the way back southwards to our boats and put to sea again immediately. A dreadful thought. But Murphy was on our side because, despite several attempts, we never managed to get through to the Task Force or receive any acknowledgement to our transmissions.

Indeed, luck had been doubly benevolent to the Argentines. It was fortunate they did not reach the top of Sapper Hill because a Royal Marine single-man observation post had been deployed there since 02.00 (05.00Z). But Murphy's abstinence did not last long.

We were gathering ourselves for our advance northwards to a radio antenna located on a hillock south of, and above, Government House. Once there we would split up into our sections. Then suddenly we realised that Alvárez and Mansilla were missing from Blue. But time was against us. First light was nearer and indistinct shapes a trifle more defined. Thus reduced in number, the assault group moved off Sapper Hill. Another kilometre – and we reached the antenna. There Giacchino issued the orders we already knew by heart.

"You, Orange (Lugo), the left (west) flank is yours. Green (me), cover my movements from here while I approach the objective and recognise it. Follow when I call you."

At only fifty percent strength, Blue was not now a viable section. Therefore the two remaining members were instructed to follow my section. Giacchino started to climb down the slope's covered approach with his section while Orange followed. They soon split, and I was unable to see Orange any more. After some ten minutes or so, I began to feel restless because of the lack of signals from Giacchino's Red. A mist made it even more difficult to spot distant figures. Smelling a rat, I set off down the slope slowly, followed closely by the rest of my section that included Blue's two orphans. We had not gone twenty metres when heavy gunfire was heard from the direction of Moody Brook. So this is the "stealth" operation of the *Comandos Anfibios*? I thought, but checked myself immediately. And so, how well do you think you're doing?

As if by magic, vehicle movement in the town began immediately. Two trucks (one of which contained Royal Marines) drove towards our objective and parked at its rear. Still 400 to 500 metres away, I was positioned on relatively high ground. Everybody was hyped up. One of my men rested the barrel of his gun on a rock and, aiming at the back of the truck offloading the Royal Marines, shouted, "I've got them in my sights. I can easily shoot them!"

"Don't!" I ordered, sure that the range was too far for a certain hit in that murky gloom. It was also crucial to retain the advantages of surprise. They did not know we were here!

He fired. I cursed.

It was about 05.45 (08.45Z). Their initial positions outmanoeuvred, these Royal Marines had been redeployed to Government House. At the most, thirty-one Royal Marines and Royal Navy sailors would defend Stanley's Alamo. They outnumbered Giacchino's assault group, however, by two to one.

Luckily enough we were virtually on the run towards Government House because, as soon as the Brits pinpointed our sniper, they began to return fire. While all this was happening, I heard Giacchino shouting, "Green! Here! Hurry up!"

Checking that my guys were following behind (they were), I tried to run faster, but all the way fought a creepy notion that we could be dashing into an ambush if Giacchino was unlucky enough to spring one.

Through a frightful amount of gunfire and thud of bullets striking the ground around us, we raced towards Red and finally reached them at the south-east outer corner of a low stone white wall. This surrounded a small patch of grass at the back of the house. The soccer field was nearby. We took cover briefly in the bushes, from where we fired bursts aimed in the din's general direction, hoping for a lucky hit. But the Royal Marines were shielded from us by the bushes around the house, making it impossible to see where they were actually located. Nonetheless I knew, despite being plagued by the bolt on my machine-gun jamming twice, that their movement would be discouraged by our fire.

The excitement magnified my impressions of everything happening around me: the product of unusually high amounts of adrenaline rushing through my blood. It explains the radiant surround to each of my memories.

Urbina left us shortly afterwards to run onto the soccer field 100 metres distant and convert it into a helicopter landing pad. His task there was to mark the wind direction with a pair of long johns that would resemble an arrow once the legs were spread and pegged down. Moving towards Giacchino with Cardillo closely behind, I was informed somehow that Alvárez and Mansilla of Blue had finally caught up and were trying to approach the house from its western end.

Seeing me, Giacchino snapped, "Talk to him!"

With cupped hands over my mouth to allow my voice greater range while hoping to be heard over the din, I shouted with a voracious power, "Mr Hunt! We are Argentine forces. The Island is taken. Amphibious vehicles have landed and are on their way towards here. Your communication lines are severed. We request that you exit the building immediately, unarmed and holding your hands up, in order to avoid greater damage. I can assure you that your rank and dignity, as well as those of all who are with you, will be respected."

There was no immediate answer.

On Giacchino's prompt, I repeated the message. Still no answer.

"Throw them a grenade!" ordered Giacchino.

I grasped one of three M2 high explosive hand grenades hanging from my webbing and threw it over the foliage onto the building's opposite seaward side.

Then a voice answered, "Mr Hunt is coming out."

After what may have been no more than two or three minutes, but seemed an eternity in the circumstances, Giacchino lost patience and urged me to make them hurry up.

Becoming angry with these fellows inside, I yelled my increasingly parrot-like message again. It was answered this time with an increase in the rate of fire from the building and isolated shouts of, "Don't go!" We could understand this language.

The shooting was reaching serious proportions and I glanced around looking for a clear field of fire. Flores and Alegre of Red with Ledesma of Orange were around Giacchino and me when a sudden orange-coloured blanket of light hurtled towards us. After a micro-second of idiotic surprise, I realised these were tracer rounds showering over us and pinpointing our position for snipers as well as illuminating the direction of our attack. They came from a machine-gun firing from the edge of town – surprisingly enough, I thought – across the soccer field. To make things worse, my machine-gun jammed again after a couple of bursts of fire. I took my pistol out of its holster and swore never to trust my life again to such trash.

We hit the deck together as fast as if we had rehearsed the reaction. Then I yelled to Giacchino, "Sir, either we get in or they'll fry us!"

"Yeah, we should go in now," he answered.

Simultaneously he jumped up, vaulted over the low stone wall and headed straight for the building. Immediately Cardillo charged after him. I followed suit. Behind came Flores and Ledesma. We gained entry at the first door encountered, only to find ourselves in a narrow hallway with no apparent exit except for another door close by on the right. Opening this was vital because tracer rounds were already beginning to hit the hallway's walls. Cardillo tried to kick it open, but only acquired a sore ankle. Then Giacchino swiftly drew a grenade from his webbing, smashed one of the door's panels, put his arm through the hole and felt for the key in the lock. But on opening the door from the inside only revealed a room without any further exits.

They had made a cardinal error. Rather than a Stanley Alamo rear entrance, this one belonged to a separate building – the servants' annexe. The time was now about 06.15 (09.15Z), fifteen minutes before the main Argentine landings at Yorke Bay.

Then everything happened incredibly quickly. Retracing our steps, Giacchino went out of the building through the first door exclaiming, "We'll have to go around!"

I followed him immediately.

Almost bumping into each other and instead of heading back to the stone wall, we turned right at the building's corner to enter the small grassy patch at the rear.

I had taken two steps into this enclosure when Giacchino, who was charging forward a couple of metres in front of me, whirled round shouting, "Christina, they got me!"

Almost simultaneously I felt a push on my belly. It had the force of a mule's kick.

My next recollection was of me lying against the corrugated iron sheeting of a tool-shed I had just passed on my left. I was looking at Giacchino lying there in front of me. He had been hit in the chest and was doubled up in pain.

Cardillo, Flores and Ledesma escaped from this killing area by sprinting around the rear of the main building to its west side and taking refuge in the maids' quarters above the kitchen. Three hours later they would be captured there by the Stanley Alamo's defenders and thus become, albeit for only a few minutes, the war's first prisoners.

I tried to move and felt a sudden burning pain on my right shoulder, as if my arm had been somehow chopped off from down there. Another shot, I thought, you're being too slow. My pistol slid out of my numb hand and I realised from then on that my right arm was useless for all practical purposes. In reality, and even though a bullet had hit and passed through the elbow, severing the nerve and artery, this was not the wound that caused my evacuation (it could probably have been treated on the Malvinas). A much more severe gunshot wound in my lower torso, where the bullet had carried away four ribs and punctured a lung, leaving a big exit opening in my back, would be the reason for my return to the mainland. The hospital in Stanley could not provide the kind of surgery needed. In addition, although I was not aware of it at the time, a third British bullet had found Diego García Quiroga on 2 April. All came from different weapons.

There were more urgent things to think about. Although feeling pleasant, an ominous warmth grew on my lower back. Painfully [...] slowly [...] I slid down until [...] presumably [...] I lay on my back. This could only be verified by the dark sky which had now materialised directly before my eyes. Any other movement was becoming extremely difficult. Everything was happening in a weird, quieter rhythm. There was Giacchino's voice. He was trying to tell me something. But although he was very close, it was still difficult to hear anything above the din of gunfire. It finally dawned on me that he was calling for a medic. Unbeknown to both of us, Urbina had already rushed back from the soccer field and, on hearing the shouts, had tried to get through the bushes and onto the grassy patch. Then a burst of gunfire hit him in his hips and, with a cry of frustration, the unlucky Sergeant was thrown spinning onto a tree trunk. I started to call for a medic – but was later told I continued to speak in English, managing to maintain a dialogue with the Brits who had gunned us down.

"Medic! Please send a medic! We're bleeding out here!"

"OK! We will, but you've first got to tell your people to stop firing and surrender their weapons."

"You ask too much. I can't do that, and you know it."

"Pity then! It'll be a long morning..."

This exchange of pleasantries was repeated a couple of times more or less along the same lines. Then another voice spoke.

"That bloke at your side. He has a grenade in his hand. Tell him to put it down. I'll count to five, and then I'll shoot!"

I translated this to Giacchino. He replied, "I can't let go of the thing. I've already removed the pin!"

I told this to the Brit, but he repeated, "I'll count to five!"

Giacchino then removed his image-intensifying goggles from his neck, passing the leather strap over his head. He tied this around the grenade lever, leaving the grenade on the ground at his side and explained to me that he would prevent the lever from tripping by pressing his body against. It was clear that all these movements were costing him an enormous effort. But continuously he kept telling me to try and get out of the line of fire and shoot back at the windows.

The Royal Marines mistakenly believed Giacchino was pleading to be disarmed and given medical assistance so that, if they approached, he could hurl the grenade at them. This was not the case, as Diego told me more than twenty-five years later, adding, "He never pleaded for mercy. Not even to the bitter end." The Green Section Commander's ordeal continued:

My memories of these moments, which were probably exceptionally grave and dramatic, are not very clear. But I can recall some of the things that happened and what was going through my head. They were mixed with, of course, flashes of family and personal memories and thoughts that belonged anywhere but on that patch of grass. Nevertheless there is the feeling of having seen them all from a distance through a gauze curtain. But most of my thoughts were monopolised by things happening there and then, as if having entered a reality with its own separate urgencies. Big questions like life or death were not on my mind at all. I appreciate these types of thoughts torture the minds of men unlucky enough to be under heavy shelling or bombing. This mind-shattering nightmare did not apply to me. I was incredibly lucky.

Behind the building I tried to loosen my belt, only to feel the stickiness of blood everywhere that was touched. I loosened the scarf around my neck, trying to move as little as possible and breathing very slowly to save as much energy as possible. My sight became blurred, then tunnelled, like the time I almost poisoned myself for lack of oxygen during a diving exercise that seemed to be ages ago. I was dying, and it was taking too long. Perhaps I was not dying at all?

"Be aware," said Giacchino to me suddenly. "I am close to losing consciousness. If I go, I have a grenade under my body. Tell those who lift me up that it will go off."

He had effectively moved over, covering the grenade with his body. I entertained my thoughts by imagining what a grisly sight the two of us would make if the thing went off.

There were sounds on the grass close to my head. I moved my eyes and saw the Governor's geese – fat, white, matron-like geese – waddling clumsily around us. But they were apparently oblivious of the continuing gunfire, me and Giacchino, who was breathing noisily over there. These geese were definitely out of place. I wondered what reaction open wounds could trigger in these animals. There was a lot of shouting, too.

Concurrently the drama continued elsewhere. Ignoring the incoming Royal Marines machine-gun fire, López from Orange ran across the soccer field to stop the advancing Argentine Marine column of Amtrac amphibious assault carriers on the road to Moody Brook from firing mortar bombs over Government House. Had it not been for him physically barring them by standing in front of Lieutenant-Commander Santillán's vehicle, we would probably have been blown to kingdom come.

I slid gradually from fantastic excitement into a peaceful quietness. The sun was rising quickly. Unable to move, I could still hear the voices and gunfire, but was speeding away fast.

I heard a chopper, but could not see it.

It was Lugo, the Orange Section Commander, who had assumed overall command of the reduced eleven-man assault group. His revised concept of operations was most effective. Like the Scots Guards' successful diversionary attack at Pony's Pass seventy-four days later, it equated to Sun Tzu's tenet of deception that "the military is based on guile, acts due to advantage, transforms by dividing and joining" (Sun Tzu, 2002, chapter 7). The defenders' initial assessment of eighty attackers laying siege to Stanley's Alamo had remained unrevised prior to the arrival at about 08.20 (11.20Z) of sixty-six reinforcing *Comandos Anfibios* from their fruitless mission against an unoccupied Moody Brook Barracks (of the original sixty-eight, two dropped out during the approach march to Moody Brook. One sustained a foot injury and was assisted by the other). Correspondingly the defenders' next assessment rose to more than double the actual total of seventy-seven enemy now surrounding their fortress (Ramsey, 2009, 35). At 09.20 (12.20Z) the Governor surrendered.

Sudden silence raised me from my reverie. Then I heard a voice calling Giacchino's name, "Pedro! It's me, Tito!"

Giacchino made a movement, tried to raise his head up on his elbows and said weakly, "Hurry up, Tito, or otherwise I'm not going to make it."

His words were followed by a lot of voices, and people materialising over us. It had taken more than ninety minutes before we could be assisted by these medics once the firing had stopped and the area was secured. By then I had reviewed my entire life several times and was still most surprised at being offered another chance.

They began to lift Giacchino up into a sort of stretcher. The moment they did this, an enormous amount of blood poured out of his parka jacket.

It made me think of waterfalls.

He sighed, fell limp into the arms of those assisting him, and was then carried into the back of a vehicle and driven to Stanley hospital.

An enormous guy suddenly appeared at my side, looking down on me. His clothes told me he was not one of us. He was a Royal Marine. I was a little confused, and felt weird rushes of pain coming from my injured back. My right arm was hurting terribly. Shortly afterwards he disappeared from my sight, and then I realised with a sinking feeling that he had crouched down. He was leaning over me, putting one hand into his combat jacket while, with the other, he was patting my chest.

This is it, I thought in an endless moment. Here comes his combat knife. This guy is going to slit open my throat without my being able to move at all. And just now, when we had made it. [...]

The uniformed giant touched my forehead and threw a blanket over me. As in a movie, his face was off the picture and then, with no apparent transition, another face filled the limited scope of my vision. This one I knew. It was Rear-Admiral Carlos Büsser's, the top cat of the amphibious force. He was telling me something that I could not hear. But I managed to tell him, though, "Don't touch my arm! Not my arm!"

I began to feel very faint. There was also growing desperation, with an inability to draw enough breath into my lungs. I would later learn that the Brit who had leaned over me had actually pulled out a morphine syringe from his pocket, injected it into my arm, and then marked my forehead with the preventative letter M (for "morphine") using the fresh blood he had collected from my wet vest. Then he threw a blanket over me, for I was already shivering uncontrollably due to the loss of blood. It was also extremely cold. The fact that he made that M sign on my forehead warning others of my morphine injection undoubtedly saved me from a second morphine dose that could have been fatal. Smart. Field smart.

I do not remember being lifted into a vehicle, but can recall the hospital in Stanley.

By my side is a body. It is Giacchino's. There are three doctors around me. Two of them are female. One runs an enormous pair of scissors over my clothing. It cuts open from the boots to my neck in a single cut. One of the girls touches my hip and looks into something.

A wound there?

She makes me roll over a little, looks at me and says, "You're through, baby." They confer at my side.

The diagnosis is confusing.

"You're through?" I want to ask. Through with what?

Through with combat? Through with life?

98

Through with a careless existence? Through with what?

But I cannot speak.

I can barely breathe – and even this simple reflex is becoming more and more difficult.

I must be moved.

Nothing more they can do for me here.

Diego was convinced that Giacchino had expired when the latter was lifted up into a blanket-cum-makeshift stretcher at Government House to be driven away in an Amtrac to the nearby King Edward VII Memorial Hospital. Nonetheless, his CO was still alive – just. It was both a strange yet uplifting paradox, therefore, that an Anglo-Argentine medical team comprising a British female nurse, Royal Marine medic and two Argentine military doctors, fought like lions in the operating theatre, trying to save him. But Giacchino was defeated in his final hour-long battle while Diego's trauma continued:

My next recollection was of my stretcher being tied to the side of the chopper. Off we flew into the sky, the blades hitting the air soothingly, bound for the icebreaker-cum-hospital ship ARA *Almirante Irizar* lying at anchor in the bay.

Something then happened that I cannot recall. Months later, the discovery of a reasonably clean scar on the inside of my left arm puzzled me as to its cause. The responsible person visited me one day in hospital. He was with me on that flight, a medical officer assigned to the vessel. After realising I was losing blood extremely rapidly, he thought of giving me an in-flight blood transfusion but did not have any equipment available. So he decided to be pragmatic. Climbing over my stretcher tied to the chopper's skids, he made an incision in my arm and reached for a blood vessel. This was connected to the spout of a blood sachet and then the officer pressed the liquid into my system while simultaneously it kept pouring out through the other openings. In that short flight my saviour used three sachets. He was impressed because the massive bleeding had been due to the severing of both the radial artery in my right arm and a branch of the lung artery.

We landed on the ship. I was still tied onto the stretcher and this caused difficulties for the sailors carrying me through the narrow passages to the infirmary. So blood poured from the stretcher whenever it was tilted at every door. This also messed up the deck. Faces were talking to me, but I could not hear them. Once more I speculated about whether Diego García Quiroga was still amongst the living. One of my former classmates, Sub-Lieutenant García Neder, who was now an officer on board the ship, did not recognise me initially with my face covered in camouflage cream, the bloody M, and everything else. Then suddenly he grabbed my wounded arm passionately. It hurt like hell. But being unable to speak, I could not tell him to let go. Also a *Buzo Táctico*, Lieutenant Ramiro, appeared. Praising our action and reassuring me that we would get to drink champagne together in celebration over this, he was most moved by events.

Lieutenant Dr Gatica inspected my wounds. There was nothing they could do for me there. So I was awarded the dubious distinction of becoming the first serviceman on either side in the war to be evacuated from the Islands. It was easily done. Several of my *Buzo Táctico* unit, including the CO, were looking on as my stretcher went by and then lifted up the steps and into an aircraft. Their faces were grey with exhaustion. Their eyes were lowered. None spoke. None moved. Neither could I, being absolutely sure now that death had occurred. It didn't feel too bad, I thought, but those guys look really tired.

While in the Fokker F47 stripped of its cabin seats, I was saved from dying once again by someone I will always remember with gratitude, even though he is still unknown to me. Obviously entrusted to prevent me from sleeping, a deadly condition when weak and on morphine, the man achieved his mission by gently slapping my face while saying, "Wake up, Rodríguez!"

Somehow during the flight I managed to tell him, "I'm not Rodríguez. I'm García!"

But the guy's mindset was inflexible. Ignoring my protest, he kept on slapping me frequently and continued to insist, "Wake up, Rodríguez!"

Perhaps it was all a dream?

On arrival at Comodoro Rivadavia we were met by a pleasant Army medical officer who accompanied us on an onward helicopter flight to the Regional Hospital. Comodoro had – and still has – a big place in my heart, because it was the place where my father used to work when he was an active logging engineer, and we used to visit him in the summers. I loved the roughness of the place, permanently wind-ridden, and the heavy smell of sea coming from the coast. But now I was feeling very faint, dizzy and tired with everything coming at me through a dense and ever-darkening fog.

When my stretcher was being carried through the hospital's main entrance, I heard a muffled comment, "It's the cyanosis!" It made me painfully aware that in my appearance I probably looked like hell. Suddenly I was in a dark room and noticed other people also there. It was the X-Ray Centre. Somebody asked me whether I could sit up.

"Sure," I replied, but would have fallen on the floor had not a couple of arms reached out and laid me on the table.

"It's better lying down. It's okay like that," one voice assured me. They were taking pictures of my chest.

A female voice called out, "What's this guy's name?"

Wanting this clearly on the records, I stated weakly, "My name is Diego Fernando García Quiroga."

Out of the ever-intensifying dark, a man's face materialised in front of me. It was the smiling, serene face of the radiologist.

"Are you a relative of Julio's?" he asked.

"He's my father," I replied.

The smile broadened at the unexpected coincidence. "Relax," the face said. "I can see no damage done to the vital organs."

As if I had been waiting for these words, somewhere inside me an electricity switch was turned off. And only on waking up more than eleven hours and two successive surgeries afterwards did this event make me reasonably sure that I was alive.

My wife and parents were there, having been flown in by the Navy. Later that day Carlos Robbio, my XO, arrived, still wearing his combat dress. News of Giacchino's death and the successful result of the operation was accompanied by his presentation of a complex little piece of metal he had collected from the grassy patch behind Government House. Still in one piece, but partially bent over and with the plastic covers gone, what remained of the Swiss Army Victorinox penknife that hung from my belt in a pouch over the left groin now bore the precise hole of a 9mm bullet in its centre. Without it, my femoral artery would have been severed with the inevitable consequence that implied. So good can life be.

There was much sleeping and dreaming. When deemed strong enough, I was interviewed by some journalists at my bedside. It was a mistake. A regimen of strong painkillers had made me confused and unaware of the war's latest developments. This condition continued for some time. The Brits had already landed at San Carlos (21 May) when I was transported further north to the naval hospital in Buenos Aires. But by then I had begun reading the newspapers, only to learn from them of friends not going to come back from the war. After receiving the visit of an officer who had lost an eye in combat, I became angry with myself for being unable to return to the front. The war was certain to end soon, and my opportunity of experiencing it had vanished by being shot on D-Day. Furthermore receiving a decoration for valour was, and remains, an undeserved honour. Some tried to explain that a nation needs heroes. But those who died in the war were much braver than me.

Finally hostilities ended, but my useless right arm prevented me from returning to service. It was not until November that I was declared fit and rejoined my unit. Immediately I completed two parachute jumps to be sure about my recovery. Life went on with only a few negative post-war effects. One was that almost every new experience encountered became dull in comparison to that Malvinas fling. I write "almost" because of my new over-sensitivity to situations and things that, before, would not have triggered a reaction from me at all. Another was that some of my memories became quite scrambled, while others have disappeared without trace. To the list can be also added enhanced scepticism, downplaying of urgency, and diminished competitive interest.

It is widely accepted that the effects of combat on men have a direct relationship with several factors: heredity, upbringing, the way in which the serviceman and his immediate group "feel" about the war, the relations with his comrades or in his private life. Some of these factors can be overshadowed by those instruments of collective influence that are used in the military such as unit discipline, structure, routines and procedural matters. I was well equipped in these areas and this fact – along with my short-lived combat experience – provided no possibility of my foundations fracturing. On the contrary, my existential self has been strengthened.

Diego's tale has many postscripts. One was his inability to lend the precious smashed penknife donated to his old unit at Mar del Plata for temporary display at the 2007 Imperial War Museum Falklands War Exhibition. The disappointing *Buzos Tácticos* refusal was mitigated by an invitation to that event's opening. In addition to his Margaret Thatcher encounter, Diego was reunited with the Naval Party 8901 Royal Marines Commander who, after the British surrender in Government House, assisted the Argentine casualties outside. In 2010 I obtained retired Major Mike Norman's email address for Diego. The latter's subsequent message to him was beautifully worded: "Though in reality that was our second meeting (in London), it was the one which gave us the opportunity to properly shake hands. I hold a warm memory of that encounter [...] how glad and thankful I (am) for having been able to meet again with fellow soldiers who I had once fought against, and confirm that our professionalism allowed us to appreciate the human beings under our uniforms" (email, 23 January 2010).

But Diego's message also contained a mission of reconciliation. This concerned Señora Delicia Rearte de Giacchino. Now in her eighties, the Mother of Giacchino lived in Argentina's Mendoza province and, as Diego explained to Mike Norman, they had been exchanging emails for some time. There had been an indication that she might want to communicate with "the British officer who was commanding the Royal Marines at Government House on that fateful morning [...] This lady is indeed a lively character, very lucid and currently very much engaged – should I also say outraged – with Argentina's political decline and the sorry corner into which our country has increasingly managed to paint itself" (email, 23 January 2010).

Mike Norman was willing to participate in any possible dialogue via Diego's translating skills. I hope this occurred. Nonetheless, there would be another more personal communication after nearly twenty-eight years: an eagerly awaited letter sent to Señora Giacchino by the British nurse who had attended Pedro Giacchino's last hour on that day of days when the British lost their Falklands, being the extraordinary event which would, in turn, trigger the Argentine 5th Marine Infantry Battalion's preparations for deployment into the South Atlantic Theatre of Operations.

References

Bicheno, H. (2006). *Razor's Edge: The Unofficial History of the Falklands War*. London: Weidenfeld and Nicolson.

Ramsey, G. (2009). *The Falklands War: Then and Now*. Old Harlow: Battle of Britain International.

Sun Tzu. (2002). *The Art of War: The Denma Translation*. Boston: Shambhala.

2nd Battalion, Scots Guards: The Tumbledown Legacy

Alan Warsap

Introduction

It is close to twenty-five years since the Falklands-Malvinas War. My personal, retrospective observations are made not only from the events of 1982, but are influenced by fifty years of involvement with the British Army from 1954 until 2004. This contact has included time as an Army General Practitioner, Regimental Medical Officer (RMO) and, lastly, as the President of an Army Medical Board responsible for examining, grading and sometimes medically discharging many men and women from service. An increasing number of boards involve at least some element of mental ill-health, mainly in men who had served in Bosnia and the Gulf War. Even today, working for The Tribunals Service, I still have contact with the medical and social problems of ex-servicemen.

At the time of the Falklands War I was, in addition to being the 2nd Battalion, Scots Guards' RMO, on the staff of the Royal Army Medical College. The Professor of Military Psychiatry at the College was the then Colonel Peter Abraham. He guided me as to what might be possible with regard to the recognition and management of immediate battle shock casualties. This information I shared with my Commanding Officer (CO) and, having just been warned for Falklands duty, it focussed our minds.

The Falklands

On Tumbledown during the night and morning of 13-14 June 1982, eight Scots Guardsmen and a Royal Engineer were killed or reported missing and forty wounded. Psychological casualties at that stage were virtually invisible, or at least battle-shock had not led to defeat. I recall only three possible battle-shock casualties at this early stage, one not of our unit, and one who recovered so quickly that he was an efficient soldier for the rest of the battle and afterwards. The third cannot be discussed – even now. He did not engage with any part of our unit medical team, but may well have been such a casualty. After post-tour leave I recall one Junior Non-Commissioneed Officer (NCO) who exhibited classical symptoms of post-battle stress adjustment reaction. He declined psychiatric referral – I hope he did well.

Recently I was encouraged to hear from retired Commodore Toby Elliott from the Ex-Servicemen's Mental Health Society and "Combat Stress" organisation that of the eight hundred servicemen from the Falklands conflict known to him, only four were ex-Scots Guardsmen (Elliott, 2006). However I am now aware that everyone, including myself, probably sustained a highly variable permanent mental scarring. In many this is dormant, but can be activated by life events in the future. What hides this scar is the great variability of individuals' capacity to cope with the mental damage sustained.

The natural tendency in many to deny or unconsciously suppress the psychological effects of battle trauma is what medical and command authority is unwittingly endorsing (and I understand this). As a result, stoicism is mistaken for absence of mental scarring and only manifest psychiatric illness is acknowledged. Variability in individual soldiers' reactions to the same battle trauma is mistakenly seized on to deny that mental scarring has occurred. For example, a heavy mortar round bursts near to and equidistant from two soldiers. One with poor resilience has a life dogged by intermittent mental ill health and dependency, often with a war disability pension to help support him. His comrade may appear at first successfully to have avoided mental scarring only to suffer partially hidden handicaps of suppressed symptoms which may or may not break through into mental ill-health later in life. Variability is such that it is not unknown to me that some soldiers claim traumatic events in their careers that they have not witnessed themselves but heard about from comrades. They cannot identify what makes them now feel different but feel altered by their experiences compared to the person they used to be.

I emphasise the great importance attached to the psychotherapeutic benefit gained by everyone in the Battalion from the opportunity to "wind down" collectively after the battle as the unit rested up in the sheep sheds at Fitzroy. Here, all ranks were jammed together out of the wind for about three days. We then spent long weeks, less closely confined, but still very much together in sub-units on a ship, and then on garrison duty on West Falkland at Port Howard. We travelled back to the UK, still all together, by ship to Ascension Island, and then flew back to post-tour leave.

The dominating medical condition we had to deal with after 13-14 June was, for many, the pain and disability of trench foot. All through that time until we returned from leave "sick parade" numbers were very low indeed, apart from the trench foot. There were no psychological casualties at this time – that is, none were evident. Late on 14 June, after the ceasefire, our Regimental Aid Post (RAP) treated some dozen Argentinian soldiers for minor injuries on their way back to a holding facility in Stanley. I saw many acts of spontaneous kindness shown to them by our Guardsmen.

From the RAP on Goat Ridge on the morning of 14 June, during hostilities, elements of the RAP staff and I went forward in a Navy Sea King helicopter to start the casualty pick-up. As we took off we crossed the Gurkha mortar line which was close by and preparing to fire on a forward target, probably Mount William. The mortars erupted, and at least one mortar bomb must have passed through the helicopter's rotor blade motion. We picked up, I believe, seven or eight Gurkha casualties. All were semi-comatose, sleep deprivation combining with the pain of their wounds. They were typically stoical, and we took them to the 16 Field Ambulance Advanced Dressing Station at Fitzroy. At this point helicopter evacuation formally ceased. Friendly fire incidents, inevitable in war, take their own special toll – and we had been lucky to escape such a fate on this occasion.

Lessons learned

Medical first-aid training for everyone, bolted on to all the pre-operational work-up training, was most important. It was realistic and often confrontational, including the practising of burials and watching uncut films of casualties from the Vietnam War. This latter was the idea of the then Captain Tim Spicer, our Operations and Training Officer. With this the men were made first-aid reliant in pairs and small groups. However, it is important to de-select for combat any soldier with unresolved mental health or drugs problems, and also only fair to inform recruits about the full military significance for them of voluntary service in the Army.

Casualty evacuation plans must be very flexible and always a primary command responsibility. Delayed evacuation was inevitable, depending as it did on scarce helicopter availability. Here, the sustaining treatment given by the Pipes and Drums Platoon first-aid trainers was of key importance, embedded as they were in all sub-units. The extent of long-term mental scarring and acute shell-shock, that is, battle-immediate casualties, is directly related to the number of physical casualties and the intensity and character of the conflict.

Following the initial shock-effects of battle from fear, fatigue, explosions and sights, there follows a degree of "post-battle adjustment reaction" for weeks and months afterwards, characterised by over-arousal feelings, family and social maladjustment, anger and aggressiveness. Our CO warned the Battalion about such difficulties before we all dispersed on leave. It helped us recognise such reactions as almost normal, and to be expected, when irrational anger welled up in the post-battle months. "If you feel angry you have nothing to prove," I remember the CO saying. After battle and trauma you cannot help but experience irrational extreme irritation to the point of violence with the seemingly trivial concerns of those at home in the UK.

I now know, years later, that there is further, hitherto hidden mental damage for some to live with when post-battle mental damage leads to a tendency to develop ordinary mental illness in those vulnerable: I mean depression, suicide and even violent and criminal behaviour. Other burdens include alcoholism, drug misuse, family breakdown, nightmares, flashbacks, unemployment and destitution in extreme cases. Long term, past exposure to battle seems to facilitate the early development of mental ill-health which might, anyway, have surfaced in the fullness of time in some subjects.

I recommend that the way to reduce battle stress in all its forms, short and long term, is to be found in the example of 2nd Battalion, Scots Guards: that is, allowing for a wind-down period to be made possible after high-intensity warfare, perhaps along the formula of three days' whole unit close-proximity living, resting, hearing how others got on, how they feel and their worries, talking through guilt and blame together, self-directed and in no way structured. This should be followed by three weeks' less intensive interaction and debriefing. It would be helpful at this time for officers to brief the whole unit on how the operation or battle worked out (or otherwise) overall. Let everyone view the big picture so that the individual can understand how his contribution fitted in. At the same time, reassure the men that their contribution did help their fellow soldiers.

There should then be a total period of three months away from the end of hostilities, to include post-tour leave, in which soldiers should be relieved of any serious military responsibility and activity. There should be no enforced or organised counselling for all – especially not by non-unit personnel. In any large body of men, closely confined, there are always enough talkers and listeners to guarantee lively discussion and thought.

Long term

So, long term, what should be done? Of course, emerging mental ill-health should come under the care of military or veterans' mental health teams with welfare back-up. For those whose lives are faltering as the result of their mental scarring, value is likely to be had, not from opening the mental wounds of past traumas, but by helping those affected to climb a tower, as it were, above their troubles and be motivated to look out toward a series of personal goals, aiming to relaunch them into stable life.

This type of therapy, or something much like it, was first proposed by Captain Arthur Brock of the Royal Army Medical Corps. He was a psychiatrist in the Great War at Craiglockhart, a wartime military hospital for officers in Edinburgh. Apparently the building still exists. It had been a Spa Hotel and is now student accommodation. Here were treated officers, most from the Somme era, who were suffering from battle neurasthaenia or shell-shock, which was the terminology of the time. This is a key part of the history of battle-induced mental ill-health, and famous among its patients were Wilfred Owen and Siegfried Sassoon, the Great War poets. As patients they were visited by Robert Graves, the poet and author, who also had post-war neurasthaenia. He finally attempted to put his past on record and behind him when, ten years after the war, he wrote his autobiography, *Goodbye to All That*, and headed for a new life abroad (Graves, 1957).

One way to help deal with post-battle mental adjustment once and for all is to write down one's experiences, good and bad, and one's reactions, whether in the form of a notebook, tape or book, and, as it were, lock it away in the past before moving on. As such, it could be suggested by units after returning from action. The Craiglockhart trio, as we can now regard them, remain the great communicators from their war generation, with messages which will endure for Great Britain. I met Robert Graves very briefly just before he gave his first lecture as Professor of Poetry at Oxford University in the 'sixties.

As you get older the past has a curious quality of becoming closer to your own life. I can well remember London match-sellers on street corners, often with a crutch and Great War medals; being told that a neighbour had "shell-shock"; being taught to fish by a man who had been gassed on the Western Front. At a recent Parochial Church Council meeting, of the eleven souls present, two had had fathers who survived the Battle of the Somme. With such reminders is it not reasonable in our more psychologically vulnerable age to make long-term military mental health and support provision for those affected by combat?

Practical help must include money. The current compensation for losing a finger in battle is £2,559 (single payment). Soldiers should not receive lump sum payments. They will need the money later in their lives and long term, regardless, and rightly so, of whether the victim shows his hand proudly to his grandchildren or to the examiner for incapacity benefits. We all cope differently. There is no logic in giving compensation for a little finger and not for mental scarring. The scar must be compensated for, not allowed to develop into some long-term mental illness which the scarring may predispose the soldier to. How do we do this? A war pension based on the number of days in combat and intensity of that combat as judged from measures such as physical casualty rates, death rates, ammunition expenditure, etc.? In this way, retrospectively, scores are produced for each day, the worst possible day being 100 points, e.g. the first day on the Somme (but no day will ever equal that).

An agreed formula calculation could be arrived at so as to produce a modest pension increment to retirement pay for those exposed to agreed significant battle-trauma.

Practical help might also include regular, if brief, long-term follow-up of those becoming the mental health casualties of battle or those with high "Somme" scores, e.g. by internet or text, and organised by the Veterans Welfare Organisation with Regimental and British Legion input. This idea was, in part, promoted by a conversation I had with Lieutenant Robert Lawrence, who was very badly wounded in the Tumbledown attack. Robert went furthest forward of any officer before he fell. I know also now that his Company, led by Major Simon Price, carried out an exemplary night attack in mountainous terrain, the worth of which I only recently came to appreciate.

Recently I have had a glimpse of medical advances which indicate a possibly more sound method of diagnosing and treating different types of mental health illness with the help of brain-scanning and imaging. There is hope here for the future casualty. However, I have two postscripts.

What is the Tumbledown legacy of the 2nd Battalion, Scots Guards? It is the intense low murmuring roar that was so distinctive and memorable as the Battalion wound down during the time in the Fitzroy sheep sheds, exchanging their experiences, worries and fears. I shall never forget it and neither should the Army Medical Services. This points the way to bringing practical clarity of action to the part-prevention and long-term military medical care and support for those damaged by war.

Finally, about five years after the war I was doing a short locum duty with the United Nations Forces in Cyprus (UNFICYP). Along the camp road I encountered the first Argentine serviceman I had seen since the war. His unit was newly arrived in Cyprus. I was unsure of his rank and no doubt he felt the same. Each off us saluted early, only to salute exactly together. We were very much on the same side. For me the war was over.

Note
The main suggestions in this paper were first touched on during a briefing to the Treasury Solicitors' Council in the Spring of 2001 on another matter.

References

Elliott, Toby. (2006). Personal communication (November 2006).

Graves, R. R. (1957) *Goodbye to All That: an Autobiography*, London: Jonathan Cape.

Who Cares about the Enemy?

Jeremy McTeague

> To be prepared is half the victory.
> Miguel de Cervantes Saavedra (1547-1616)

Introduction

Training soldiers to operate effectively in combat is the core activity of the British Army. Indeed, in the latter half of the twentieth century the priority placed on training by the Army's high command was (and may still be) the single most critical factor for its success. It is this almost religious dedication to preparation that has enabled the Army to fulfil the numerous demands made upon it without losing a war.

The Army spends enormous time and resources selecting, assessing and developing the strengths of young men and women to make them "fit for purpose". Soldiers in the "teeth arms" such as the infantry must therefore be "battle ready". From a practical perspective this means that they must be highly competent in handling their equipment and weapons. They must know, understand and be able to act according to standard operating procedures (routines that permit men to operate in a logical way when, under extreme pressure and duress, their rational thought processes may be slow or unreliable). Finally, they must be supportive of the command structure and have the self-discipline to sublimate self-interest and act in the best interests of their sub-units.

British Army training is staggeringly effective and it reaps some important side-benefits such as the widespread development of *esprit de corps*. Nevertheless, in my experience, there are several "soft" areas where the training of leaders for combat could, and should, be improved and where failure to do so can, and will, have hard and durable personal consequences for the potential combatants. The first improvement is giving advice on what to expect regarding the emotions and concerns that arise before and during combat, and the second is dealing with the appearance of unpalatable emotions post-combat.

Emotions and concerns arising before and during combat

Dealing with indecision caused by concerns about being wrong – when the stake may be life itself or otherwise

The idea of being frozen into indecision by the fear of being wrong is neither new nor complicated. Indeed many people are able to relate to such an experience. But what most people have experienced is the need to decide on an issue in the absence of critical urgency or where the penalty of error is not death or injury to self or comrades.

Just prior to the last fourteen days of the Falklands-Malvinas conflict in late May 1982, my unit, 1st Battalion, 7th Duke of Edinburgh's Own Gurkha Rifles, still at sea on board the Cunard liner RMS *Queen Elizabeth 2*, received its warning order to land at Blue Beach 2, San Carlos Water on 1 June. The orders given to the Battalion, and down through the organisation whilst on board our subsequent ship MV *Norland* on 31 May, the night before the landing, were scant. As illustrated here (fig. 1), my orders book clearly reports: "Action on beachhead – no idea".

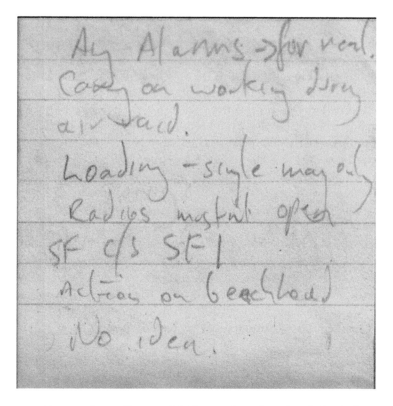

Figure 1. Extract from Jeremy McTeague's orders book depicting notes for the Battalion's landing at Blue Beach 2, San Carlos Water.

This caused my men and me real concern. We were about to enter a battle-zone and the plan to effect that act of entry was non-existent. A plan is always better than no plan, and while initiative is rightly a valued trait, it cannot and must not be relied upon as the sole factor/contributor to define courses of action. All officers and non-commissioned officers should be trained to understand why they should never use the words "no idea" in formal orders.

How to deal with being utterly powerless when under duress
On our long night-approach march along Goat Ridge on 14 June towards our Company Start Line (the location from which a company deliberate attack is launched) on the eastern end of the Tumbledown, we were in single file moving through a suspected minefield when, suddenly, we came under heavy artillery and mortar fire that lasted for nearly an hour. The standard operating procedure (SOP) in such a situation is to fall to the ground, seek cover and await orders. As the Platoon Commander, I was aware of my responsibility to get my men into safety. We could not just scatter, and yet to make an orderly exit, we would have had to keep close together in single file – a perilous action indeed in the context of the current situation. But falling to the ground was only a marginally better solution, as we remained within the target area of the accurate Argentine artillery and mortar fire.

Having decided that we should remain in cover, I was still without any other options and so felt powerless to protect my men further. In that situation the realisation that there is nothing one can do is not easy to accept, and one feels a corresponding overwhelming sense of inadequacy. Indeed for some time after this frighteningly intensive and prolonged bombardment had ceased, I worried that my men thought of me as being ineffective. This was a poor state of mind for a young officer preparing to participate in the launching of a deliberate company attack on an enemy defensive position that had been prepared for sixty-seven days beforehand.

My message is crystal-clear. It is simple to teach young commanders and soldiers alike that instances of powerlessness will occur on the battlefield. So merely having that knowledge in advance will allow soldiers in a similar position to deal appropriately with it.

How to handle new, unexpected and intense emotional states personally and in one's men
No matter how long the time one has known the men under one's command, there will, in my experience, always be a change in the way that they behave and in how one behaves as combat becomes imminent and the danger grows or, indeed, is experienced. We all react in different ways and, in many instances, I was surprised by how much and in what unexpected directions my men's behaviour changed. Interestingly it was not that the men's behaviour changed for the worse *per se* – it just simply became erratic and intense.

This presented problems in command and created the need to be super-understanding and empathetic on the one hand, and firmer and occasionally more authoritarian on the other – depending on the individual and specific circumstances. Vitally, it became clear to me that I had also to examine my own behaviour to ensure that this remained as consistent as possible. I should stress that this did not mean my pretending to be unaffected by the situation – just that the manner of my being affected was consistent with the Lieutenant McTeague my soldiers knew from before. Being recognised as having a good sense of humour is invaluable in this respect.

How to manage fear in oneself and in others

Since I was a small eight-year-old boy on the rugby field, I have had to deal with fear of enemy and injury – as have most of us. It is nothing new in itself, and normally we go through life without being overly perturbed when we find that we are afraid of something since our control of fear from an early age has been mastered.

What we do not normally have to face is a rapid escalation in the threat and to manage the realisation of its new enormity. At the Royal Military Academy Sandhurst we were not trained in how to deal with fear of a threat that was so large that one's death (and that of most of one's men) appeared (quite rationally) to be the only logical outcome. My orders book again (fig. 2) provides insight into my thinking on the eve of the Battalion's battle, and the D Company attack on Mount William in particular. This was to be a frontal attack across nearly 1,000 metres of absolutely open and barren terrain. There was not a tree, bush or rock in sight along the projected path of our advance to attack three Argentine Marine platoons totalling 157 men who were dug in both on Mount William itself and just to the north-east and north-west of this objective respectively. This enemy force outnumbered D Company and was similar in number to those facing the Scots Guards. The only hope of success was that the darkness of night would cloak us and our movement, and supporting fire from A Company's fire base of Browning heavy machine guns, Milan anti-tank missiles, general purpose machine guns in the sustained fire role, our Battalion 81mm mortars and the artillery would suppress the enemy whilst we were exposed in the open.

The scene is set with an uncertainty: *Phases 2 and 3 of the attack will be together, or one after the other?*

Then the tasks: *11 and 12 Platoons will be the first attack platoons. 10 Platoon (my command) will initially be in reserve (sigh of relief). But then: 10 Platoon will commit sections piecemeal to support 11 and 12 Platoons. And one section is to look after prisoners.*

Then as a third task: *another section is to evacuate the wounded until it is committed for the assault* (this was verging on the impossible, since the section could be one kilometre to the rear at the time I was meant to be putting it into the attack. Also for the record: at this point all three of my sections had now been committed to various tasks!)

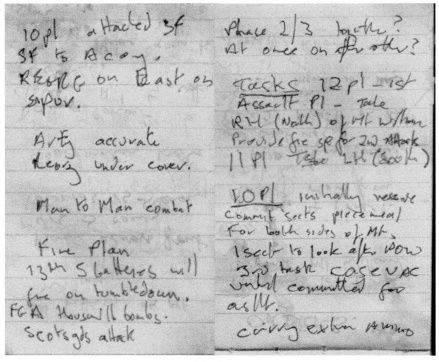

Figure 2. Extract from Jeremy McTeague's orders book depicting notes for D Company's deliberate attack on Mount William.

Then it gets worse: *Carry extra ammo.* Ammunition is very heavy and carrying it for other soldiers, when attacking, is like sending a boxer into the boxing ring in handcuffs.

And even worse: *attached SF (general purpose machine gun in the sustained fire role) has to go to A Company* so I had also lost my only integral fire support. I was then told that the enemy artillery is very accurate and that we must reorganise ourselves after the attack under cover. In effect this meant treating wounded, re-supplying and dealing with prisoners whilst under artillery fire.

Finally Major Mike Kefford, my Company Commander and a man warranting great respect, advises that the fight is going to be "man to man combat".

114

Without overstating the case, this set of orders describes a desperately difficult set of circumstances with a level of complexity that was bound to result in massive casualties, if not outright failure. The level of fear and hopelessness I felt was shared by my men and our fear was palpable, yet there was full acceptance of my orders. As I shook hands with my section commanders half an hour before crossing the Start Line (now in broad daylight because of the delay imposed on the Scots Guards' attack by fierce enemy resistance), I wished that my training had included guidance on how to alleviate the obvious fear that we all felt. It was a really unpleasant final thirty minutes whilst we waited to move.

In later life: dealing with unpalatable emotions

How to control violent fantasies and the desire to inflict violence
This issue has been well documented and become a somewhat over-emphasised cliché. Despite this, it is a real phenomenon and remains inadequately understood by people who have experienced it, and entirely misunderstood by those who have never experienced it – rather like men knowing what it is like to give birth. When I discovered that my fellow officers also suffered from similar experiences, it was a huge relief and I immediately found myself better able to view such fantasies more objectively, so limiting their impact.

Military training establishments should explain how these fantasies come about and how they can be dealt with. Such knowledge is enough to allow many individuals to help themselves or, in more extreme cases, to provide the impetus and "permission" to go and seek help.

How to diminish feelings of shame or humiliation

War for the combat soldier is likely to be a humiliating experience. He is on an emotional rollercoaster. He has to open himself up and prove himself to other men to such an extent that it can be, in retrospect, humiliating – rather like a teenage boy boasting or flexing his biceps in the vain hope of impressing a girl. His comrades see him terrified, hugely aggressive and even feeling guilty. Indeed they see him in a wider range of unpalatable emotional states than should his mother or wife. They witness his basest behaviour which, at its worst, is him having to kill another. The immediate reaction to such behaviour is normally positive and this can last for some time. But in the end, years later, feelings of shame and humiliation come to the fore as we judge our memories against the standards of the mature individual. Dealing with these emotions requires fortitude, and the worst thing is that they are unexpected. Forewarned is forearmed.

The emotional effect of combat and its anticipation

Combat and the anticipation or expectation of combat, unsurprisingly, causes us to experience a wide range of emotions – many for the first time, and often in a far more intense way than previously. For example, (fig. 3) anxiety is a common, balanced emotion that we often experience and which performs a useful function in our everyday lives. However, in near and actual combat situations, anxiety is heightened to fear and, *in extremis*, is intensified to outright terror. As stated earlier, fear is not uncommon. It is much rarer than anxiety but we have all generally experienced it at some time. Terror, on the other hand, is rarely experienced.

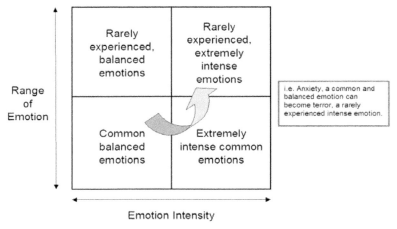

Figure 3. Combat and its anticipation create and intensify emotions.

The effect of experiencing fear for prolonged periods, or terror for even short periods, creates an emotional disjunction, with the victim losing his sense of emotional perspective in the short to medium term. Matters of routine or the mundane become beneath contempt, unworthy of consideration as they are "totally unimportant" in the victim's world, where "survival" is deemed the only issue of any importance. This is an entirely natural response. Survival is a key instinct and somebody who has cause to be extremely fearful must be able to focus on surviving to the exclusion of all else. To that end, everything else is properly relegated to irrelevance.

This phenomenon became blindingly apparent when my Battalion returned to peacetime soldiering, and officers and soldiers alike found themselves having to deal with boredom and self-discipline issues for the first time in their careers.

Emotions in the aftermath

Within a couple of days of the war ending, D Company was flown to Fox Bay on West Falkland. There we were able to keep to ourselves, rest and relax in one another's company. It was, in retrospect, an important time which allowed us to talk together about our personal experiences in an unstructured, and yet safe and comfortable way. Yet this was not the purpose of the exercise, which was to clear up the mess left by the Argentines and to mark out and clear minefields. I sometimes wonder what the effect on us all would have been if we had been taught how best to use such a period of respite.

When we subsequently returned to the UK, much of our excitement of being at war had worn off. In particular, we no longer experienced such a range of emotions. Nevertheless I was still experiencing intense emotions and mood swings. These quickly diminished, but in recent years I find that a pattern of behaviour has re-emerged (fig. 4). Common balanced emotions, such as irritation, can flash into anger with little provocation, a negative question or statement can be interpreted as an insult, causing strong reactions of insecurity, aggression or even the behaviour associated with victimisation. Feelings of low personal esteem also surface with some intensity.

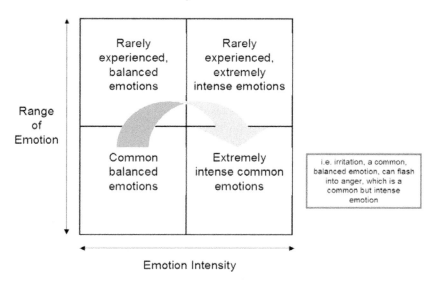

Figure 4. In the aftermath and beyond, emotions intensify erratically.

Finally, I have found recently that my ability to accept authority has weakened considerably. This may be tied up with natural ageing but, since my return from the conflict, I recognise my internally questioning the right and qualifications of each of my superiors to tell me what to do. It is very simple. They have never had to manage under the circumstances that I have experienced, and I am convinced (wrongly I am sure) that they know little about *real* management of people other than what they have been taught on courses. They have not had the ultimate hands-on experience of exercising high-stakes leadership.

The emotional intensity gap

Like many veterans, I experienced intense emotions and managed men in such heightened emotional states that their demeanour, words and actions were unacceptable to civilian society (fig. 5).

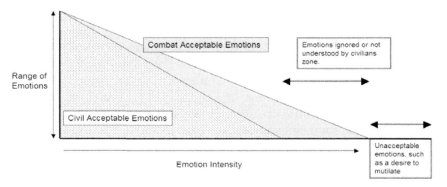

Figure 5. In the aftermath, emotions that were experienced in combat are no longer acceptable, thereby creating an emotional "gap".

As stress builds and emotions intensify, the actions and attitudes of soldiers reach a point that is generally deemed unacceptable in civilian society. Aggression is a common and relevant example. In a combat zone, aggression is not only acceptable – it is required. Even then, aggression can become so intense and unbridled that it becomes unacceptable even in military situations. An example of this might be the savage mutilations witnessed in Rwanda and Kosovo.

The gap between what is and what is not acceptable in civilian life is, in my opinion, at the root of the problems soldiers face in the aftermath of combat. The soldier who has experienced the requirement of "jumping" this gap must work hard to re-orientate his values and is likely to need assistance to do so. Once again, if soldiers were advised on this issue and taught how to identify it, they could develop coping strategies that would reduce their confusion, worry and alienation caused by their being unable to bridge "the gap".

Conclusion

If in possession years later of even a minute amount of knowledge as to what I would feel and how my reactions would be in normal interaction with others, then perhaps I would have been able to deal effectively with a number of issues, or at least seek advice. To my regret I am only now becoming aware of the many long-term effects of facing combat. To add insult to injury, it seems that many of the things described by me are well documented and a plethora of coping strategies exist.

I was on the winning side in the Falklands-Malvinas conflict and have generally dealt well with the experience and its aftermath. However, if we had lost, I hesitate to contemplate what the effects on me would have been. To have to deal with the unpalatable reality of defeat layered on top of the impact of combat must be a heavy burden indeed. I therefore strongly commend and respect those many Argentine veterans who have subsequently made a success of their lives, and sympathise with those who have suffered. It is time for all veterans of the Falklands-Malvinas conflict to look at how we care for those who have yet to regain their emotional balance – even if this means in the final analysis caring for "the enemy".

British Army officers are brought up to maintain a "stiff upper lip". That is good so far as it goes. However, stiff becomes brittle over time, and more comprehensive training policies on how to deal with the emotional issues surrounding combat and other high-stress military operations such as peace-keeping must be explored. Our society owes it to its veterans not to brush aside the issue of post-traumatic stress and its associated conditions with platitudes and parades.

With the training I advocate, it would be hoped that young commanders might be better equipped to deal with the horrors visited upon them in current non-conventional conflicts. I therefore urge the British Government to invest heavily in preventative emotional preparedness training and curative specialist post-combat care. This is definitely not a job for the National Health Service for the simple reason, of which I am personally convinced and which informal anecdotal evidence has confirmed, that people suffering from trauma require to be treated by people who have been exposed to, and suffered from, trauma.

The Life, Passion and Death of a Rumour

Lucrecia Escudero Chauvel

The Story of the *Superb* Submarine

What happens when two orders of verisimilitude, i.e. official and unofficial sources, meld together using the press as their crucible? A possible media world is created of such strength and mastery as to be able to modify the course of the "real world".

On 31 March 1982, the reader of the newspaper *Clarín* sees an article date-lined London. The piece is based on two telex reports sent out by Spain's EFE and France's AFP. The information contained in the telexes originates from ITV, Britain's privately owned television station. According to the televised report, "The British Navy has sent a nuclear submarine to the Southern Atlantic".

The announcement, reported by the war correspondent, includes the information that the submarine left its military base at Gibraltar for an unspecified destination. *Clarín* prints the story with the headline: "London has sent submarines".

This initial chain of inter-media back-and-forth, which is a characteristic form of legitimising the press, uses the media itself as its source. The report prompts the British Foreign Office to hold a press conference. The Office's press secretary announces that there is no official comment regarding the story: "We have nothing to say about the reported version." In response to journalists' questions about the submarines armament status, the press secretary responds that it is not armed with nuclear warheads.

This first declaration by the Foreign Office during the construction of the *Superb*'s possible media world highlights the issue of presuppositions in press information. Consequently, all belief about the truthfulness of the information is suspended and, so, the reader can consider it to be a "version".

The report, however, has already entered into the arena of media circulation. The reader, thus, has at least four pieces of information:

1. a submarine called the *Superb* exists;
2. it is a nuclear submarine;
3. it is not currently equipped with nuclear warheads;
4. it has left its base at Gibraltar for an unspecified destination.

The possible media world has supplied its model reader with a series of properties necessary for the correct identification of the semantic unit "nuclear submarine". It thus transforms it into a textual topic, and at the same time, it transforms the empirical reader into a model reader, because simultaneously the reader is now in a position to exercise "conjectural thinking" (Eco 1990, 236) and can clearly infer four pieces of complementary and intertextual information. This information will begin to delineate a media world through which will navigate the reader's belief that:

1. the nuclear submarine *Superb* is heading towards the Malvinas-Falklands;
2. no information has been published about its exact armament status because it is a military secret;
3. the news story is treated as a "version" precisely because it is a leak of classified military information;
4. something important must be in play if the British Foreign Office is making statements concerning the report.

The reader can also generate an interpretative or hypo-codified abduction such as "given the diplomatic escalation of the Argentine-British conflict, it's possible that nuclear submarines are being used". The reader might also decide to subscribe to an explanation strongly supported by the media's inter-transmission: "If British television, an Argentine newspaper and two international press agencies from countries not even directly involved in the conflict are giving out the same report *that no one denies*, then there's a good chance that it's true."

On the following day, 1 April, while awaiting the Argentine landing on the Malvinas-Falklands, *Clarín* increases the tension level with an article entitled "Worsening of the crisis with Great Britain". The newspaper credits itself with the 31 March news-piece:

> Sources consulted by *Clarín* have confirmed that Williams (the British ambassador to Argentina) has been called by the Argentine Chancery. Referring to the report that the British government has sent a nuclear submarine to the conflict zone, he stated: "I can only respond to questions concerning diplomatic matters, not military operations."

The suspense signal emitted by the newspaper gives the model reader a preview of the future development: either the possible media world will be confirmed or refuted. Either action will carry with it corresponding propositional attitudes.

Confirmation is not long in coming. In an article appearing on page four on the very same day, *Clarín* uses unofficial sources in its article

"The deployment of British ships to the Malvinas-Falklands is confirmed". The paper reports that five telexes date-lined London indicate that AFP and EFE's 31 March cables had been picked up by three other international agencies: Italy's ANSA, the US's AP, and Britain's Latin Reuters. The reader has no reason to doubt that these world famous information agencies have already checked corresponding sources.

The reader goes on to see that these agencies confirm the *Superb* as being "a nuclear fuelled submarine, which has left its base in Gibraltar and is heading for the Malvinas-Falklands". An important piece of information is added: the submarine weighs 4,500 tons and its crew of 97 is specialised in submarine detection. The submarine's possible media world is then furnished with new elements: it is also reported that "a second Hunter-Killer class submarine, as well as several other frigates and aircraft carriers, may accompany the *Superb*" (*Clarín,* 1 April, "The deployment of British ships is confirmed").

At this point, the experts intervene. From the International Institute for Strategic Studies in London, top British specialist Mayor Elliot deems the deployment of Hunter-Killer class nuclear submarines to be a highly efficient measure: "With government authorization, the *Superb* would be capable of rapidly sinking two to three Argentine naval units."

Another newspaper, Britain's *Daily Telegraph,* also steps in. While relating the characteristics of the submarine's crew, the paper hints that the ship *is currently in the area of the Malvinas-Falklands*: "The submarine crew stationed in the islands' waters pertains to an 'élite' group of the Royal Navy" (*Clarín,* 1 April, "The deployment of British ships is confirmed"). Using the original two telexes from EFE and ANSA date-lined London, it affirms that: "Yesterday, all British newspapers reported the deployment of a nuclear submarine to the Malvinas-Falklands" (*Clarín*, 1 April, "Bellicose language in the British press").

The nuclear submarine delineated by the possible media world does not pertain to the real world experience of the reader, who has probably never seen a British nuclear submarine. It can, however, enrich the reader's intertextual and encyclopaedic experience as a model media reader: "A narrative world borrows properties from the real world. In order to do this without wasting energy, the narrative world activates individuals already recognised as such. The narrative or possible world does not necessarily reconstruct these individuals element by element. [...] A possible world greatly overshadows the real world of the reader's encyclopaedia" (Eco, 1979, 131).

As such, technical verification of the story becomes momentarily unnecessary. The story has been amply guaranteed by the experts. The possible media world constructed need only be sufficiently probable and credible for the model media reader to accept it. At this point, he is already capable of interpreting the totality of information received about the submarine and can thus filter it into a personal frame of reference as a "small world".

Within twenty-four hours the initial story has entered the category of certainty. The story becomes credible not only because of the amount of identifying signs that allow the reader to imagine the submarine in detail, but also because of the resonant echo from other media which reconfirm the reader's initial abductions. To these abductions must now be added the reader's fear that the submarine, which has advanced destructive power and speed, is practically on Argentina's doorstep. These inferences place into motion not only a system of logical expectations but also, and above all, emotional ones.

What truly strengthens the model media reader's belief in the existence of the submarine are official statements by British Defence Minister John Nott. Asked by journalists to confirm or deny the *Superb*'s presence in the waters surrounding the Malvinas-Falklands, Nott states: "I do not comment on rumours" (*Clarín*, 1 April, "Absolute silence"). Herein is one of the paradoxes of strategic information: any other statement made by Nott would have been considered as false. But the very act of qualifying the story as a rumour highlights and strengthens the information without the necessity of overtly confirming or denying its veracity. Such is the power of lexical presuppositions.

The Argentines still had not landed on the Malvinas-Falklands when the British *counter-information strategy* was set in motion. This Argentine escalation, which permits a strategic production and diffusion of the rumour, parallels the intensity of the British retreat from the islands: on 2 April, not only was Port Stanley surrendered, thus signalling the high point of the British retreat, but the British flagship – the icebreaker *Endurance* – was the one to lead the withdrawal (*Clarín*, 2 April, "The British fleet operating in the Malvinas-Falklands"). Does this action, which organises factual history in a particular way, signify the death of the rumour and the dissolution of the possible media world? Absolutely not. In the meantime, the rumour has already entered Argentina and now not only do newspaper sources contribute to its construction but so does "information from certain sources associated with the Argentine Defence Ministry, which state that nothing is known about the location of a nuclear submarine called the *Superb*, which London situates as being in the waters of the South Atlantic" (*Clarín*, 2 April, "The British fleet is operating in the Malvinas-Falklands"). The press, busy covering the Argentine landing on the islands, momentarily loses sight of the submarine's precise location. The model media reader has, though, already registered this new existing presupposition on the Argentine side, and the reader can legitimately become more and more nervous.

By 4 April, after the political-military shock of the Argentine invasion had lessened, the submarine returns to comply faithfully with the dictate that all creatures born in a possible media world must be fed and cared for:

> According to reliable military sources cited by AFP, a nuclear submarine, which may, or may not, be the *Superb*, has been sighted in international waters off the coast of Mar del Plata. It is sailing in the direction of the Malvinas-Falklands. (*Clarín*, 4 April, "Two British ships?")[1]

Given the seriousness of the report, an Argentine reader exercising the power of critical interpretation could begin to feel that checking the "reliable military sources" is urgent: are they Argentine or British? How can a British nuclear submarine be only 600 kilometres from the Argentine capital? And furthermore, are there now two submarines? The possible media world offers nothing in response to these questions, but does momentarily calm the model media reader: safety measures have been ordered by the Argentine navy in all major sea resorts.

London, meanwhile, continues to carry out its strategy of planting presuppositions. Defence Minister John Nott repeats that he cannot confirm or deny if the *Superb* is carrying out operations off the Argentine coast: "I have no intention of giving any information about the location of our submarines" (*Clarín*, 4 April, "Two British ships?"). This is the third case of presuppositions that the British possible media world has presented. By maintaining his refusal to comment, Nott nourishes the suspicion that British submarines are actually off the Malvinas-Falklands. As opposed to the previous presuppositions conveyed by the Foreign Office and Nott, both of which characterise reports about the submarine as "versions" or "rumours", Nott's present intervention as an *active official source* closes the British information strategy circle in the construction of a possible media world and in the cooperative response to it awaited from the reader.

It seems clear that Nott's presupposition is meant to be inserted into the already woven semiotic fabric as a pre-constructed discourse. If

---

[1] Mar del Plata is an Argentine coastal resort, which could accommodate three million tourists annually. It is located approximately 600 kilometres from Buenos Aires.

presupposition is always considered to be an anaphoric transmission, then it can also be considered to be the starting point of a cataphoric process. Nott's statement is a case of existential presupposition because it depends on a particular enunciation strategy. [2] As such, Nott's statement acquires a particular power, in as much as the statement's objective is, as shall be seen, effectively to convince the public that the British government has sent submarines to the Southern Atlantic. This enunciative power can be exercised not only because Nott has specifically referred to the rumour, but primarily because of his special position as an information source. The entire socio-semiotic network supports him. His presupposition thus becomes highlighted information and is picked up by the papers, thereby activating the interpretative mechanisms of its model media readers.

A telex from London on 3 April disseminated by AP, EFE, Latin Reuters and American UPI – which up until now had not placed itself in the hunt for the submarine – throws the submarine's whereabouts into question. The report affirms that the *Superb* can be currently found at the head of a blockade Task Force navigating towards the Southern Atlantic (*Clarín*, 4 April, "The British government sends an air-naval force to the Malvinas-Falklands"). The story, published by *Clarín* on on 4 April, throws the model media world which the reader has patiently constructed into turmoil: if the *Superb* is, as UPI reports, presently sailing towards the south, then what submarine is, as AFP reports, off the shores of Mar del Plata? Just how many submarines are there? British Prime Minister Margaret Thatcher intervenes in the possible media world indirectly to explain why a discursive fleet of phantom submarines is necessary and thereby to curb all possible doubt on the part of the model media reader as to the submarine's existence. On 3 April, Thatcher is attacked by the Labour Party during a session in the House of Commons immediately following the Argentine landing. While defending herself, the Prime Minister states: "It would be absurd to send the entire fleet every time Buenos Aires speaks aggressively" (*Clarín*, 4 April, "The British government sends an air-naval force to the Malvinas-Falklands"). While awaiting the British Task Force's arrival in the islands' waters, a fleet of obviously swifter rumours and presuppositions can be deployed.

Only two days have passed since the Argentine landing. Why hasn't Argentina organised – either through official or unofficial media information sources – its own counter-information strategy? Because to

---

[2] "Existential presuppositions have the power of making their referential object existent, regardless of whether or not their existence has previously been known. The very act of mentioning it creates a propensity for existence" (Eco 1990: 300).

respond to a presupposition one must first construct a complex counter-presupposition. The Argentine government, which lacked even a basic information strategy, simply failed to do this. Regardless, the possibility for the Argentine official sources to carry out a meta-discursive intervention existed. This intervention could have situated itself outside of the communication interaction, framing it: we have already seen how textual sources "talk" with each other. It could have attempted correctly to identify the nature of British information.

On 5 April Argentine forces from the recently created Malvinas-Falklands Theatre Operations Command militarily reinforced the islands. Meanwhile, at Portsmouth, the British government moved her troops into its largest battle fleet assembled since the Second World War, and the DAN press agency tagged along in the hunt to find, and identify, the submarine. A DAN telex, published by *Clarín*, reports that the *Superb* is 250 kilometres from Buenos Aires and is heading directly towards the Malvinas-Falklands. In the possible media world, the story contributes to the construction of the submarine's identity as a textual topic by adding new characteristics:

1. the submarine has a particular speed;
2. it can remain submerged for long periods of time;
3. it has a special type of highly destructive torpedo (*Clarín*, 5 April, "A strong naval contingent leaves Great Britain today").

On 6 April the Argentine Navy decides to enter the possible media world: they attempt unofficially to locate the submarine's position and identify her characteristics. Tracking the submarine through news pieces published after 31 March, and confirming its presence in the waters off Mar del Plata, the Navy signals that "As of two days ago, the submarine should be in proximity to the islands." This temporal and spatial localising function ("as of two days ago" and "in proximity to the islands") includes an additional piece of information: an Argentine submarine, the *Salta,* is being deployed because of the *Superb*'s presence in international waters (*Clarín,* 6 April, "Military preparations off the Argentine coast").

To conclude the rumour's first week of life, Rodolfo Terragno, London-based correspondent of Venezuela's *El Diario*, intervenes in the international dialogue. In Caracas, *El Diario* publishes his report that the 4,500-ton nuclear propelled submarine called the *Superb* is presently in proximity to the Malvinas-Falklands; but this titbit of information is one with which the Argentine model media reader is already familiar.

The Proliferation of the Rumour

The conflict's second week begins with the introduction of the United States on the scene. Brandishing United Nations resolution number 502, the US assumes a negative diplomatic policy towards Argentina. The resolution requires that Argentina withdraw its troops from the islands. Secretary of State Alexander Haig begins travelling back and forth to Buenos Aires. The rumour's second week is rich in information about the submarine: there are now two of them, the *Superb* and the *Oracle*. This time, the possible media world binds itself to its previously constructed script and the model media reader need only activate the already delineated topic "nuclear submarine". Although the *Superb* still maintains its "nuclear" semantic property, the *Oracle* is a conventional, diesel-propelled unit.

The telex which heralds the news is simultaneously published in London, New York and Madrid by the AFP, ANSA, AP, EFE, Latin Reuters and UPL. To the existing data about mother *Superb* – 4,500 tons and a crew of 97 – must now be added the telexed information that she travels at a velocity of 30 knots per hour (explaining her speed in reaching the Malvinas-Falklands coastline after passing Mar del Plata only two days after her deployment from Gibraltar), and that she carries five 533-millimetre torpedoes. Her daughter, the *Oracle*, weighs 2,410 tons, has an underwater speed of 17 knots, and a modest crew of 68. Despite her smaller size, the *Oracle*'s battle capacity is greater: she has eight 533-millimetre torpedoes. Evidently not satisfied with this little family, *The Times* affirms that four of the Royal Navy's nuclear submarines "are sailing to the islands of the South Atlantic" (*Clarín*, 8 April, "The advance of the British fleet continues").

Twenty-four hours before Alexander Haig's arrival in Buenos Aires, the submarines were identified by journalist Jacques Isnard of France's *Le Monde*. The report comes to the aid of the media world which has been created up until this point. *Clarín*, entitling Isnard's story "A submarine fleet!", also cites information from the *Times*' new article. *Superb*'s other children are called the *Sceptre,* the *Spartan* and the *Splendid*. Each weighs 4,500 tons and is armed with torpedoes valued for their silence. The model media reader, who has been following events daily, is alerted: "With such a submarine force, London will be using military means to implement the threatened blockade approved by the House of Commons on April 7th" (*Clarín*, 9 April, "A submarine fleet?").

The multitude of identifying signs, the testimony of the experts, the international agencies that simultaneously dispatch new information, the different telex date-lines, the dialogue between newspapers and, finally, Argentina's unofficial statements alongside Britain's official ones, makes doubting the existence of British submarines in the South Atlantic difficult. The possible media world and the inter-media system that has sustained it have managed to construct something extremely tangible, real and credible: a family of nuclear submarines. The model reader has no escape.

Altered states

The newspaper itself starts to doubt the existence of the submarines at this point. *Clarín* leaves the evidence aside in order to conjecture:

> According to information from expert sources, the majority of the units in question could not reach the waters off the Malvinas-Falklands Archipelago for 10 days (after their deployment from Gibraltar). Despite this, all information leads one to suppose that Hunter-Killer nuclear submarines can already be found in the region. The British press frequently refers to four such units. (*Clarín*, 10 April, AFP, EFE and Latin Reuters, "British troops are reinforced")

Clarín's statement is important because it signals a weak point in the construction of the *Superb*'s possible media world (PMW): for one part, a hard nucleus of identifying signs continues to circulate. These signs assign properties given by British sources: nuclear power, speed, and crew. These signs, which will continue to circulate in the media, can be called PMW 1. For another part, PMW 2, in which certain properties of PMW 1 can be already found in the Malvinas-Falklands, are "narcotised".

If PMW 1 and PMW 2 are both states in the same possible media world ("the nuclear submarine *Superb*") then this point of temporal dysfunction in the newspaper ("in ten days") permits the model media reader to distance herself from the reported information and carry out a doxastic disconnection: "The possible submarine that has been delineated as an inhabitant in my world of beliefs may be the same entity within a real world or may be a different entity in a different world".[3]

Argentina's Minister of Foreign Relations, Chancellor Nicanor Costa Méndez, its President, General Leopoldo Fortunato Galtieri, and the other two members of the Military Junta, Admiral Jorge Anaya and Brigadier General Lami Dozo, are unable to reach a negotiation agreement with U.S. Secretary of State, Alexander Haig. Haig travels to London on 11 April with Argentine's official proposal. The pause created by PMW 2 dissolves along with the possibility of a diplomatic solution. On the same date, *Clarín* offers new information:

[3] For an analysis of abductive phenomena, see Eco, 1990, 22ff. They are mechanisms which create worlds.

The British press echoes the analysis of some military observers who point out that Great Britain is likely to initiate a blockade with five nuclear submarines, four of which are presently to be found in the waters off the Malvinas-Falklands. These submarines will act alone while awaiting the British Task Force, which comprises 36 ships, and which was deployed five days ago from Portsmouth and Gibraltar. (*Clarín*, 11 April, "Thatcher ratifies the blockade")

While the United Kingdom hardens its position in response to the Argentine conditions brought by Haig to London, the submarines become legion. *Clarín,* basing itself on its own sources, reports that, "According to certain rumours, and as London has warned, Soviet and U.S. submarines will be patrolling the waters off the Malvinas-Falklands" (*Clarín*, 12 April, "A peaceful vigil").

The Argentine reader finds herself in a submarine war film. Historical events relate to the situation at hand: who can forget the *Graf Spee,* the German pocket battleship which, at the outset of the Second World War, came to die on the shores of Montevideo, scuttled after unrelenting pursuit? The reader already has so many analogous intertextual models. The possible media world sustained by *Clarín* permits the reader to select a group of interpretative hypotheses which operate like an economic principle. Given the persistence of historical imagery, the reader can expect the *Superb* to have the ability to unleash the Third World War as "there are those who remember that Germany's decision on 1 February 1917 to declare 'submarine war without restrictions' ultimately determined the United States' entry into the First World War" (*Clarín,* 12 April, "Britain begins a naval blockade in the Southern Atlantic").

But the reader must also contend with 12 April, the key date of both Alexander Haig's trip to London and the beginning of the British blockade. The reader can propose a group of hypo-coded abductions according to which "the interpretation has been selected as being the most plausible among others, but it is still uncertain whether it is or isn't correct. An explanation can only be given in consideration of successive verifications" (Eco, 1990, 237). The reader can suppose, for example, that the story about the quickly identified British submarine fleet, which has been furnishing the possible media world, is being circulated simply to intimidate the Argentines. If this supposition is correct, then why has no Argentine information source unmasked the British strategy, by calling its bluff? Doing so would constitute an Argentine defence counter-information strategy.

From the British point of view, the issue was to construct a credible and effective information strategy. To do this, unofficial information had to be given out in London and then picked up and "owned" by the Argentine press. The model media reader, however, cannot discern the British counter-strategy, because no textual index in the possible media world has informed the reader about it. The reader might also implement a group of meta-abductions. Through these they can decide if the possible media world delineated by preceding inferences coincides with their universe of experience. The reader, however, cannot, *a priori*, brand *Clarín* as a traitor for having disseminated information that favoured the enemy's information strategy, precisely because of the presence of an external media contract which: (a) includes a media trust construct permitting the newspaper's sale and consumption; and since (b) the newspaper includes other sections, such as editorials and articles about diplomatic negotiations that clearly signal the paper's support and defence of Argentine interests. So what can the reader do?[4]

Hypothesis 1 or the negotiation supporters: some British and Argentine political sectors are interested in reaching a diplomatic solution. Nourished by newspaper articles published for approximately two weeks, which are based on the rumour that a submarine fleet is being deployed, and which alert both British and Argentine public opinion about the military, political, and life-costs implied by a frontal encounter, interpretative hypothesis and plausibility is strengthened by the rumours' systematic persistence and by the lack of Argentine control over them. Here, there is a nuclear arsenal of such potency that it can only be vanquished by a peace agreement; it is fundamentally an invisible entity, a dissuasive and mythological submarine:

As of daybreak four nuclear submarines have been operating in the blockade zone. The submarines have begun to send information to their admiral ship, the aircraft carrier Hermes. According to a British specialist, the submarines are a threat to the Argentine fleet. Their main advantage is that they can remain submerged for two months at

---

[4] The reader can, for example, stop reading *Clarín* and switch newspapers. *La Nación* published only three stories about the *Superb* during the same time-frame. A small box on page 10 in their 3 April edition entitled, "At liberty to sink aircraft carriers" specifically refers to the *Superb*. Another small article on page 4, 13 April, entitled "So many submarines" counts the possible nuclear submarines circulating in the region, but makes no specific reference to the *Superb*. A final story on 20 April, published on page 2, "Alarm in the British fleet because of submarine", is dedicated to an unidentified submarine sighted thirty nautical miles from the British fleet.

a time and can navigate underwater at a speed above 30 knots an hour. The same expert affirms that this speed cannot be matched by Argentine surface ships. According to sources consulted, the British submarines' radars are highly superior to those of the Argentines. All of them are equipped with Tigerfish Mark 241 torpedoes that can hit targets up to 17 miles away. Their radars benefit from the enormous energy of nuclear reactors and have a wider operating radius than that of Argentine surface ships and Argentine anti-submarine heli-copters. The experts are convinced that the Tigerfish are capable of easily sinking Argentine vessels. (*Clarín*, 12 April, AFP, ANSA, AP, EFE and Latin Reuters, "The British fleet reaches Ascension Island")

Hypothesis 2 or the war supporters: other British and Argentine political sectors are uninterested in a United Nations-sponsored negotiated solution to the conflict. They want to construct a powerful counter-information strategy (disqualification of the enemy) that can be manipulated (proper qualification) in order to defeat the British.

The rigid position of both these sectors can be better understood in light of the fact their hypotheses were voiced between 12 and 14 April, i.e. exactly when Alexander Haig was in London delivering the Argentine peace proposal and ascertaining the British negotiation position.

A press secretary for the Ministry of Defence confirmed yesterday that British submarines have been sent to the Malvinas-Falklands islands. This action is consistent with the reinforcement of the British blockade which began at daybreak on 12 April. Several reports, though, fail to coincide about the number of submarines in the blockade zone. [...] Hunter-Killer submarines, whose presence has not been denied by the British government, are among the most modern of their class. According to the British Admiralty, these submarines are practically undetectable. Their radar system can locate enemy ships up to 40 miles away. Experts, however, do not underestimate the strength of Argentine forces, which is superior to that of any other Latin American nation. (*Clarín*, 13 April, AFP, ANSA, AP and Latin Reuters, "London confirms that submarines are patrolling the water off the Malvinas-Falklands")

According to a high-ranking naval officer, Argentine defence forces have located British submarines off the Malvinas-Falklands. Their presence is not affecting regular airdrops to Argentine troops defending the island. Qualified naval sources indicate that four British submarines are enforcing the naval blockade. Of these, only two are nuclear units from the Hunter-Killer class. These units can be used to both detect and attack Argentine vessels. The Argentine Armada possesses a thousand planes, including Trackers and Neptunes, as well as ships which can locate enemy submarines. According to our sources, the enemy submarines have orders to blockade a highly defined and reduced area. (*Clarín*, 14 April, "Air-carrier deployment to the islands is confirmed, submarines have been detected")

The media holds a cancerous viewpoint, which can be labelled Hypothesis 3. It is possible that unverified information was passed back and forth within and between media and press agencies. Like a diseased cell, this information set off a multiplication process that became impossible to arrest. If this hypothesis is correct, then news was produced on the basis of published conjecture, instead of hard facts. The reader, accepting Hypothesis 3, would be freed from the ingenuous position which had been delineated for them, and would be placed instead in a critical extra-semiotic position. The reader would run the risk, however, of placing the established media contract with the press in general, and *Clarín* in particular, into crisis. Is it worth running such a risk?

The Death of the Rumour
Clarín was silent on 15 April. Coincidentally, this was the day that Haig arrived in Buenos Aires to deliver the official British response. On 16 April, telexes from AFP, ANSA, UPI and Latin Reuters begin to "narcotise" the submarine's aggressive profile, attributing simple "patrol" functions to it (*Clarín*, 16 April, "The British fleet undergoes exercises on the open sea"). On 17 April, an official Argentine Navy source commented that the British had excellent submarines "precisely because they cannot be located" (*Clarín*, 17 April, "Argentine ships sail towards the Malvinas-Falklands"). Given the amount of identifying signs that the *Superb* had left in her wake, the reader could now begin to suspect that she was a fake.

On 18 April, TELAM issued a telex. Date-lined Rio de Janeiro, it reported that a Brazilian commercial airline pilot had sighted and photographed a submarine navigating in the Gulf of Santa Catarina, "but it is doubtful that the vessel can be correctly identified as poor meteorological conditions affected the quality of the photograph" (*Clarín*, 18 April, "Spotted in Brazil"). A rare event: a photograph of a rumour. The *Superb* deteriorates to the category of the Loch Ness monster, another often photographed rumour.

The submarine lost itself in the mist and failure of the Haig mission.

The report on the 18 April was the last piece of information that the Argentine reader would have about the *Superb*. The presence of phantom submarines was now unnecessary as the British task force was only eighty kilometres away from the Georgia Islands. On 22 April, *Clarín* published the submarine's obituary, date-lined London, on page 6:

> A British submarine which was previously reported as patrolling the waters off the Malvinas-Falklands has been sighted in Scotland. The submarine appears to *have never been* in the South Atlantic. Defence sources confirmed today that the nuclear submarine *Superb* was presently returning to its home base of Faslane, off the river Clyde. (*Clarín*, Latin Reuters, 22 April, "It showed up in Scotland")

On 23 April, both the *Daily Record*, Scotland's most widely read newspaper, and regional television reported that the *Superb* had never left her home base. The British Defence Minister "is obliged to admit that a bluff has been discovered on the part of the British" (*Clarín*, 23 April, "The *Superb* bluff"). The submarine died as it had been born, through media intra-transmission.

Media Truth

The rumours and stories that circulated about the *Superb* step outside the bounds of journalistic propriety and enunciation. The question is not if the press did, or did not, knowingly lie. What must be analysed are the elements which permitted the *Superb* story to circulate as non-fiction, when it was really a fictional work. The story was framed in a kind of discourse which did not prevent the introduction of fictional elements. Let us look at some of these elements:

(a) The enunciator's viewpoint: the identity charade
     The submarine story's identity is originally classified as "a reported version". In the construction of the possible media world of the *Superb*, it has already been seen how a group of indices which were fundamentally related to press agencies' textual sources allowed carrying out a precise identification: the submarine's identity is a "fact" because it was labelled as such by a varied group of social actors from different places.
     A second level of analysis deals with the identity of the constructed object, instead of the type of information which contributed to that construction. The official and unofficial textual sources which were repeatedly circulated throughout press agencies, as well as the expert opinions and statements collected about the submarine, agreed on a

huge amount of semantic traits and qualitative identification elements assigned to the submarine.

A third level of analysis focuses on the identity of the object in relation to the power position of sources who made statements about it. The statements of the Foreign Office, British Defence Minister John Nott and Prime Minister Margaret Thatcher contain a special authoritative ring – they are, after all, "official" sources – which contribute to frame the story as truth.

For a story to circulate as truth there must be social agreement about it. Because the *Superb* lie had a pragmatic value, constructing a consistent possible media world for it was essential. As such, a media contract became necessary.

(b) The reader's viewpoint: the possibility of proof

How strong is the argument that the information presented to the reader was credible? In other words, what guidelines did the reader use to decide to believe, or to not believe, the submarine identity statements made by the media? Classical research on media reception indicates how much the reader will trust information presented across different media formats as truthful. In relation to the analysis of true information presented about the *Superb*, it seems obvious that the reader was capable of developing personal verification hypotheses that could, or could not, be utilised. Although the media left some room for doubt, it did not give the reader decoding elements, nor did it assign the reader a precise physical location in which both the *Superb* and the reader's belief in it could reside.

It seems clear that any attempt by the reader to verify the *Superb* story implied, at the very least, an extra-semiotic operation in which the reader had to leave aside the report that the submarine had been found in Scotland. Such an operation, however, is a Epimenidian paradox: the operation is impossible because the 22 April report about the "real" *Superb*'s location inhabits the same possible media world as the rumour. In other words, the media world was transformed into a vicious circle: if the reader believed in statements which indicated that the *Superb* was off the Malvinas-Falklands coast for twenty days, then how could the reader simultaneously believe in statements by the same enunciative newspaper sources (the press agencies, John Nott, etc.) that throughout that same period, the *Superb* was in Scotland? How could the reader decide if the press was lying at the beginning or the end or vice-versa? From the reader's point of view, deciding what to believe and when was undecidable.

The *Superb* case is a salutary example of a rumour used in a psychological war strategy. It can also appear to the reader to be a case of "false information". Italian researcher Carlo Marletti, a well known specialist in analysis of fake information, writes of new journalism:

> Questioning the frontiers between reality and fiction [...] the new journalism has failed to give us any clue what is truly news or relevant for the redefinition of exchange relations and for the reciprocal relationship between fiction and reality which is in crisis. [...] The sociology of knowledge indicates that no manipulation or falsification can be effective in and of itself, but can only be viewed in relation to a defined "irreality construction" within which it acquires its own significance. [...] A falsehood, in other words, is "valued" only when conditions exist which make duplicity difficult. (Marletti, 1984, 60-62)

Asked about why *Clarín* backed for over twenty days a story which was later discredited, journalist and editorialist Ricardo Kirschbaum, who authored one of the most incisive books about the Malvinas-Falklands conflict, responds:

> "On the one hand, this was an intensely psychological war. Serious newspapers acted pragmatically. As information enterprises, they clearly knew how the war would probably turn out, but they also thought that Argentina should play the game. On the other hand, the only source of information about the story was Britain. What could they do? Call London? How could they verify those sources?" (Interviewed at the *Clarín* offices in Buenos Aires, 17 December 1990)

Retired Vice-Admiral Fernando Millia, director of the oldest Latin American publication about naval strategy, *El Boletín del Centro Naval*, held the office of Press Secretary for the Argentine Navy during the war. He gives his viewpoint about the *Superb* phenomenon:

> "I have a very particular view about the *Superb* case. When NATO moved from a 'flexible response' strategy to one of 'assured destruction', the weapons needed to implement the strategy also changed. Submarines, which usually use short range torpedoes, had to have nuclear warheads. The *Superb* was supposedly at Gibraltar when its deployment to the South Atlantic was announced. One week it was in Scotland at a U.S. submarine base where nuclear warheads are kept! I suspect that the *Superb* went to change its conventional torpedoes for nuclear warheads, thus preparing for the eventual

necessity of delivering a massive response in Argentine territory. The objective was the continent."

Do you believe that the submarine reached the waters off the Malvinas-Falklands?

"No, I don't think that she went farther than Ascension Island. The submarine's location was never pinpointed in technical terms, that is to say, with radar. An espionage operative told us that there were two submarines in the area. I think that British intelligence services promoted a certain idea to the media, but I have no reliable information. The European press had the information first and reports influenced each other. As in every war there were different versions of the story. In war, information is always foggy." (Interviewed in Buenos Aires, 16 December 1990)

Horacio Verbitsky, one of Argentina's most important opinion-makers and editor-in-chief of the leftist *Página/12* newspaper, summarises the information strategy surrounding the *Superb* in the following manner:

"The *Superb* was an exceptional case. The whole incident was mostly about generating an Argentine psychological response. It was an imaginary war; it was never really planned to go to war. What was planned was a gigantic, psychological operation. The *Superb* episode, for example, resulted in the Argentine fleet's being unable to operate comfortably because of fear or phantom submarines." (Interviewed in Buenos Aires, 18 December 1990)

In a research report about a New York City crime-wave which had been covered by several New York papers, Fishman postulates that the press itself created the crime-wave:

"I discovered something that made me wonder whether the entire news production process was creating the crime-wave it was reporting. [...] As I checked with other journalists, I found that many had doubts about the reality of the crime-wave. Still, no one could resist reporting it. The crime-wave was a force which weighed heavily on their judgment of what constituted news, and it simply could not be ignored. Clearly, some kind of system was operating. Something in the news production process was creating the crime-wave. What was it?" (Fishman, 1980, 5)

The newspapers organised a frame of reference which converted a few news stories into an entire belief system. This internally nourished system was sufficiently stable to allow the story about the submarine to acquire a life of its own. In the media continuum, the story simply became a stabilised element in a flux of rumours.

Were, or were not, British and Argentine submarines present in the area blockaded by the British? To answer this question we must turn to historical documentation and reconstruct, *a posteriori*, the entire interpretative circuit. Of course submarines were present in the area, but not the ones indicated by the press. Furthermore, their manoeuvres did not even take place on the dates stated by the press. The six submarines employed by the British Task Force were:

1. The *Spartan* and the *Splendid* from the Swiftsure class with a weight of 4,500 tons, a crew of 93 and a speed of 30 knots. Each carried five modified Tigerfish torpedoes and began operations on 12 April.
2. The *Conqueror*, the *Valiant* and the *Courageous* from the Churchill and Valiant class; each 4,500 tons, a crew of 103, and a speed of 30 knots. Equipped with six modified Tigerfish torpedoes, they commenced operations on 16 April, 16 May and 30 May respectively.
3. The *Onyx* from the Oberon and Porpoise class; 2,410 tons, 69 crew members on board, a velocity of 12 knots and eight modified Tigerfish torpedoes. She started operations on 28 May. (Hastings and Jenkins, 1983, 374)

Up until 10 April, the press continued to construct and furnish a possible media world for the *Superb*. The *Spartan* and the *Splendid,* however, were the first British submarines to enter the operation zone, and they did not enter the zone prior to 12 April. Argentine submarines such as the *Salta* or the *Santa Fé* – highly damaged during the battle for the Georgia Islands at the end of April – waged intense attacks until the Argentine surface ship *General Belgrano* was sunk on 3 May by British forces. The reader, though, could only be apprised of this "extra media" information after the war from specialised British and Argentine publications.

Returning to the possible world, after 10 April, and above all after 12 April, two media information constructions melded together: one, the survival of the fictional story of the *Superb* in the PMW 1; the other, fictional and non-fictional information about the other submarines that made up the British expedition in PMW 2. From the point of view of the model media reader, the construction of news credibility appeared sound and the possibility of deontic ascription remained indeterminable.

The statements of unofficial textual sources from the Argentine Air Force and Navy were later revealed to be the closest to the actual truth. Despite their accuracy, however, they were unable to produce an information rupture that was sufficiently potent to recontextualise the frame of existing presuppositions which the model media reader had been given to construct over the passing days. No Argentine statement had the positional power to produce a communication catastrophe in the British strategy.

The rumour's evolution curve in relation to political and military events during the first month of the conflict indicates that the point of major information tension in the *Superb*'s possible world occurred on 31 March, 1 and 2 April; moments before the landing of the rumour in Argentina and of the Argentines on the islands. Reports dedicated to the rumour on those dates averaged four a day. The rumour's second wind occurred during the period of Haig's London-Buenos Aires trip, with an average of three stories a day. The date 12 April 1982 is the epicentre of the maximum point of information tension about both the rumour and negotiation attempts; on this date *Clarín* simultaneously published PMW 1 and PMW 2.

What makes the *Superb* case especially interesting is that on 13 April, after Haig and the Military Junta's statements that diplomatic attempts to reach a negotiated solution had collapsed, and after the arrival of the *Spartan* and *Splendid* in the blockade zone, the *Superb* rumour was thrust into crisis. This crisis continued until the submarine's profile was totally eclipsed, thereby marking how the entire construction of the small world of the submarine formed part of the great world of strategy of the war. At this point the analyst, a "privileged" reader, in as much as he has simultaneous access to textual and extra-textual evidence, become another type of model reader, able to test interpretative hypotheses and formulate a sufficiently cautious group of meta-abductions:

1. On the one hand, the rumour, as has been accurately noted by Kapferer, always functions as a simplified explanation system through its provision of an organisational frame in which to place daily perceptions of events (Kapferer, 1987, 80). In this sense, the rumour is viewed as a narrative not far from myth. The *Superb* story filled the first page of the first week of the conflict. The *Clarín* reader could hold onto a series of cognitive hypotheses which could easily be accepted in such a small – and easily manipulated – world.

2. On the other hand, the possible media world which circulated because of the rumour forced official textual sources from both

countries to take a position about the accuracy of the reported information and about the accuracy of the entire communication interaction.

The *Superb* story demonstrates the inverted importance that unofficial textual sources have over official ones: unofficial sources, entering the information scene to confirm or deny the media-invented phenomena, exalted it to the status of "event" simply because it had been referred to by official sources. The entire information circuit is thus legitimised. The extant presuppositions of British and Argentine official textual sources act as a counter-legitimisation discourse. They become one more element in the construction of the *Superb*'s possible world. Viewed from this perspective, the *Superb* story is not very far from the genre of historical novel which intertwines historical persons with fictional ones in the same textual scenery.

It is very possible that British intelligence sources, who had to gain time until the actual arrival of the Task Force on the islands, created the rumour so that it would be picked up by the media. The media system, however, is the entity which effectively produced the rumour. Official British textual sources confirmed the story indirectly with a conglomerate of textual strategies which produced "false information" that acquired the status of "news report" the moment it is embraced by the press. While the British Navy was being deployed, these official sources were supposed to fill the time-lag with an opportune story capable of capturing the reader with the same type of suspense present in a mystery novel. As such, the rumour had to have a carefully timed life-span in order to be effective.

A construction of the rumour which categorises it as a kind of media verisimilitude placed the Argentine official and unofficial textual sources who espoused it in a position which is, at the very least, uncomfortable. Deprived of a meta-discursive strategy aimed at defusing the *Superb*'s possible media world, Argentine sources joined the rearguard of the British strategy. Although this posture gave the Argentines the opportunity of double-crossing the British strategy, they failed to sink the British communication plan. When British nuclear submarines truly began to operate in the area, the Argentine media opportunity had already passed. And the newspaper? *Clarín* established a double media pact with the reader: one, the constructed possible media world legitimisation and identification system, was internal to the media; the other, external to the reader, played with a fictional and factual double register. Everything that was publishable got published, without discrimination, just like the great book of the world.

The news information strategies failed to escape the logic of their own internal production system and their main loyalty – their Great Pact – is not so much to their readers as to themselves. Perhaps because of this, the antagonistic categories of telling the truth or lying – as John Searle would say – as they adhere to a particular extra-textual reference source, are not sufficiently operative inside a media world. In the dichotomy, the press creates, through its articulations – which are based on its own information sources – and through its production of possible worlds, such an effective form of unreality that it can step beyond the bounds of the actual events. This process confirms the way that the media legitimises itself and its version of factual events, i.e. media truth. What comes into play in the consumption of information discourse is not verification, but credibility.

Many Years Later

An analysis of the British role in the Malvinas-Falklands War by Lord Franks for the British Parliament, known as the Franks Report, was published on 18 January 1983. Article No. 331 states:

> In conclusion, we believe that action should have been taken during the first phase of the Georgia Islands crisis which was consistent to the deployment of ships in the sector. The opinion of Lord Carrington is that the use of surface ships would not have gone unnoticed and would have implied serious threat precisely at the time that the government sought to avoid any action which might cause provocation. An intervention could have caused a series of attacks by the Argentines against the Falkland Islands, in the face of which the government would have been forced to respond. This objection is not the same as that to the deployment of a submarine, because the possibility existed of obscuring her movements. The decision to deploy the first nuclear submarine was taken on Monday, March 29th, 1982." (*Franks Report,* 1983, 235)

Lord Franks's report raises a final question: Was a secret submarine deployed on 29 March, hidden from radar and from the media who were focused on describing the *Superb*? Was the *Superb* a dupe, a British intelligence strategy, meant to obscure the existence of the "real" submarine which was deployed on 29 March and whose identity and qualities remain unknown? To date, the question is unanswered, but does point to the vertigo created by information disseminated during conflicts: A wants B to believe that C, and so on to infinity.

References

Eco, U. (1979). *Lector in fabula*. Milano: Bompiani

Eco, U. (1990). *I limiti dell'interpretazione*. Milano: Bompiani.

Franks Report. (1983). *Falkland Islands Review: Report of a Committee of Privy Counsellors. (Cmnd 8787)*. London: Her Majesty's Stationery Office.

Fishman, M. (1980). *Manufacturing the News* (Austin: University of Texas Press).

Hastings, M., and S. Jenkins. (1983). *The Battle of the Falklands*. London: Pan.

Kapferer, J. N. (1987). *Rumeurs*. Paris: Seuil.

Marletti, C. (1984). *Media e politica*. (Milan: Angeli).

Malvinas-Falklands Revisited:
Prelude, War and Aftermath

María Cristina Fra Amador

The Malvinas Islands have always been more desired than loved. In 1592 Samuel Johnson described them as "a bleak and gloomy solitude, an island thrown aside from human use, stormy in winter and barren in summer, an island which not even the southern savages have dignified with habitation" (Kirkpatrick, 1989/90, 11).

Argentina had been trying to resolve the dispute since the mid-1960s, but without success. In 1964, Argentina raised the question of the Malvinas Islands in the Subcommittee on Small Territories of the UN Special Committee on Decolonization.[1] The British position was that sovereignty was not negotiable but the questions of the welfare of the islanders and contacts with Argentina should indeed be discussed. The report of the Special Committee resulted in the General Assembly of the UN approving Resolution 2065 in 1965. In this resolution, the Assembly recognised the existence of a dispute, and invited the two governments to "proceed without delay" with negotiations to find "a peaceful solution to the problem, bearing in mind the interests of the population of the Falkland Islands" (Freedman and Gamba-Stonehouse, 1991, 8). However, this progress was cut short through effective lobbying by the Falkland Islands Committee in the Houses of Parliament in 1968.

Argentine governments, ignoring demands by nationalists for immediate and drastic action, continued with the negotiations. In 1969, the first steps were taken to open a line of communications with the Islands. The Communications Agreement of 1971 introduced a weekly air service with the mainland. However, in 1975 it appeared that Britain was even going back on this integrative trend when an expedition was sent to determine the economic potential of the Islands (the Shackleton Mission). There were also military incidents such as the one involving the *RSS Shackleton* in February 1976 (Freedman and Gamba-Stonehouse, 1984, 9).

After the 1976/77 crises, the British Government appeared to be again willing to negotiate seriously. Argentina now understood that the only possible approach that remained was that of a leaseback arrangement, through which Argentina would receive titular sovereignty

---

[1] See Resolution 1514 (XV), in which the General Assembly declared the need to change the situation of all those countries under colonialism.

but allow a British administration to continue. In 1977 bilateral negotiations resumed, and a leaseback proposal was studied as well as possibilities for a joint Anglo-Argentine economic programme for the exploration, exploitation and development of the region. The Conservative government of Margaret Thatcher continued with this approach through 1979 and 1980. But once again the islanders required the Government to add their representatives to all future delegations discussing the Islands with Argentina and to freeze the sovereignty issue, thus channeling all trilateral negotiations into exclusively peripheral matters. What was curious was that the islanders had demanded Britain provide them with defence of the Islands, but Britain refused their demands. Of particular significance was the decision to withdraw *HMS Endurance* from service by April 1982. The Defence White Paper of June 1981 suggested abandoning the British naval presence in the South Atlantic and in Antarctica.

Analysing the facts, Argentina felt that it had received mixed signals. On the one hand, three years of work on the possibility of a leaseback had been abruptly abandoned, and the islanders had become a third party to the negotiations with power to veto any progress on the sovereignty issue. On the other hand, the British showed no interest in increasing their economic and military position as an alternative to serious negotiations with Buenos Aires.

At that time, Argentina was governed by a military Junta and the analysis made by them suggested that the British Government should be encouraged to follow the logical position reflected by the *Endurance* decision, and reactivate negotiations. The immediate Argentine objective was to return to the original negotiating framework of 1965/67. For the Junta, if Britain refused to negotiate seriously, Argentina could break diplomatic relations or cut communications links to the Islands. Their understanding was that the extra cost of defending and supplying the Falklands would impose a considerable burden on Britain just as it was trying to cut back on this sort of expenditure. Therefore, the Junta decided in January 1982 to follow a double policy. It resolved to "reactivate to the fullest extent all negotiations for the sovereignty of the Malvinas, South Georgia and South Sandwich Islands" and, at the same time, "prepare a contingency plan for the employment of military power should the first alternative fail" (Gamba-Stonehouse, 1984, 12). At the same time, the special Joint Armed Forces study on the military contingency for the failure of the negotiations started its planning phase. The essence of the military operation would lie in surprise. Minimum force would be used and there should be no islander casualties whatsoever. The world would be presented with a *fait accompli* and Britain given no emotional stick to wave at the United Nations.

Late in 1976 "scientists" were put ashore on South Thule in the South Sandwich group. Argentina described its objective as establishing a station on South Thule for future scientific investigation "within the jurisdiction of Argentine sovereignty" and hinted that the presence, if the case were to be reported to British officials, would not be permanent. Hence, this was done with no publicity and initially with a flat denial that any such landing had occurred.

During 1982 in Buenos Aires, there were a series of articles written by a well informed journalist, Iglesias Rouco, for *La Prensa* newspaper, which anticipated a military attempt to resolve the dispute. Rouco said, "it is believed that, if the next Argentine attempt to resolve the negotiations with London fails, Buenos Aires will take over the Islands by force this year (1982)" (Bunge, 1992, 49). As the Argentine newspaper *La Prensa* had prophetically remarked a month earlier, "the only thing that can save this government is a war".

On 26 and 27 February 1981 another round of the New York talks began, but the British had little to say on sovereignty. Nevertheless, the British were considering a 99-year lease, and the settlement that was to commence the lease was to be finalised somewhere between the years 2000 and 2081. The negotiations continued and in February 1982 the Argentines decided that the British proposal was their own best alternative. The instructions to the Argentine delegation in New York were to obtain a regular schedule of meetings, to include sovereignty in the list of negotiable items, and to establish a permanent negotiating commission. However, the dispute was intensifying because Argentina had decided that the time had come for a breakthrough, which the British could not provide as long as the Falkland Islands Council insisted that the sovereignty issue should be frozen. The diplomats lacked any freedom to manoeuvre. While rumours and press speculation on the invasion reached a crescendo, a scrap-dealing company working for a private Argentine company ("Georgias del Sur S.A."), and run since 1978 by Mr Constantino Davidoff, was ready to leave the continent for the Islands. Davidoff had a contract that had been awarded by a British firm in Edinburgh for the removal of what was left of the old whaling stations at Leith, Stromness and Husvik on the island of South Georgia. The British Embassy in Buenos Aires knew of the four-year contract. Davidoff needed help to get to South Georgia. He inquired whether *HMS Endurance* might be able to provide passage, but this was refused. In August 1981 he then applied to the Argentine Ministry of Foreign Affairs and to the Argentine Navy for permission to use its Antarctic transport ships to the Islands at a favourable rate. This opportunity offered an

Argentine presence for the next four years, under a legal contract between a British and an Argentine company, and a way of strengthening the Argentine position in the disputed territories. The Argentine Ministry of Foreign Affairs therefore recommended to the Argentine Navy that it agree to Davidoff's request. The advantages for the navy were obvious and the arrangement would allow for at least two stops a year for its ships on Antarctic duties to provide supplies. It seemed "preferable to a covert attempt to establish a base on South Georgia, which might be precluded because of the fragile state of the negotiations with Britain" (Freedman and Gamba-Stonehouse, 1991, 40-41).

"Project Alpha" was formed in September 1981, just after the first request had come from Davidoff for passage on a naval transport, under the previous regime. The plan was to infiltrate Davidoff's workforce with military "scientists" who would then be part of the "legal" landing party on South Georgia.[2] They would later be joined by a group of marines who would embark on a ship on the re-supply route to Argentina's Antarctic bases and establish a more permanent military base of some fourteen men from April onwards. This would be just after *HMS Endurance*, as announced by Britain, had departed the South Atlantic for the last time. In this way the *de facto* sovereignty would be asserted through the broadcast of weather and navigational reports (Freedman and Gamba-Stonehouse, 1991, 42).

With its navy at sea and only two days away from the Islands, the temptation for the Junta to take the historic step at the end of March 1982 seemed irresistible. When the invading forces arrived in Port Stanley on 2 April, the British marines were in no position to resist and were soon surrounded. Argentina had recovered its possession of the Islands. Hence, Argentina would negotiate any issue with Britain "except sovereignty" (Coll and Arendt, 1983, 89).

President Galtieri assumed that the British would accept a *fait accompli*, but Great Britain responded with force equal to the Argentine escalation. The war cabinet ordered the recapture of the islands of South Georgia. The prospects for the success of the invasion were enhanced when, after Galtieri had rejected Haig's last peace proposal, the United States imposed economic sanctions on Argentina and began to supply aid to Britain in the form of fuel, ammunition, missiles and signals intelligence (Dockrill, 1989).

---

[2] Years later, we spoke with Mr Davidoff and his lawyer, who denied that the *Junta Militar* entered into a trade-off to infiltrate marines. Davidoff is still suing the British and the Argentine governments.

The task force was sent to re-establish British administration with the minimum loss of life and to control the exclusion zone. Here, we have to consider the extent to which one's defensive measures are proportional to the degree of aggression suffered. Vitoria and Grotius, theorists of classical war, insisted that no matter how justified the use of force was, it had to be guided by the principles of proportionate objectives and proportionate means: "the *ius ad bellum* and the *ius in bello*" (Coll and Arendt, 1983, 45). The breakout from the beaches began on 27 May. The battle of Goose Green was a devastating demonstration of Britain's absolute will to achieve victory at whatever cost in blood and treasure. This was one of the decisive actions of the war. The battle also dispelled some British hopes that a mere military demonstration would provoke the enemy to collapse.

Cecil Parkinson went on television on 6 June to declare that there would be "no place for the Argentinians in those islands or in the future administration of them" (Hastings and Jenkins, 1984, 260-61). The Goose Green and Darwin battles inflicted some 600 British and 1,000 Argentinian casualties. The battle of Tumbledown and Wireless Ridge on 14 June led to the Argentine surrender at Port Stanley, but Galtieri ordered his troops on the Falklands to "fight to the last man". On the evening of Monday, 14 June, the British and Argentine commanders, Moore and Menendes, signed the document that ended the war in the Falklands, with the surrender of all Argentine forces on the islands. The Junta in Buenos Aires publicly announced Argentina's surrender with its "Comunicado No. 66 del Estado Mayor Conjunto" (*La Nación*, 17 June, 1982).

Since 1945 and the San Francisco Conference, the Argentine government has filed claims through its delegates for the restoration of Argentine sovereignty over the Malvinas. This claim had been repeatedly explored during eighteen years of negotiations between Britain and Argentina under the auspices of the United Nations Special Committee on Decolonization. Argentina had relied on the fact that, in 1965, the General Assembly had passed Resolution 2065 (XX) recognising the character of the islands "whose removal from that status should be negotiated as part of the process of implementing Resolution 1514 (XV)".

In the years preceding the conflict, the United Nations passed resolutions in 1965, 1973, and 1976 calling for negotiations between Britain and Argentina within the framework of UN guidelines on deco-lonization. The pre-crisis negotiations between Britain and Argentina led to a stalemate on the issue of sovereignty and self-determination of the Islanders. After the Argentine invasion, Great Britain won the support of the UN Security Council for a resolution demanding an immediate cessation of hostilities and the withdrawal of all Argentine forces from the Falklands. On 3 April, Resolution 502 calling on the governments of both countries to refrain from the use or threat of force in the region of the Falkland Islands was passed. After Resolution 502, Resolution 505 bid Pérez de Cuéllar to seek settlement and called for a cease-fire, but it proved ineffective. Based on Article 5, this was a case in which the Security Council tried but failed to take measures to maintain international peace and security.

Ambassador Jeane Kirkpatrick, a long-standing Latin American expert who was the U.S. ambassador to the United Nations, and a member of President Reagan's National Security Planning Group, said in her Commentary Essay of October 1981, that "U.S. Security in Latin America, had warned that America was paying insufficient attention to the deterioration of the U.S. position in the hemisphere, which has already created serious vulnerabilities where none previously existed" (Gerson, 1991, 114). For Kirkpatrick it was therefore "in the strategic interest of the United States to maintain good relations with Argentina. If it did not, Central and South American support could no longer be expected for U.S. policies aimed at containing the spread of Communism in the Western hemisphere" (Gerson, 1991, 114-116). Kirkpatrick's point of view was dismissed by the State Department as unmindful of the strategic importance of strong Anglo-American ties. It is said that her role during the crisis was very important for Argentina, as she was a "very good friend" of the country and "prided herself on being an Americanist". Contrary to Haig's position, Mrs Kirkpatrick urged a U.S. policy of neutrality or semi-neutrality because it was consistent with the Monroe Doctrine and the Pan-American alliances, which aimed at keeping the European powers out of Latin America. [3]

Great Britain broke diplomatic relations with Argentina, froze Argentinian assets in London, and asked partners in the European Economic Community (EEC) and the United States to impose financial

---

[3] Noam Chomsky's reflection on Kirkpatrick being a very good friend of Argentina was that "She was no doubt a very good friend of Argentine neo-nazis. Was she a good friend of the people of Argentina?" (personal letter to the author, 2 February 1996). It is also interesting to consider Chomsky's argument that "Haig thought that Argentina was guilty of aggression, tacitly suggesting that Haig thought there is something wrong with aggression. But that can hardly be true because he was actively engaged in U.S. aggression against Vietnam and strongly supported completely unprovoked Israeli aggression against Lebanon" (personal letter to the author, 2 February 1996).

sanctions and a trade embargo. The Thatcher government stated that it would not permit either appeasing a dictator or appeasing an invasion, much less the two combined. Although diplomacy was preferable, force could and would be used to re-establish sovereignty. Thatcher, indeed, took a very strong position, giving the House of Commons assurance that her government would not yield on the question of British sovereignty over the Falklands, and that the wishes of the British citizens resident there would be paramount in deciding the future of the Islands.

Argentine diplomacy had the advantage but also the constraint of being single-minded. The goal of sovereignty had been instilled for 150 years in the national consciousness. The Argentine position was widely known to be firmly held. Argentine diplomacy in the pre-invasion years had been a relentless but creative pursuit of one goal through such diverse means as naval gunfire, the establishment of weather stations, and the agreement to supply oil and education for the islanders. In the crisis stage it became cautious, inflexible, and a prisoner of its own consistency. First abandoned in favour of force, diplomacy was then called on to prevent counter-force, inconsistency, and self-defeat.

As pointed out by R. N. Lebow, "the actual management of the crisis is all important in determining whether or not it is resolved" (1981, 267-268). In crisis, political leaders must cope with an enormous volume of incoming and frequently threatening messages in an environment characterised by severe time constraints. Hence, it is important how policy-makers perceive crisis and whether or not they respond in time.

If ever a nation was tired of grappling with colonial issues, it was Argentina. Centuries of patient diplomacy lay close to ruins with Argentina's "recovery" of the Malvinas. The invasion would not stifle Argentines' internal dissent, but at least it would unite the nation for a time. Re-establishing its sovereignty on Malvinas would have served as a vindication of military rule and cleansed the reputation of the armed forces after the horrors of the "dirty war". It would have also elevated the Junta to renewed authority, which was certainly required to enforce Economic Minister Alemann's economic package.

The truth was that the Argentinians did not take the threat of British counter-attack seriously enough. They also thought that the United States would maintain neutrality and withhold intelligence and logistical support from Britain. Besides, Argentinian leaders did not read British reactions, British military capabilities, and especially the character of the British Prime Minister (Curtis, 1995). In addition, the British did not appreciate the depth of Argentinian feelings about "a few rocky islands" in the South Atlantic. And the United States, preoccupied with great events elsewhere in the world and with its own economic problems, failed to see that the conditions were ripe for a war between two of "its friends" in its own hemisphere. Thatcher's objective was to demonstrate that Britain was still Britain, and that the 1,000 sheep-herders on the Falklands were effectively Englishmen and, therefore, in accordance with the long tradition and fearless practice of the British crown, safe from the threats of a military-led government.[4] This was Thatcher's expressed purity, right or wrong, concerning democracy *versus* dictatorship.[5]

Once the British decided to use force, the real choice for the Argentinians was not their goal of sovereignty, but the solution offered by the United States or that offered by Mr Pérez de Cuéllar. The Junta had great difficulty realising this and, insofar as it did, it consistently failed to take this reality into account in its decisions. We should remember, though, that despite the fact that peace was possible, and the basis for peace was evident to everyone, as Haig noted, war was the conscious choice of the Argentinian leaders. It has been suggested that Galtieri saw the invasion essentially as a distraction to take his people's minds off political repression and economic calamity (Freedman, 1982, 196). He used the Argentine dream to gain power but failed. Instead, Argentina lost the war, as well as years of diplomatic negotiations based on claims to sovereignty. The lesson is that future Argentine governments should negotiate the issue of Malvinas from a diplomatic and jurisdictional point of view rather than that of sovereignty.

References

Bunge, W. (1992). "Malvinas: De una Victoria Diplomática a una Derrota Militar", *Actualización Política* 5.

Coll, A., and A. Arendt. (1983). *The Falklands War: Lessons for*

---

[4] Chomsky wrote in his letter the author (2 February 1996), "A more accurate picture of Britain's long tradition is given by Winston Churchill, speaking to the British cabinet 80 years ago: 'We are not a young people with an innocent record and a scanty inheritance. We have engrossed to ourselves [...] an altogether disproportionate share of wealth and traffic of the world. We have got all we want in territory, and our claim to be left in the unmolested enjoyment of vast and splendid possessions, mainly acquired by violence, largely maintained by force, often seems less reasonable to others than to us.' That's a much more accurate description of Britain's long tradition, as people throughout much of the world can testify."

[5] On this matter, however, Chomsky adds, "Thatcher raised no objection to the standard British practice of overthrowing democratic regimes that were in its way (e.g. Cheddi Jagan) or sending troops to support brutal dictatorships (e.g. Dhofar)" (personal letter to the author, 2 February 1996).

Strategy, Diplomacy and International Law. Boston: Allen and Unwin.

Dockrill, M. (1989) *British Defence Since 1945*. Oxford: Blackwell.

Curtis, M. (1995) *The Ambiguities of Power: British Foreign Policy Since 1945*. London: Zed Books.

Freedman, L. (1982). "The War of the Falkland Islands", *Foreign Affairs* 61, 1, 196-210.

Freedman, L., and V. Gamba-Stonehouse. (1991), *Signals of War*. New Jersey: Princeton University Press.

Gamba-Stonehouse, V. (1984). *El Peón de la Reina. Buenos Aires*: Editorial Sudamericana.

Gerson, A. (1991). *The Kirkpatrick Mission. New York*: The Free Press, New York.

Hastings, M., and S. Jenkins. (1984). *The Battle for the Falklands*. New York: Norton.

Kirkpatrick, J. (1989/90). "My Falkland War and Theirs", *The National Interest* 18, 11-20.

Lebow, R. (1981). *Between Peace and War*. Baltimore: Johns Hopkins University Press.

RETROSPECT

A detail from the official 1888 Map of Gobernación de Tierra del Fuego y las Islas
Malvinas (cartographer anonymous), Archivo General de la Nación Argentina.

The Anglo-Argentine Post-Conflict Common Ground: the Combat Veterans' Aftermath

Eduardo C. Gerding

Introduction

The Malvinas conflict lasted seventy-four days. There were thirty-three days of combat that caused 649 Argentine fatalities, 255 British fatalities (and 777 wounded), and three civilian fatalities. This short but intensive multi-dimensional war contained maritime engagements, air-to-ship combat, aerial combat, and land battles such as Darwin and Goose Green, Mount Longdon and Tumbledown, that were exceptionally bloody and culminated with fixed bayonet and hand-to-hand fighting.

My aim is to examine, by using an extensive bank of statistics, some of the Argentine and British somatic and psychological injuries from this conflict and, in particular, to compare these to the American experience in the Vietnam War. I shall limit myself to describing two effects on sailors and soldiers of the extreme climate experienced during the conflict, namely hypothermia and trench foot, and then attempt to analyse the post-conflict effects of post-traumatic stress disorder that, in some cases, led to suicide and comorbid diagnoses. Other issues such as post-traumatic growth, existential authority, prevalent diseases, unemployment and family violence which can affect war veterans are also discussed. Finally, I shall describe the role and tasks of the War Veterans' Sub-Management Area at the *Instituto Nacional de Servicios Sociales Para Jubilados Y Pensionados (INSSJP)* in Buenos Aires, where I am the Malvinas War Veterans Medical Co-ordinator.

I would like to stress from the outset that, in the Malvinas conflict, the bulk of the Argentine forces were made up of conscripted servicemen, whilst the British fought with regular troops. Much has been written and talked about the war's teenage Argentine conscripts. However, both sides had young soldiers and, for example, it also should be noted that two seventeen-year-old, two eighteen-year-old and three nineteen-year-old British paratroopers of 3rd Battalion, Parachute Regiment were killed in the fighting on Mount Longdon. The underlying age factor therefore should not be forgotten in this presentation. This factor's consequences have been succinctly highlighted:

[T]he Vietnam veteran was our nation's youngest soldier. Whereas the average age of the World War II combatant was 26 years, the average age of the Vietnam veteran was 19. One can readily appreciate the monumental impact the brutality resulting from

153

combat in Vietnam would have upon a 19 year-old, an adolescent with a barely formed identity still searching for suitable roles in adult life. At an age when most young men are typically forming lasting ideas about intimacy and relationships, soldiers in Vietnam were losing friends in painfully horrible ways, and perhaps learning that closeness hurts too much. (*Veteran*, 2005)

Little research has been carried out on the veterans of both sides in the Malvinas conflict. There have been a few isolated and limited projects. In 1991 a study was carried out on a group of sixty-four British Army serving Falklands War veterans. Their mean age was 27.5 years, they had 9.2 service years, eighteen had married in 1982, and fourteen suffered the death of a near one since the conflict. A significant number exhibited post-traumatic stress disorder symptoms associated with their experiences (O'Brien and Hughes, 1991). Similarly, a group of 171 Argentine Malvinas War Veterans was studied in 1995. Twenty percent had lost one or more teeth, forty percent suffered some kind of accident after 1982, seventeen percent had a blood cholesterol over 240 mg %. In many cases the father died during the conflict, enhancing their sense of guilt.

It could be said of these projects that, when they analyse information with strict statistical methods, their conclusions are perhaps too fragmented to have real and lasting value (Emerson *et al.*, 1983). Both countries have missed opportunities to implement long-term comprehensive empirical research projects on their young combat veterans from this small war in which the total number of combatants was not excessive. In the decades after the conflict, the planning and implementing of follow-up studies on these veterans could have been conducted relatively easily. Indeed, the only true common denominator pertaining to both sides is the combat veterans, their problems and need for effective psycho-social support. Much could have been learned from a pioneering study of veterans from both sides who had fought in the same war.

Hypothermia

In extreme South Atlantic autumn and winter weather conditions, hypothermia can quickly become a killer when an individual's core body temperature drops to a dangerously low level. This became a major problem for a large number of Argentine sailors after their ship had been sunk by enemy action. Moving at thirty-five knots, the cruiser ARA *General Belgrano* (formerly USS *Phoenix*) was hit outside the Total Exclusion Zone by two torpedoes of the British Royal Navy submarine HMS *Conqueror* on 2 May 1982. This engagement would result in a total of 321 fatalities (thirty percent of a 1,091-man crew), representing fifty percent of all Argentine casualties in the war. Thirty percent who died were eighteen-year-old conscripts, with eighty-four per cent of them being killed as a direct result of the torpedo explosions (Sethia, 2006).

However this was the only engagement during the conflict that had a prolific number of casualties caused by the extreme climatic conditions. As the vessel began to sink, the prevailing weather was of most concern to the survivors, there being gales with wind speeds in excess of 100 kilometres per hour, nine-metre-high waves, and a wind-chill factor of minus twenty degrees centigrade. Approximately twenty-five percent of the survivors had to plunge into the sea, that had a temperature of two degrees centigrade. Men dressed in water-permeable clothing can be considered almost "nude" when immersed in the cold South Atlantic waters, and some survivors were covered by slippery oil, which made it difficult to haul them into the rafts. Ten percent of these caused great difficulties to the survivors (Gerding, 2002) and, for most, it took twenty-four hours before they were rescued. It is important in combating such conditions that clothing is layered, e.g. silk over the skin, then wool, polyester fleece and a nylon garment. But the statistics of this second phase of the disaster are grim: sixty-nine of the survivors suffered from hypothermia and eighteen died from this condition (Gerding, 1996).

Trench foot

It was Baron Dominique Jean Larrey (1766-1842), a military surgeon, who classically described the role that trench foot played in the 1812 defeat of Napoleon's Army in Poland. This non-freezing cold injury results from prolonged exposure to cold at temperatures from just above freezing to ten degrees centigrade, wetness and immobilization of the feet (Gerding, 1998). A graphic description of the condition has been provided by a First World War veteran, Sergeant Harry Roberts of the Lancashire Fusiliers:

> If you have never had trench feet described to you, I will tell you. Your feet swell to two or three times their normal size and go completely dead. You could stick a bayonet into them and not feel a thing. If you are fortunate enough not to lose your feet and the swelling begins to go down, it is then that the intolerable, indescribable agony begins. I have heard men cry and even scream with the pain and many had to have their feet and legs amputated. (Webb, 2014)

Fourteen percent of all casualties on both sides in the Malvinas conflict involved trench foot. The main reasons for British troops succumbing to this condition were a combination of the land high water table, inclement weather conditions, and appalling quality of the standard issue Direct Moulded Sole (DMS) boot, which leaked like a sieve. In such a climatically hostile environment, high quality boots were vital in this classic infantryman's war. The table below is revealing with respect to the boots issued to the 707 Marines of the Argentine 5th Marine Infantry Battalion, which was dug in on the Tumbledown, Mount William and Sapper Hill. The unit had trained extensively in southern Patagonia the preceding year and was well versed in the requirements of foot hygiene to counter bad weather conditions:

Average exposure days	Cases
Argentines 65	290
British 24	70
5th Marine Infantry Battalion 71	1

There were 173 Argentine trench foot cases treated at the Puerto Argentino Military Hospital. Thirty-four trench foot cases were treated at the end of the war at the Puerto Belgrano Naval Hospital with a hyperbaric chamber. Fifteen were severe cases, and twenty-three did not require amputation (Campana, 1987). Afterwards typical foot deformities could be observed. In third-degree injuries, the shedding like a cocoon of the shrunken gangrenous shell of epidermis leaves a pink sensitive skin similar to a baby's foot. A group of Royal Marine Commandos who were examined at the Institute of Naval Medicine suffered demyelination of medial and/or lateral plantar nerves of one or both feet. The best prognosis indicator of trench foot is the degree of damage to the peripheral nerves (Ungley et al., 1945). As a result of this pathology many British soldiers who took part in the 1982 conflict suffer from cold sensitivity and will never be able to deploy to a cold environment again (Marsh, 1983).

The lessons of the past were re-learned. A good quality boot and rigid hygiene standards for feet in the field are crucial to avoiding trench foot, which has the potential to cripple infantry units before they can engage the enemy.

Post-traumatic stress disorder (PTSD)

When men (and increasingly women) go to war, some are killed, some return home physically injured, whilst others return with invisible yet often equally damaging psychiatric injuries. The desirable notion that a military force deployed on operations might avoid taking somatic casualties is a totally utopian one. This is also the case with psychiatric casualties. War provides an exaggerated, perhaps extreme, version of the entire range of human experience – not just fear, hate and guilt, but also excitement, love, friendship and achievement.

There is no single "experience of war", for good or ill. There are some for whom active service remains the best thing that ever happened to them, and for whom life afterwards is dull and monochrome. For many, though, especially those who are not part of a modern professional and volunteer military force, war is not the "best days of their lives". On return from war they appear healthy in body, but not in mind. In order to diagnose PTSD, the patient must have been exposed to an extreme stressor or traumatic event to which he or she responded with fear, helplessness or horror, and have three distinct types of symptoms. These are:

- re-experiencing the event in the mind;
- avoidance of reminders of the event;
- hyper-arousal for at least one month.

Symptoms of the latter manifest themselves physiologically in insomnia, irritability, impaired concentration, hyper-vigilance and increased startle reactions. The diagnosis is easily missed, as sometimes there is an overlap with depression or other anxiety disorders.

About thirty percent of men and women who have spent time in war zones experience PTSD, whilst an additional twenty to twenty-five percent have had partial PTSD at some point in their lives.

It is estimated that between twenty-five to thirty-nine percent of Argentine Malvinas War veterans suffer from PTSD, and eighty-eight percent of them have never attended a health centre. The concept of veteran peer support presented at the 2006 Nottingham colloquium might well be of benefit to them. Indeed, the supposition that PTSD can persist for fifty years after a conflict (Herrmann and Eryavec, 1994) is of particular significance. More than half of all male Vietnam War veterans and almost half of all female Vietnam War veterans have experienced PTSD. The latter has also been detected among veterans of the Gulf War, with some estimates running as high as eighty percent.

Depression is more common than post-traumatic stress disorder in UK war veterans. However, only about half of those who have a diagnosis are currently seeking help, and few see specialists (Iversen et al., 2005). With eighty-six years of experience in treating PTSD, the UK has Residential Treatment Centres at Ayr, Newport, and Leatherhead. The two main treatments used by psychiatrists are Cognitive Behaviour Therapy and Eye Moving Desensitisation and Reprocessing (EMDR). According to the Ex-Services Mental Welfare Society (Combat Stress), more than 85,000 veterans and their families have been helped, with forty-six percent of the referral sources coming from self, friends and families, and thirty-six percent from service charities, welfare, and so on.

Post-traumatic growth (PTG) and existential authority

War veterans can also be affected by the influences of both post-traumatic growth and existential authority. The former is an inner phenomenon which grows steadily during the remainder of the veteran's life when, with continued drive and initiative, there is constant application of the many lessons learned and truths revealed on the battlefield. Whilst this is a positive effect, there are traps and, for some, it can lead to chronic fatigue syndrome and other problems. With existential authority, however, there is throughout the life of the veteran a continual negative inner questioning of external authority and its capabilities. The veteran has experienced war, a major life-event that relatively few have witnessed or participated in first hand. So the veteran's subsequent query, particularly after he has become a civilian once again, is a natural one. Could my current superior have dealt with that past situation in which I was placed? If the answer is no, the subsequent attitude might lead to reduced respect for the superior which could cause eventual problems between employee and employer.

Suicide

Suicide is a multi-dimensional concomitant of psychiatric diagnoses, especially mood disorders, and is complex in both its causation and treatment of those at risk. There have been an *estimated* 350 suicides amongst Argentine Malvinas War veterans (*La Nación,* 2006) and, according to the British Falklands veterans' South Atlantic Medal Association 82, in excess of 255 British Falklands War veterans are estimated to have committed suicide, which is more than the British servicemen who were actually killed during the conflict. This is claimed to be a conservative figure, but it is emphasised again that this, as well as the Argentine figure, are only most unsatisfactory estimates. Indeed, the results of estimating veterans' suicide figures can vary wildly, as the following American experience demonstrates. According to one study "no more than 20,000 Vietnam Veterans died of suicide from the time of discharge through the end of 1993" (Bullman and Yang, 1995). However, Deans (1990) states that "Fifty-eight thousand plus died in the Vietnam War. Over 150,000 have committed suicide since the war ended". The lack of comprehensive surveys both in Argentina and UK which might produce reliable sets of figures for Falklands-Malvinas veterans continues to be a major drawback to understanding the problem fully. In order to measure these figures more accurately, an adequate and preferably longitudinal sample would be required.

Suicide prediction results in thirty percent false positives and, although suicide prevention is ideally primary, the reality is that most treatment is either secondary or tertiary (Maris, 2002). A report from Sri Lanka (Kim and Singh, 2004) described possible reasons for persons committing suicide:

- conflict between collectivism and individualism;
- rigid hierarchical structure;
- repressive education;
- influence of foreign cultures through cinema and television.

Efforts must be made to avoid normalising, glorifying, or dramatising suicidal behaviour, reporting "how-to" methods, or describing suicide as an understandable solution to a traumatic or stressful life event. Inappropriate approaches could potentially increase the risk for suicidal behaviour in vulnerable individuals, particularly youth. Applicable protective factors are:

- an individual's genetic or neurobiological makeup;
- attitudinal and behavioural characteristics;
- environmental attributes;
- measures that enhance resilience;
- effective and appropriate clinical care for mental, physical, and substance abuse disorders;
- easy access to a variety of support mechanisms.

Comorbid diagnoses

Eighty percent of people who commit suicide have comorbid diagnoses, fo example substance abuse. Fifteen percent of depressives who are admitted to hospitals will eventually commit suicide, and eighteen percent of alcoholics will die by suicide (Roy, 1986).

According to a 1981 report of the Centre for Policy Research in the USA, the rate of alcohol problems among veterans as a whole is significantly greater than the rate for non-veterans. The association of self-reported excessive drinking in Vietnam combatants during military service, and in the first year following discharge, was acknowledged in 1985, whilst six years later it was maintained that exposure to heavy combat more than doubled a Vietnam War veteran's risk of post-discharge alcohol misuse. But according to one report (McFall *et al.*, 1992), the widespread incidence of substance abuse amongst Vietnam War veterans is attributable to PTSD, not simply the degree of exposure to combat. These statements are contradictory and illustrate the need for even more research.

Despite these experiences in the USA with war veterans and use of alcohol (and also drugs), there are no Argentine war veterans registered at SEDRONAR (Secretaría de Políticas Integrales sobre Drogas de la Nación Argentina).

Prevalent diseases

As a result of the average age (forty-five) of Argentine war veterans, awareness must also be raised of prevalent diseases which will affect them. Such is the case with Chaga's disease, a tropical parasitic disease that has infected 2,300,000 Argentines, mostly in the north and north-west provinces. Coronary heart disease is the most common cause of death in the UK (125,000 deaths in 2000) but, by 2010, will also be the leading cause of death in developing countries. Thirty-five percent of the Argentine population are heavy smokers, and it has been observed that the current prevalence of smoking, with all its implications for the increased risk of contracting lung cancer, was higher for veterans than for non-veterans (McKinney *et al.*, 1997).

Unemployment

In the 1995 survey, war veteran unemployment in Argentina was exceptionally high at seventy percent. This is also a deep-rooted cause of many of the subsequent problems for veterans. Long-term unemployment can cause severe depression to the affected individual, which might have fatal consequences. Unemployment amongst the veterans still remains high and compares most unfavourably with Argentina's unemployment rate of 10.9 percent, according to the *Instituto Nacional de Estadísticas y Censo* (INDEC). It should also be noted that, in August 2005, the USA's unemployment rate among the 3.9 million veterans of the First Gulf War era (from August 1990 onwards) was 5.2 percent. Yet this was only marginally higher than the rate for non-veterans, which stood at 4.7 percent.

Furthermore, a veteran exhibiting post-traumatic growth combined with existential authority can be perceived by the civilian organisation that employs him as a significant threat. In other words, the veteran has simply become too strong or unruly for the organisation's prevailing system and, in extreme cases, this can lead to dismissal (sometimes by devious means), unemployment and further negative consequences for the veteran concerned.

Family violence

According to the Argentine Judiciary, the cases of family violence have increased four-fold. Sixty-six percent of those women involved in family violence are married. Families of veterans with PTSD experience more family violence, more physical and verbal aggression, and more instances of violence against a partner (Byrne and Riggs, 1996). This represents yet another challenge for the War Veterans' Sub-Management Area at the INSSJP.

The War Veterans' Sub-Management Area at the Instituto Nacional de Servicios Sociales Para Jubilados Y Pensionados (INSSJP)

The INSSJP was founded on 13 May 1971 (Law 19.032). It has 3,200,000 affiliates (1,800,000 are older than sixty-five years of age) and represents sixty-two percent of Argentine elderly people. There are thirty-six delegations and 550 nationwide offices. On 16 March 1989 (Resolution 494/89), the War Veterans' Division was founded at the INSSJP in accordance with Law 23.109 promulgated on 23 October 1984. The INSSJP tasks have been:

- establishing the mission, objectives and personal responsibilities of the War Veterans' Sub-Management Area;
- conducting a national programme of Social Sanitary Control;
- running a Health Promoters' course at the University of Buenos Aires;
- running self-knowledge workshops;
- providing free psychological assistance (at John Fitzgerald Kennedy University in Buenos Aires);
- maintaining a free emergency telephone helpline.

About 150 war veterans are employed at the INSSJP and, at the Sub-Management Area, not only deal with war consequences but also the challenge of providing adequate assistance to veterans' wives and children, sometimes in poverty-stricken areas. The distribution of Argentine war veterans affiliated to the INSSJP is as follows:

Province	War Veterans	Wives	Sons	INSSJP War Veteran personnel
Córdoba	1083	795	2189	10
Lanús	1061	810	2226	10
Chaco	927	677	2454 *	10
Corrientes	871	673	2298	10
San Martín	738	538	1390	10

Capital city	603	372	697	6
Morón	544	405	1101	10

* Fifty-six percent of these sons are below twelve years of age.

There is no doubt that we still have a long road ahead. Paraphrasing military terminology, I would like to name our activities "Operation Healing": a true national debt repaid to all the brave men who went to the conflict.

References

Bullman, T. A., and H. K. Yang. (1995). "Suicide Among Vietnam Veterans". *Federal Practitioner* 12, 3, 9-13.

Byrne, C. A. and D. S. Riggs. (1996) "The cycle of trauma: Relationship aggression in male Vietnam veterans with symptoms of post traumatic stress disorder", *Violence and Victims* 11, 213-25.

Campana, J. M. (1987). *Revista Argentina de Cirugía*, 52, 1-2, 59-65.

Deans, C. (1990) *Nam Vet*. Portland: Multnomah Press.

Emerson, J. D. *et al.* (1983). "Use of Statistical Analysis in *The New England Journal of Medicine*", *The New England Journal of Medicine*, 309, 709-13.

Gerding, E. C. (1996). "Accidental Immersion Hypothermia in the South Atlantic", *International Review of the Armed Forces Medical Services*, 69.

Gerding, E. C. (1998). "Trench Foot: The South Atlantic Experience", *International Review of the Armed Forces Medical Services*, 71.

Gerding, E. C. (2002). "The 1982 South Atlantic Conflict's Aftermath", *International Review of the Armed Forces Medical Services*, 75.

Herrmann, N. and G. Eryavec. (1994). "Delayed Onset Post-Traumatic Stress Disorder in World War II Veterans", *Canadian Journal of Psychiatry*, 39, 439-41.

Iversen, A. *et al.* (2005). "'Goodbye and good luck': The mental health needs and treatment experiences of British ex-service personnel", *British Journal of Psychiatry*, 186, 480-86.

Kim, W. J. and T. Singh. "Trends and dynamics of youth suicides in developing countries", *The Lancet* 363, 9415, 1090-91.

La Nación. (2006). "La Plata Islas Malvinas' War Centre", 28 February.

McFall, M. E. *et al.* (1992). "Combat-related posttraumatic stress disorder and severity of substance abuse in Vietnam veterans", *Journal of Studies on Alcohol* 53, 4, 357-63.

McKinney, P. *et al.* (1997). "Comparing the smoking behavior of veterans and nonveterans", *Public Health Report* 112, 3, 212-18.

Maris, R. (2002). "Suicide", *The Lancet* 360, 9329, 319-26.

Marsh, A. R. (1983). "A short but distant war – the Falklands campaign", *Journal of the Royal Society of Medicine*, 76.

O'Brien, L. S. and S. J. Hughes. (1991). "Symptoms of post-traumatic stress disorder in Falklands veterans five years after the conflict", *British Journal of Psychiatry*, 159, 1, 135-41.

Roy, A. (1986). *Suicide*. Baltimore: Williams and Wilkins.

Sethia, N. (2006). "Hit by two torpedoes", *The Guardian*, 18 October.

Ungley, C. C. *et al*. (1945). "The immersion foot syndrome", British Journal of Surgery 33, 129, 17-31.

Veteran (Vietnam Veterans Association magazine). (2005). March-April.

Webb, Sarah. (2014). *The First World War*. London: Hodder Education in association with Imperial War Museums.

Seeking "The Other" in the Post-Conflict, 1982-2006

Mike Seear

On the eleventh day after cessation of the Falklands-Malvinas War, I was on duty at 04.00 hours in the small Goose Green operations room set up in the bunkhouse for bachelor shepherds. The previous day, 24 June, was a dreadful one for 1st Battalion, 7th Duke of Edinburgh's Own Gurkha Rifles. Whilst back-filling some Argentine trenches north of the settlement, Lance-Corporal Budhaparsad Limbu had hit his spade on an unexploded, but buried, M-79 grenade that a paratrooper of 2 Para had fired during the battle there on 28 May. The grenade now exploded, killing the Lance-Corporal and wounding two other Gurkha soldiers. Indeed Budhaparsad was the formal two hundred and fifty-fifth and final British Task Force fatality of the war. As the Battalion's Operations and Training Officer, I had been on duty in the operations room at the time and became fully involved in the immediate crisis management of this unpleasant incident.

More than twelve hours later there was little to do, but even at this "dead-man's hour" thoughts about the accident kept me fully alert. It was also the event that started a long-term project, as I turned over a pad of signal message proformas and began jotting down on the rear blank page a few notes of my experiences in the previous tumultuous twelve weeks which represented and still remain, in my view, the greatest single-nation crisis management operation since the Second World War. I had been in the category of "last in, last out", having landed on the Islands for the war's final fourteen days, and would depart in nearly three weeks time. But on this night that single page would become the embryo of a book manuscript that would require an accumulated period of eight years to complete and publish (Seear, 2003). Even on that particular night, as the idea grew, I decided that there had to be an Argentine dimension to my book, that it must include a particular representative of "the other" we had confronted in the war.

Corporal Nicolás Urbieta, an Argentine 4th Infantry Regiment support section commander, was the natural choice. His helmet, weapon, webbing, large pack, kit bag, training manuals, five unposted letters and roll of film had been found by my Battalion Tactical Headquarters' British radio operator, Corporal Chris Aslett, and some Gurkha soldiers when, upon the cessation of war, they had been scouring the Two Sisters' and Mount Harriet battlefields for Argentine souvenirs. In the kit bag was also half a sheep's carcass that indicated the extent of the Argentine soldier's predicament: a desperate shortfall of rations. All these items, less the carcass, were brought into my little Goose Green operations room. I intervened when one Gurkha was about to throw the letters into my wastepaper basket. Although they were written in Spanish, I rescued them and, indeed, they would become my personal souvenirs of the war. Thus, a couple of nights later, when starting to write those book notes, I remembered the Argentine soldier's letters. There was no hesitation. The letters had to be incorporated into my book project.

My initial writing was combined with the interesting task of editing for many hours the two Gurkha Battalion post-operational reports of the war: one at the settlement of Goose Green and the other on board the British Task Force's former Naval Ocean-going Surgical Hospital Ship SS *Uganda* en route back to the United Kingdom. But those untranslated letters still intrigued me, as the book's first draft manuscript of fifty-five pages, typed up by two ever-faithful Gurkha clerks in the makeshift Battalion orderly room on board, was completed by the time of our arrival at Southampton.

In the autumn, I visited my Aunt Nancy at her flat in London to tell her of my book plans and ask for help in translating the letters. Otherwise known as the Baroness Seear of Paddington and soon to be leader of the Liberal Peers (1984-88) in the British Parliament's House of Lords, she sought a Spanish-English translator from her impressive network. When the English versions of the letters were eventually returned to me, they were accompanied by a note from the translator. She opposed my idea that these letters be published, commenting that they described a terrible situation which faced the Argentine soldier, who was suffering so much. I shrugged at these objections of a civilian who would never be able to understand the thought processes of any combat veteran and, instead, avidly read Urbieta's letters. I could empathise immediately with this graphic account of how one Argentine soldier was waiting at the end of May in his section defensive position on Wall Mountain, East Falkland, for the British to attack.

His moods ranged from bravado to downright depression. As a war veteran I sympathised with "the other's" roller-coaster emotions. I also had his roll of film developed. Some of the photographs had been ruined by the hostile wet Falklands' climate, but some were of surprisingly good quality and showed the young Nicolás Urbieta as a section commander in training with his men at Río Gallegos. The Regiment had been sent south from its Monte Caseros base in the sub-tropical northern province of Corrientes to counter the threat posed by Chile against Argentina's southern border. But plans had changed suddenly and the 4th Infantry Regiment were to be deployed direct from Río Gallegos in civil aircraft to the Islas las Malvinas.

Dark and short, but stocky in build, Urbieta seemed to have a charismatic leader's air about him. In November 1982, I mailed the originals to the British Red Cross, requesting that they be returned to Urbieta. A few days later I received a letter informing me that they had been forwarded to the International Committee of the Red Cross in Geneva for eventual onward transmission to Argentina and Urbieta.

In the next two years of my Gurkha secondment from the Light Infantry, which included a Battalion move to Hong Kong in April 1983, I continued with my writing. However, at the end of this final fourteen-month period with the Gurkhas, it was obvious that the manuscript was not of sufficient literary quality to be published. I was posted to Norway and that imperfect 200-page manuscript of my war experiences from the worm's eye-view of the Gurkha Operations and Training Officer was put in a shoebox. Storing this in the cellar of my home on the outskirts of Oslo, I concentrated instead on my new staff appointment at the Kolsås NATO headquarters and my young family, which now included my third daughter born in Hong Kong the previous year. A baby of my war's aftermath, she had Downs Syndrome. There were greater priorities in my life than writing, with her two open-heart surgeries during the two successive years and the beginning of turbulence within the family. Nonetheless, I adopted a philosophical attitude: my book project remained alive, and patience would be required to realise my ultimate publication aim.

In 1988 I became a civilian in Norway and Head of Security and Emergency Response at Scandinavian Airlines. The start of this latter venture had remarkably similar parallels to my Gurkha secondment six years previously: the requirement to grow into a new culture, language, job and become acquainted with new people, albeit civilians. I threw myself at the challenges. The only difference was that my next "war" would come years later in this job. With the benefit of hindsight this was also a subconscious second bite at the "Falklands-Malvinas apple" which might rectify my non-optimal performance during that war. At an early stage in my emergency response training with airline personnel I enlisted Professor Lars Weisæth, a world authority in traumatic stress, to assist. He was to teach me, in an enlightening yet simple way, the theory of traumatic stress and psycho-social support after my experiences in the Falklands-Malvinas War.

My home life deteriorated. My marriage survived two separations. Burning the candle at both ends, with additional demands on account of my daughter's condition, I collapsed at Easter 1993. The diagnosis was chronic fatigue syndrome, the prescription six months' sick leave. Yet on return to my job I continued at the same reckless work pace as before.

There were more crises both privately and professionally: another short separation in my marriage, and an aircraft hijack successfully crisis-managed. But by then my post-traumatic growth and existential authority had begun to grate on some airline superiors. I knew too much, certainly more than them, and was therefore being perceived as a "threat" to the system. The climax came in May 1996 at a London international civil aviation symposium where two questions I posed in open forum were interpreted, incorrectly, by a Norwegian with power and less than perfect English, as being too provocative towards him and his organisation.

Within two months I was jobless, victim of an "unlawful dismissal". My second bite at the "apple" had turned rotten, completely crushing my professional ego. Refusing to accept the fact that, in reality, I had grown out of my job, this event also proved to be that much talked-about war veterans' "trigger in later life" which re-awakens past battlefield traumas. I endured a prolonged sense of powerlessness, just like that on the last night of the war when we came under intensive enemy artillery and mortar fire behind the Tumbledown. My current predicament resulted not only in twenty months of unemployment, but a severe depression combined with multiple symptoms of post-traumatic stress disorder. Eventually this culminated in a nervous breakdown, an ensuing three-week hospitalisation, eventual marriage breakdown and loss of my family home. It is what psycho-traumatology experts label a "multi-event". However, this implosion of my professional and personal life did have one positive effect: it produced a subconscious cathartic need to re-examine my life. That twelve-year-long objective to publish a book was resurrected with a return to the old shoebox in which lay my uncompleted project. It was to bring back a much needed focus amidst all the personal wreckage in my life, as the rewriting of *With the Gurkhas in the Falklands: A War Journal* started to gather pace.

All this increased the need to seek out in a more active way my chosen "other" of the 1982 Falklands-Malvinas War. But was Nicolás Urbieta alive? I decided to attack the problem on two fronts. One was the formal route. A letter was written to the International Committee of the Red Cross in January 1997, with a reply from Geneva on 13 March 1997 confirming that Urbieta had been repatriated to Argentina after the war. (He was one of the 4,144 Argentine prisoners of war transported by the P&O cruise liner SS *Canberra*.). Although not normal practice, attempts would be made to locate him in Argentina.

I had also chosen an informal route. Amongst other items I had retained from Urbieta's kit was a piece of toilet-paper. On this he had written the names and addresses of the ten men in his section. So I also

167

wrote a letter asking for Urbieta's whereabouts in Argentina and had this translated into Spanish. Then, rather like Robinson Crusoe throwing bottles containing hopeful messages into the sea, these ten identical letters were posted to the ten toilet-paper addresses. I succeeded with only one. But it was enough. The recipient obviously thought that the contents were unusual and passed it to Marcela Bordenave, an Argentine National Congress representative whose political advisor asked for an interview about my connection with Urbieta and the war in view of the forthcoming fifteenth anniversary of its cessation. I received Urbieta's address and a one-page article written about Urbieta and Seear that was published on 15 June 1997 by *Clarín*, the largest national newspaper in Argentina. The main theme of the article was that the British officer wanted to meet "the other", whilst the Argentine Sergeant (Urbieta was still serving in the Army with the 24th Mechanised Infantry Regiment at Río Gallegos in the southern province of Patagonia) most certainly did not. Indeed "the other" did not seem to want to talk about the war at all, and most definitely not to his former enemy. Curiously, there was one phone call from Nicolás to me a week or so after the article had been published. Alas, our conversation did not last long as he did not speak English, nor I Spanish.

The article hit a raw nerve elsewhere in Argentina. *Clarín* had also published a letter I had written in May 1997 to Urbieta which displayed my address in Norway. Many Argentines subsequently wrote to me. Some were Malvinas War veterans. Others were civilians. One was María Emilia Bosio, a student of English who helped me considerably by translating many of these letters and the *Clarín* article. Another was Alberto Peralta Ramos, a freelance TV producer of the cultural programme *Astrolabio* (Sextant). He informed me that he had produced a TV programme on the Gurkhas, and had also given a briefing to the Argentine Army HQ in Buenos Aires about the Gurkhas when it was made known that the latter would be deployed to the South Atlantic in May 1982. He became an invaluable and generous ally in my quest to find out more about "the other" and Argentine culture during my subsequent three visits to Buenos Aires in 2002 and 2003. Sadly he died in June 2006.

Late in 1997, an angry letter came from an Argentine woman who lived in the little country town of General Roca in Córdoba province. María Isabel Clausen de Bruno berated me severely for belonging to the Gurkha war machine which had been intent on killing the young conscript boys of the Argentine Army in the Malvinas War. However, this bad start did not last long. I was now living on my own in a thirty-five square-metre basement flat in Oslo, had been unemployed for sixteen months, and was still licking my wounds after a most difficult time. "Marisa", as she liked to be known, was a staunch supporter of the Malvinas War veterans and, paradoxically, also provided me with much written psycho-social support after I sent her several long letters explaining my predicament.

By now I had worked up a head of steam in writing my book without having secured a publisher and, at last, acquired a job in April 1998 as a security and crisis management consultant. I deemed that more material for the Argentine dimension to my book was needed, as publishing Nicolás's letters did not give my potential readers enough information about "the other" and his war. A meeting between Nicolás and myself was therefore imperative. But first my life-reconstruction would continue, with marriage to another Norwegian in 2000. I made a comeback in Scandinavian Airlines and was engaged as a part-time crisis management consultant in a project that lasted thirty months with rewriting plans, holding seminars, and designing, writing and implementing a number of major exercises, mainly at the Head Office in Stockholm, Sweden. The project was closed in June 2001. But its results would be put to the acid test in a uniquely horrifying way nearly four months later at Linate Airport, Milan when 118 people were killed in the airline's early morning aircraft accident there on 8 October 2001. I heard the news at lunchtime, and the remainder of my day was inevitably one of many personal reflections and reactions to the tragedy.

Another four years had passed by before the time seemed right for me to travel to Argentina. Many friendships were to be made in this surreal odyssey. My two facilitators on that first trip at the end of March 2002 were Alberto in Buenos Aires and Marisa in General Roca. Alberto met me at the airport and hosted me with much generosity in the capital. He engineered my meeting, in a Buenos Aires restaurant over a cup of coffee, with retired Brigadier-General Mario Benjamín Menéndez, the former 1982 Malvinas Military Governor who was also the Commander of the Argentine Land Forces on the Islands. A second meeting was arranged with Lieutenant-Colonel Tomás ("Tommy") Jorge Fox in the latter's Buenos Aires apartment. He was the artillery forward observation officer perched on top of Mount Harriet in the war who directed that Argentine 155mm artillery fire against the Gurkhas for nearly three days when we were dug in at a place called Wether Ground on the southern coastline of East Falkland. After four hours of swapping stories about the war, "Tommy", his wife, who was an English teacher, Alberto and I enjoyed a delightful midnight meal at a Buenos Aires restaurant.

I also met Marisa and her husband, Roberto, at the iconic Plaza de Mayo, scene of General Galtieri's speeches from the balcony of

Government House, otherwise known as the Casa Rosada (Pink House), to the Argentine crowds during those heady post-Falklands invasion days of April 1982. From there we visited the impressive pink stone Malvinas War Memorial in the Plaza San Martín, where inquisitive Guadalupe Barriviera, a *Clarín* journalist, interviewed me about my quest for Nicolás.

The *Clarín* article was published the following day, forty-eight hours before the veterans' Malvinas Day on 2 April, and Marisa's and Roberto's home where I was staying was besieged by the local media. A national radio programme conducted a ten-minute live interview between Nicolás in Río Gallegos and me. Nicolás seemed a solid person who, despite his previous hesitation, did not appear during the broadcast to have an aversion to speaking to me. But there was to be no meeting with "the other" on that particular trip. Nonetheless a breakthrough had been made. I returned to Buenos Aires to watch the impressive Malvinas War Veterans' Day military parade with Alberto. That evening, before my flight home on the following day, I received a phone call in my hotel room from a Jorge Pérez Grandi. He had read the *Clarín* article published a few days previously and wanted to meet me as soon as possible. He had been Nicolás Urbieta's platoon commander in the war.

An hour later I met Jorge in the hotel lobby, and for the next three hours he told me about his platoon's experiences and the fighting at the Battle of Two Sisters against the Royal Marine 45 Commando unit on the night of 11-12 June 1982. He also gave me some startling information about the modest Nicolás Urbieta. An extract from my book is pertinent:

> After they ran out of ammunition Pérez Grandi ordered Urbieta to lead his platoon off their position. Not shirking his responsibility, the officer then covered their withdrawal alone. But, as they began to move down Moody Valley, a mortar bomb exploded by Pérez Grandi. Shrapnel tore into his right arm, legs, and thighs – smashing bones and slicing off chunks of flesh. He ordered his men to continue their withdrawal, but one volunteered to remain with him. Pérez Grandi's men managed to escape but, on reaching an Argentine Army artillery battery three kilometres away near Moody Brook bridge, south-east of Mount Longdon, Urbieta asked for a stretcher and, accompanied by nine men, made his way back to Dos Hermanos (Two Sisters). Like frozen mutton, his platoon commander's bleeding had been slowed down by the cold. Pérez Grandi was put on the stretcher, covered with combat kit and, despite lack of morphine, survived the agonizing trek to a waiting truck at the artillery battery. Urbieta had tabbed more than nine kilometres to rescue his officer who, that

same day, underwent an emergency operation in Puerto Argentino's military hospital before being flown out on the last Hercules to Río Gallegos. Pérez Grandi contracted gangrene and was hospitalised for a year. Urbieta remained in defence around the battery, only to withdraw to Puerto Argentino's Racecourse just before the ceasefire – but would receive no decoration for his outstanding bravery. (Seear, 2003).

In December 2002 I made a second visit to Argentina accompanied by my Norwegian colleague and friend, Professor Lars Weisæth. By then I had established a further contact in Buenos Aires, Dr Eduardo Gerding, the Malvinas War Veterans' Medical Co-ordinator. There was the possibility of establishing a traumatic stress project, so Lars and I interviewed eight Malvinas War veterans, assisted by Eduardo. I was intrigued to discover that two of them had been through a similar "unlawful dismissal" process. As a result they were still unemployed. I tried to encourage them by sharing my experience.

Lars and I then travelled to General Roca to interview another six veterans in Marisa's home. The exchange was most positive, and I became convinced that veteran peer support is a most effective concept for assisting veterans who continue to suffer with traumatic stress reactions. Indeed I thought then, and still do, that a potential opportunity has been squandered by government and experts alike in not attempting to organise a unique bilateral project between Argentina and the United Kingdom on Falklands-Malvinas combat veterans' issues. Focus on the concrete challenges of humanity rather than the abstract notion of sovereignty might have brought the two countries closer together on the Falklands-Malvinas issue.

Although more material was gathered for my book as a direct result of this visit, including a subsequent valuable exchange of emails between Rear-Admiral Carlos Hugo Robacio, the former Commanding Officer of the 5th Marine Infantry Battalion which fought in the Battle of Tumbledown two nights after the Two Sisters battle, I did not manage to make any contact with Nicolás. But Marisa travelled to Río Gallegos in March 2003 to persuade him that it might be a good idea for us two veterans to meet. After my book had been published in July 2003, Marisa invited me to return to Argentina in September of that year. She had also just published a book that documented our correspondence and my initial visit to Argentina in the previous year. *Entre tu mano y la mía* (*Between Your Hand and Mine*) was the title and appropriate symbol that cultural friendship and understanding with "the other" can be successfully achieved post-conflict. The annual Córdoba City Book Fair was to be held that month and she had been asked by "La Solapa" (a cultural organisation) if we might be interested in presenting our books jointly at this event. It would be a unique occasion.

But there was something more. Alberto arranged a second meeting between Brigadier-General Menéndez and me. The aim was simple: to keep my promise and present him with a copy of my book. But the retired Brigadier-General did something for me which I was to discover during my visit to General Roca three days later. The General had arranged through the Argentine Army to have Nicolás flown up from Río Gallegos so we could finally meet. This long-awaited meeting took place in Marisa's kitchen on the morning of 20 September 2003. Through an interpreter Nicolás and I talked for a long time. It was then I learnt of the error in my book. For carrying out his rescue of the wounded Jorge Pérez Grandi from the Two Sisters battlefield, Nicolás had indeed been awarded his nation's second highest award for gallantry – the Medal for Valour in Combat.

Nicolás accompanied Marisa and me the next day to the Córdoba City Book Fair. This event also produced another highly personal meeting for him. When questions were being asked by the large audience at the end of the two book presentations, a woman raised her hand to speak. She stood up. A minute later Nicolás was embraced by her. She was the mother of Jorge Pérez Grandi. Twenty-one years after the war, she had met her son's rescuer at last. This visit will not be my last to Argentina. The next will be to coincide with the Veterans' Malvinas Day Commemoration event in Buenos Aires on 2 April 2007, and is one of numerous other journeys during the twenty-fifth anniversary year of the war that will include the veterans' commemoration parade in London, the South Atlantic Medal Association 82's Pilgrimage to the Islands, and presentation of six lectures about the war and its aftermath aboard the Cunard Liner RMS *Queen Elizabeth 2*, which had transported the Gurkhas to the South Atlantic in 1982.

My future writing will be about going to war, battlefield survival, post-conflict cultures, post-traumatic growth, existential authority, traumatic stress, life reconstruction, combat veteran peer support and reconciliation after the Falklands-Malvinas War. Maybe it might help those Falklands-Malvinas combat veterans on both sides who still suffer from the dark side of the post-conflict aftermath.

References

Seear, M. H. (2003). *With the Gurkhas in the Falklands: A War Journal*. Barnsley: Pen and Sword Books.

"Saving the Nation":
Post-Conflict from the Point of View of the "Guilty"

Sophie Thonon-Wesfreid

On 24 March 1976, a Military Junta composed of the Army, the Navy and the Air Force took power in Argentina and suspended the constitutional organs for seven years up to the elections of October 1983. Its first leader was the General of the Army, Jorge Rafael Videla, who dominated the country from 29 March 1976 to 29 March 1981. The repression led by the military and police forces was the cruellest ever imposed on Argentina and probably in Latin American history. Savage tortures were systematically applied to the people arrested and 30,000 persons "disappeared", many of the bodies of whom have never been found.[1] During the trial undertaken in 1985 against the different members of the four successive Juntas, the prosecutor, Julio Strasera, qualified the repression as being "ferocious, clandestine and cowardly".

The first task undertaken by the dictatorship was to justify the coup perpetrated against an elected government, the one led by Juan Domingo Perón's widow and third wife, Isabel Perón, and then to justify the repression. The Armed Forces denounced the civil government as totally unable to assume its mission and therefore responsible for all the national disasters, such as anarchy, corruption, lack of productivity, financial speculation, etc. which were supposed to have gangrened all state institutions. On the contrary, the military power, supposedly uncontaminated by these vices by being endowed with moral and ethical principles, presented itself as the only one able to restore order, strength and faith to the Argentine nation, and as being in charge of a divine mission: the search for the common good and national restoration.

In order to justify the bloody and clandestine repression exercised by the military forces, a concept was created called the National Security Doctrine, an expression of a new plan of domination by the United States over Latin America. This doctrine, elaborated by President Richard Nixon's administration, consisted in the reinforcement of Latin American armies for the destruction of the enemy, from inside or outside of the country, in order to assure the protection of North America's interests, in both strategic and economic fields.

---

[1] One of the methods used to eliminate people and then "disappear" their bodies was to throw them, alive but drugged with pentothal, from aircraft into the sea of the Río de la Plata.

In a famous open letter written a year after the coup on 24 March 1977, a journalist and writer, Rodolfo Walsh, drew up a balance sheet of the dictatorship: 15,000 people had "disappeared" – double that number by 1983 – through the systematic use of torture, and 400 illegal centres of detention were scattered throughout the whole country; there had been widespread destruction of productive forces and political and trade union structures; poverty had increased – in a year the purchasing power of the worker had been reduced by forty percent; unemployment had reached ten percent of the working population – and would be more than doubled by 1983; and financial speculation had replaced productivity. The external national debt of eight million dollars in 1976 had grown – and would equal forty-five million dollars by 1983. Rodolfo Walsh "disappeared" because he wrote this letter.

The combined effects of the repression and disastrous application of uncontrolled liberal economic principles [2] generated a deep frustration among the population. Marches and demonstrations were organized all over the country. On 7 November 1981, the day of the famous saint, San Cayetano, about 50,000 Argentine workers gathered to protest against the military regime, its repression, and unemployment. Five months later, on 30 March 1982, more workers' demonstrations took place all over the country on the basis of the same slogan: "The military dictatorship is ending". There was a march in Buenos Aires to the Plaza de Mayo, that is to say directly under the windows of the military power.

Three days afterwards, 1,000 Argentine troops from the Army, Marines and Air Force disembarked in Puerto Argentino on the Malvinas Islands, Argentine territory occupied by Great Britain since 1833 under the name of the Falkland Islands. The next day, the new leader of the Military Junta who had assumed power on 22 December 1981, General Leopoldo Fortunato Galtieri, announced in public the recovery of the Malvinas Islands on the basis of the legitimate right of Argentina with its national patrimony, in the name of "all and each of the Argentines without distinction of groups or flags", adding that "the place taken had been decided without any political consideration". Such a remark implied, indeed, an obvious political motivation which has been revealed by the reaction of the Argentine population.

The recovery of this Argentine territory occupied by a colonial nation was, in fact, an old claim on the part of Argentina. The aim decided on by

[2] In a speech delivered on 30 October 1980, before the Argentine Chamber of Commerce, General Jorge Rafael Videla rejected state intervention in the economy as being the germ of social and economic disorder.

the dictatorship was to remain at the head of the nation, gathering the population under the same banner and making it forget the bloody repression and the disastrous economic situation through a glorious campaign for liberation. [3] The reaction of the Argentine population was enthusiastic, along with that of several Latin American countries, for this campaign was considered a defence of national sovereignty against colonialism and a new war for independence. The Military Junta had been so devoted to the United States and its demands that it was certain of American support.

On the day of the landings, President Reagan asked Argentina to withdraw its troops immediately and, as a second step, he turned his back on the Argentine dictatorship and provided help to British Prime Minister Margaret Thatcher. The Chilean dictatorship, led by Augusto Pinochet, also provided help to the British Government and its troops, support that Margaret Thatcher would remember when the ex-dictator was arrested in London sixteen years afterwards on the basis of an arrest warrant issued by the Spanish judge, Baltazar Garzón.

Galtieri explained later that he had been indeed "expecting a reaction" from Great Britain "but had never contemplated such a mobilization for the Malvinas". He added: "I have to say that I feel a great bitterness because the North Americans know very well that, as the Supreme Head of the Army, that is to say, before being the President of the Nation, I always tried to be close to them and their Administration and to renew the mutual understanding weakened by the former Administration. I was very disappointed when Haig backed the English."

The war was short and intense. Its start was marked by two main events. [4] The first took place on 2 May when a British Royal Navy nuclear

[3] In 1985, in the trial of the Junta by the newly elected government of Raúl Alfonsín, a voluntarily retired Argentine officer, José Luis García, being an opponent of the same Junta from the first day of the coup, denounced the sacrifice of young soldiers and officers in order to save the dictatorship from infamy.

[4] A specific event has to be mentioned: on 25 April, as part of Operation Paraquet, Royal Marine Commandos landed at Grytviken on the small island of South Georgia where the Argentine naval officer Alfredo Astiz had been in command of the Argentine contingent for three weeks. He immediately "surrendered to the enemy, without due resistance" (Rattenbach Report, 1983, paragraphs 837g and 850p). His picture appeared on a national television programme, which would permit his being recognised by several mothers of the famous Argentine "Madres de la Plaza de Mayo" as an infiltrator of their group in Buenos Aires and Paris, who gathered information from group members whilst pretending, under the

submarine detected the Argentine cruiser ARA *General Belgrano* outside the Total Exclusion Zone determined by the British Government. Without warning HMS *Conqueror* torpedoed the ship, which sank in a remarkably short time. Three hundred and twenty-one Argentine sailors died. The second event occurred two days later when the British Royal Navy destroyer, HMS *Sheffield*, was hit by an Exocet missile launched by a Super-Étendard fighter aircraft flown from its base at Río Grande. In this attack twenty of the ship's company died. On 14 June, Brigadier-General Mario Benjamín Menéndez surrendered to the Commander of the British Land Forces, Major-General Jeremy Moore. The war was over after seventy-four days and nine hundred and four fatalities. The remaining days of the Argentine dictatorship were numbered.

In December 1982, the Junta established a commission to hold an enquiry into the responsibility for this shameful war. This was commonly known as the Rattenbach Commission, "as was demanded by national sovereignty and the dignity of the Armed Forces". It concluded that "the method adopted by the Junta to prepare the nation for this war has neglected the most elementary rules of organization to be implemented within the military forces. This explains that fundamental errors have been committed in political orientation and military strategy with which the conflict has been initiated and concluded."

On 15 March 1986, the three Generals, Anaya, Galtieri and Lami Dozo, were sentenced respectively to fourteen, twelve and eight years in jail by the Supreme Council of the Armed Forces. In October 1983 the Military Junta was obliged to organize elections, which were won by the Radical Party of Raúl Alfonsín. A civil trial took place in 1985 against the Military Junta, led by the Argentine Federal Court of Justice, which sentenced to life in prison the main leaders of the dictatorship for the atrocities they had perpetrated. Very few nations have committed to trial their dictators, who are more often, even if very rarely, judged by international courts of justice or *ad hoc* jurisdictions.

Hundreds of criminal enquiries were opened in the country by judges to allow the imputation and the condemnation of military soldiers or officials responsible for torture, murders, rapes, illegal detentions, disappearances and robberies. In spite of this exceptional victory in the

false identity of Gustavo Nino, that he was looking for his supposedly disappeared brother, just as the mothers were looking for their disappeared children. Alfredo Astiz has never been convicted by Argentine justice but by a French criminal court, which sentenced him to life imprisonment on 16 March 1992. However Argentina has never extradited him.

difficult fight for human rights, in 1986 and 1987, under military pressure,[5] two laws called "Final Point" and "Due Obedience" were passed by the Argentine National Congress, granting impunity to the murderers. Later, in 1992, a decree of pardon was handed by Alfonsín's successor, the Perónist Carlos Menem, to the previously condemned Generals, who were then freed. A long night of impunity fell on Argentina, impunity from which it has still not emerged despite the progress made. [6]

In 1992 trials were held on the basis of the only exception allowed in the two previously mentioned laws, which dealt with the illegal appropriation of new-born babies whose mothers had been arrested, kept alive until the delivery and then "disappeared". The generals previously condemned were arrested and committed to house arrest as they were older than seventy years of age. They have not yet been judged.

But the main fight led the victims, their families, the Human Rights Associations and their lawyers, a few judges and prosecutors, and left-wing progressive parties to demand annullment by the National Congress of the "Final Point" and "Due Obedience" Laws. Success was achieved in 2004. Hundred of cases that had been closed in 1987 were then re-opened and investigated. The first conviction was made on 17 September 2006 against a police officer, Miguel Etchecolatz, for "crimes against humanity committed within genocide": this was the first condemnation ever pronounced in Argentina on this criminal ground and, as such, it recognized the very nature of the crimes perpetrated by the dictatorship. That is to say, criminal acts, committed on a massive scale, according to a systematic plan of elimination of people because of their beliefs, and whose horror violates human consciousness.

However, the cases are numerous (one thousand and four), scattered all over the country (in fifty-two cities), and the financial means provided do not make allowance for the importance of the task. For example, a key witness in the Etchecolatz case, Julio López, recently disappeared.

---

[5] Two officers who had fought in the Malvinas War, Aldo Rico and Mohamed Alí Seneildín, formed a rebel group of soldiers called "Carapintadas", which demanded the cessation of the criminal investigation.

[6] A culture of impunity developed not only in the domain of crimes against humanity perpetrated by the dictatorship, but also in public and private finances, a great favourite through auctions of public properties and services. Financial crimes, such as embezzlement of money, bribery of civil servants, illegal royalties, white-washing of black money, and tax evasion were neither tried in a court of justice, nor were they really condemned.

Neither the political leaders, with the exception of a few, nor the police seriously considered the criminal dimension of such an event and what it implied in a democracy. The criminal investigation then took on a tragic and fatal delay. Witness protection, along with a thorough cleaning-up of the police, is required, because the fight for justice in Argentina is still a dubious battle.

Without doubt the Malvinas War hastened the fall of the dictatorship, but did not cause it. On the contrary, what the Junta achieved was the destruction of a country in which a political generation disappeared and the external debt of eight million dollars rose to forty-five million. What the four Juntas actually caused were the plagues of Argentina which survive even today: namely unemployment and poverty, lack of state control, corruption and a difficult justice.

References

Rattenbach Report (1983) (suppressed until 2012).

On the Making of the film *An Ungentlemanly Act* [1]

Stuart Urban

Publicity/background notes, written in 1992

In 1982 I sat back and watched with disbelief as we went to war for a place most Britons probably could not have found on a map a few weeks before. Although I consider myself British first and foremost, I have relatives in Buenos Aires, and spent time in Venezuela for various parts of my childhood and youth (I still have dual nationality). I not only felt torn between Britain and Latin America but was also fascinated at how two developed nations supported a war over this outcrop of rock and grass or, as some would have us believe, for the principle of it all. In 1986 I wrote my first screenplay on the war set amidst the Paras. It very nearly got made on two occasions but its would-be backers ran out of funds and its time passed. But the beginning had always fascinated me, a mini-Khartoum or Dunkirk or Singapore, yet without the degree of bloodshed that would have made the war inevitable and the story too painful to watch. This beginning proves that this was a war fought on both sides for wounded honour; the Argentines at what they saw as a century and a half of usurpation, the British at the insolence of Argentine aggression.

For the first few years not enough detail came out (*The Sunday Times* "Insight" team did a very able account, but only of the British side). Then more elements started appearing in dribs and drabs and a really fascinating film began to take possible shape. To me, the outlandish shoot-out on the croquet lawns and vegetable patch of Government House provided an ideal alternative focus to everything that had come before on television about the war. No one had seemed to depict how absurd the whole thing was, few seemed to take note of the Argentine writer Borges's analogy of "two bald men fighting over a

---

[1] In the Autumn of 1992, the BBC gave a nod and a wink to the production company Union Pictures in the UK that it might wish to make the script I was developing about the extraordinary first thirty-six hours of the Falklands War to mark the tenth anniversary of the conflict. This was a tragi-comic but true tale (or should that "but" be "and") of how the Governor, Rex Hunt, and his small party of Royal Marines, received the stunning last-minute news on 1 April 1982 that an Argentine invasion force was about invade the Falkland Islands. Some thought it was an April Fool's Day prank... Here is my production diary detailing some of my experiences preparing and making the film.

comb". I did not wish to laugh at the characters in the story – indeed, as far as I am concerned, they are very heroic. What fascinated me was the surreal sideshow in the twilight of Empire; the laughable levels of men and equipment that Britain maintained against a dictatorship that was known to be ruthless and violent; the brave Governor, whose unswerving loyalty to Mrs Thatcher never faltered and who chose to defend the undefendable Government House rather than let the wooden houses of Stanley come under fire (ironic because the Argentines, who presumed he would have vacated it, like any sensible bloke, blundered into an unexpectedly solid defence); the symbolic first death which occurred over a language mix-up – the leader of the Argentine Commandos was bleeding to death in the chicken run, begging to be relieved of the live grenade in his hand, while the British thought he was threatening them not to come near or he would hurl it. And in the midst of this crisis that began on April Fool's Day some Islanders understandably failed to come to terms with what was going on; one man tried to walk to work through a firefight while a lady offered tea to Marines firing over her garden fence.

In bringing this true story to the screen I rejected the usually po-faced approach of drama-documentary (even though this is technically the category *An Ungentlemanly Act* falls into), ignored the occasionally flashy thriller-genre techniques deployed particularly in pieces about Northern Ireland, and tried instead to begin the film boldly as an Ealing comedy and then descend into tragedy. This, I believe, is something like the way it was. I was flattered and delighted when Major Mike Norman, who conducted the defence by Royal Marines, agreed to be military advisor on the basis of the screenplay. I have met and talked with almost every major character in the script (both British and Argentine) and researched it to the best of my ability. Nevertheless, I try to tell the story through characters that we care for, whose fear and horror and laughter we understand. There are certain changes of time/place for dramatic convenience, a handful of minor characters get rolled into a slightly smaller handful, re-naming of a few supporting characters for legal reasons or by request of those involved. But, on the whole, in trying to be objective and using the methodology which earned me a first class history degree (I make this mention at the risk of sounding immodest but hoping to present solid credentials), I hope that what I am presenting is worthwhile. While making no apologies for the fact, I accept that presenting recent historical events as tragicomedy might be considered provocative. Some people will no doubt lambast me for concentrating on the first, highly embarrassing, chapter of this war (though my defence is that my 1986 script followed the whole course of the war and I was so keen to get it made that I even defended a High Court action to retain the copyright). But this invasion is after all the reason the war took place. Because we won, people in this country never really questioned how the war could have been allowed to happen and I think some people will be very surprised at seeing this. My purpose in the end is not merely or even primarily political. Hopefully people will conclude from these absurd, confused, and frightening events that history is not the neat arrangement of facts that some books and politicians offer us, that people can blunder into a war without stopping to think what on earth they are doing, and that in the case of a unique and fragile little community like this, force of arms is no solution because the peace and harmony of the Falklands were destroyed when the first shot was fired and as long as "Fortress Falklands" continues. But even though the minefields might never be cleared, perhaps if people can soften their attitudes after a film like this, a settlement can one day be reached.

An Ungentlemanly Act
Extracts from Stuart Urban's production diary

3 November 1991 – To Sunningdale, home of the Hunts, at 11.00 am on this last Sunday morning before I leave for the Southern Hemisphere. Fifi, the historic red Fiesta car, sits on the gravel, not indicating to any casual observer that she had survived sea voyages, gun battles and artillery bombardments. Her colour is a fine complement to His Excellency's maroon London taxi and official car, which I will see in the flesh down south.

Rex and Mavis kindly agreed to receive me at very short notice before my rushed departure. Rex is short, as I knew, but physically graceful and well proportioned. Like Dick Baker and his wife, years of colonial service have produced an affable, friendly and engaging couple. I took Mavis at first to be a possible cook, so different did she seem, in apron strings and rolled-up sleeves, from her photographs, as she prepared the Sunday lunch. She strikes me at first as flighty and nervous, though after a few minutes' talk she actually becomes rather camp in manner and speech ("let's have a pinkie" at 12.15 pm). Rex is as helpful as he can be in his interview but, of course, I must ask myself (and him) whether what he is telling is all that he knows. Did he (as Captain Nick Barker of *Endurance* maintains) have forewarning of the invasion? If he did, I would have to change the complexion of the film's opening. Major Norman backs Rex Hunt on this, so I am inclined to discount what Captain Barker says – Mike Norman has no axe to grind.

But I question Rex closely and his disavowals seem genuine. Both Rex and Mavis are very discreet on the matter of the former Royal

Marine garrison commander Garry Noott and why he was not asked to resume command as he knew the terrain much better than the incoming garrison's commander, Mike Norman. I think there is something I am not being told but will I ever discover what? Mavis will not admit (indeed denies very hastily) that she told Connie Baker or Major Norman that the Falklands were not worth fighting for that night: "You see, I don't know if she told you but Connie never cared for the Falklands." Connie never gave that impression to me. I conclude that Mavis expressed those feelings in a crisis in which they all feared for their lives and that the other two (both reliable witnesses) could not have made this up. The fact is that a lot of people testify to various things about Mavis that night which I intend to show in a toned-down form. I sympathise with her greatly and she will engage the audience's sympathy but inevitably the Hunts will find some things about her portrait which they will not like and I feel apprehensive about this, because they are such pleasant people. But I feel it is my responsibility to show the truth.

To Soho via the home of Franc Roddam (executive producer of this film and director of *Quadrophenia*) and Carina and their four-day old baby Flynn, and on to Union Pictures' Marshall Street base, where casting resumes. That afternoon designer Steve Hardie arrives from North Carolina, tired and jetlagged after his *Hellraiser III* but ready for the off.

Monday 4 November (extract) – Walking along Regent Street I receive a mysterious call on the mobile from someone who introduces himself as the individual who single-handedly operated the Spanish language desk at GCHQ during the first eighty-six hours of the crisis. He was monitoring the Argentine military interception, in other words. He would not say how he knew about this film or obtained my unlisted mobile number. He provides us with fascinating information which, among other things, follows the government line on not being able to be certain that invasion was imminent until it was too late. He also confirms Rex Hunt's insistence that Nick Barker did not inform him of any imminent invasion. There was only one MI6 man in Latin America even though he was stationed in Buenos Aires. *Endurance* and Nick Barker were the main source of intercepts. But because there had been Argentine naval manoeuvres of this kind in previous years, also utilising the NATO Blue codebook, the Government did not act swiftly enough. Has Rex Hunt or someone in the Government put this "mole" up to calling me? Somebody must have.

5 November (extract – preparing to fly to the Falklands from UK) – At RAF Brize Norton, designer Steve Hardie and I are greeted at the security gate with the question is our flight "duty or indulgence?". I have

to think carefully before replying. "Crab Air"[2] destinations are billed in abbreviated form to confuse the enemy and passengers. Service is brusque in the extreme, making even El Al stewards seem courteous. A hiss from the squaddies greets the tannoy request for "officers and civilians" to go forward first and take their seats on the flight. The cargo aircraft interior is "spartan minimalist", with vast steel containers and a white rope running down the starboard side in case we keel over on a forced landing or whatever. That's fine if we list to port, but what happens if we go the other way? The "cabin" is alternately freezing and roasting. There is no thermostat, only on/off (polar blizzard vs. fires of hell). I pity the "stewardess", not a conventionally attractive girl, whose safety demonstration must nevertheless be performed to a sea of leering smiles, shaved heads and ribald comments. Pork scratchings and a Penguin bar (destination: Falklands, get it?) for the snack meal, a ham roll for dinner, sausages and bacon for breakfast in a package labelled "SAS partner". Good thing I'm not kosher or vegetarian. Later, the men find amusement in portable TV gameboys. The stewardess gets her revenge by barking orders and we are all finally commanded by the tannoy to sleep before being plunged into darkness (no such thing as reading lights here).

Wednesday, November 6 (extract) – On arriving in Stanley after some twenty-four hours' travelling, Steve Hardie and I cannot resist racing round to see everything we can before the sun sets. Having written about and researched this place for so long (five years when I count my first screenplay about the war) nothing quite prepares me for the Falklands, which must be one of the strangest places on earth. You step off a plane eight thousand miles down south and here you are not quite in little England but a little English colonial outpost, situated not only physically in the middle of nowhere, but also in some unspecified past. The wind, the startlingly clear air, the tame birds, the penguins on beaches, all tell you that you are well away from any civilised land mass. Rushing round to have a quick look at the outside of Government House, it appears terribly small, so petite as to resemble a doll's house. It seems to translate on a different scale when photographed or filmed. Here, on the manicured croquet lawn at the front, and in the chicken-run and vegetable garden behind, the war began with a gun battle. Unreal.

Stanley is also very compact, almost like a model village, with its higgledy-piggledy houses with multi-coloured roofs, and in the gardens you see horses and sheep and smoking oil-drums. Almost a "toy-town",

---

[2] "Crabs" is a slang name for members of the RAF (editor's note).

as one of my characters describes it. It has a fairytale air, despite several building monstrosities that have sprung up, and ugly satellite dishes. Up to Tumbledown to catch the sunset. It is very unsettling to stand near the spot where Robert Lawrence (hero of the previous BBC drama, *Tumbledown*), whose wedding I went to, stood when he looked down at Stanley and was shot through the head in the last hour or so of the war. Birds approach us, and all around lies the fragmentary debris of war – sleeping bags, half-buried Argentine positions etc. Standing next to the memorial cross to the Scots Guards who fell here, we can see for nearly fifty miles, well past the airport. The light here is certainly most unusual and for this alone it would be worth making the film here. Steve and I decide that this is really the only place to shoot the movie because it cannot be replicated. But our mission is merely a fact-finding one, with the possibility of a second unit or reduced unit coming here after we finish the main photography in New Zealand. Back to the Upland Goose Hotel (as featured in the film!) for a surprisingly pleasant meal of steak – alas, no Upland Geese available as if you want to eat one it has to be found and executed, which requires a few days' notice.

Thursday 7 November – At breakfast I saw a man riding to work on his horse, sitting on the traditional kelper's fleece saddle. Our American waitress, who is also the owner-publisher of a local paper, informs us that he is called Dennis Middleton and pastures his transport outside his workplace during the day. Got to have him in the title sequence, which presents key images of Stanley. First stop is the kitsch chalet that the Argentines built for Vice-Comodoro Gilobert, boss of the military airline LADE and quite possibly a master spy, in Falklands terms. His former home is now the Falklands Museum, run by John Smith. We have brought him a fish tank from the UK for his whale embryo (a dead one). In return he gives us a lot of co-operation and assistance. Like other Islanders, he rightly boggles at the prospect of our attempting to recreate the Falklands elsewhere. A depressing call to London reveals that the New Zealand budget is looking way over and the project is now threatened, despite the tax shelter monies available there. Bollocks. There are so many people and places to see in our forty-eight hours on the Island that we are inevitably late for every single appointment, charging about on foot or in the Land Rover of our good-humoured guide, Tony Smith, the relentless wind buffeting at all times.

One surprising and depressing thing about the Islanders is their casual racism towards Latinos, calling the Argentines "wogs" and so on – even the most cultured and reasonable of them frequently emit such epithets. I feel personally insulted for, as I have said, although I count myself British I have relatives in Buenos Aires, have lived in Venezuela

184

and still have dual nationality. But then this ambiguity of feeling is why I set about making a film on this war in the first place. I meet Pat Peck, one of the Falkland Islands Defence Force (FIDF) men lined up outside the Bakers' house garden wall in the mock execution scene that we will have towards the end of the film. They thought the Argentines were preparing to fire but it was just posing for the cameras. I looked at the wall, and saw the still extant bullet hole in the adjoining house, caused by an Argentine heavy machine-gun round which narrowly missed Tony Hunt during the invasion. So bizarre, the wall where men thought they were to be shot and the quaint house with its symbolic bullet hole. It would be so wonderful to recreate these extraordinary scenes where they took place. After a confusing amount of bureaucracy (Government House had lost all trace of our visit and appointment) we finally gain entry to the minuscule seat of government. A brief chat with the Governor is followed by an excellent tour conducted by chauffeur majordomo, Don Bonner, who is one of the cast of our film. He still drives the maroon taxi on certain occasions but more often the conventional Range Rover (registration: GH1). We come across Roger Huxley, a short, Ealingesque Foreign Office man who keeps turning books over and denying us permission to photograph even the most innocuous secretary's desk for fear of unmasking some major secret of state. Don Bonner mutters oaths and mouths the letters "FO" behind Mr Huxley's back. Clearly a clash of parallel command structures, as Don runs the house and Roger the diplomatic side.

Roger tells Don to "stop bullshitting" about where various bullets came through but the evidence is clear enough throughout the house, with many patched up lumps in the wall and even the odd piece of antique furniture with a part missing. In the pantry the floor is still cratered from a high explosive grenade that came through, fortunately not killing any of the defenders. I did not even know a grenade had penetrated the house so I must include this incident. Then to the chicken and sheep run where the first lethal shots of the war were fired. The mind can scarcely comprehend how Captain Giacchino and his courageous Commandos simply strolled right up to the kitchen door, intending to seize the Governor before they were cut down amidst chickens, geese and sheep. Giacchino is a national hero with streets named after him in Buenos Aires, yet here was the spot he met his end in such a bizarre, sordid and unnecessary manner. Unnecessary, because he bled to death over a difference of language, a grenade clutched in his hand. The Marines would have rescued him, indeed tried to, but always thought he was menacing them (he was pleading to be disarmed and given medical assistance). I study the small potato shed behind which one of the wounded Argentines hid, including Diego Quiroga, and as per written testimony there are several low bullet holes which must have narrowly missed the wounded man's head.

In the same shed Argentine bodies were found at the end of the war. The chicken and sheep milling around are not descendants of the 1982 generation because they were eaten by the hungry defenders in the last days of the war. Next the London taxi in its garage, whose walls are also pitted with many bullet holes. Miraculously, the official car and its female sidekick, Fifi the Fiesta, survived the war intact and were liberated by the Paras on 14 June. We decide to ask the Governor straight out if he can assist us in the making of the film and to our surprise Mr Fullerton shows himself to be completely for it, saying that "this is the place to make the film", not New Zealand. He says he has complete authority (and indeed his authority here is second only to the Queen's) but I cannot believe he would not have to refer his decision back to the Foreign and Commonwealth Office, in which case we can kiss it goodbye. There is a definite embargo emanating from Whitehall or Downing Street on any co-operation being offered to this film, for example in the loan of men or *matériel* for filming purposes. Wouldn't it be fantastic to come here, if we could overcome the logistic and transport difficulties? To make a film with full-scale action sequences thousands of miles from any film facilities or industry (except Argentina's of course – but no air travel is allowed to/from the Argies).

After dinner we meet Jim Fairfield, the ex-Royal Marine who left his two infant children and his wife to fight that night at GH, fully expecting to die. When it came to the time to surrender, Jim told the Governor to "fuck off". I struggle to understand the mentality of these "Royals" as they call themselves. But then Jim at least was fighting for his family and home, whereas others who fought were just off the boat. Jim, like most of our interviewees, remains cagey on who actually shot Giacchino. Well, I've got to show someone doing it and he seems the right sort of warlike guy.

Friday 8 November – The bellicose attitude of the authorities ten years after the war means that not only is an inordinate amount of jet fuel wasted on Phantom escorts for flights across the Exclusion Zone, but travellers heading to Argentina (a forbidden air travel destination some four hundred miles away) have to endure the absurdity of a three-legged, thirty-six hour journey. It starts with a five-hour flight over the South Atlantic and Tierra del Fuego in a tiny toilet-less aircraft, staying over in Punta Arenas (Chile) whose only redeeming feature is that it is the second most southerly town in the world, then up a couple of thousand "Ks" to Santiago, change planes for the second time, and finally the one-and-a-half-hour hop across the Andes to Buenos Aires.

Sunday 10 November – On landing, my Falklands visa is carefully bordered (but not abused or obliterated) by an Argentine entry stamp. Zooming along the freeway in one of the city's ubiquitous 1990s-built Ford Falcons with retro styling, we pass the first of many signs proclaiming the "Malvinas were, are and will be Argentine".

Buenos Aires is a delight at 1.30 am when we arrive, the streets and cafés throbbing with life and excitement and vitality. A vibrant metropolis, surely one of the unacknowledged great capitals of the world. Yet this exciting mass of people joined its dictator leaders in the escapade of the Malvinas... After a few hours' sleep I make contact with Rear-Admiral Büsser and Brigadier (as he now is) Gilobert aka the Master Spy of the Malvinas. Büsser, who insists on being called "Doctor" rather than "Contraalmirante", checks up that I am who I am by ringing me back at the Hotel Claridge. The hotel name is symbolic of the Argentine's love-hate relationship with things British, like the red letterboxes and Victorian railway stations. It is wonderful and exciting to discover that these two key Argentine characters of the script, about whom I have heard and written so much, correspond with my visions of them in the first draft. Büsser is the utterly civil *caballero* I expected, but his apartment is festooned with guns, militaria and photographic blow-ups of the "recovery of the Malvinas" which he commanded.

The numerous Catholic images around the place remind me of the role that religion has played in Hispanic military oligarchies – forget the military-industrial complex, this is the military-holy alliance. Büsser shows me photographs of the troops being blessed before Operation Rosario (gotta stage that scene!), and even the secret plans and logs. His recall is pretty sharp, though, like with Rex Hunt, it is presumably a well rehearsed tale. Interestingly, he reveals that it was he who slapped the face of the Argentine NCO who was humiliating the Royal Marines and, moreover, he personally accosted and disarmed one of the enraged Commandos intending to massacre the Marines after the death of their leader, Captain Giacchino. What is more, he tells me that a male servant (by his description it can only be Don Bonner) came out wielding a shotgun at the flag-raising and eagle-eyed Büsser spotted him before he could do any damage. Büsser's personal snaps reveal the "spy" Gilobert in a peaked air force dress cap (his parka obscured whether he had the whole dress tunic, etc., or not) which would seem to confirm he had some foreknowledge of the invasion, because otherwise why would he have packed it for a short trip in which he no longer represented Argentina? Büsser also revealed (without my asking) that he had in fact shaken Rex's hand at the end of the surrender by asking, "And now I hope you will do me the honour?", something which Rex denies. But since Büsser also volunteered the very embarrassing information about their flag coming loose in a gust of wind I am inclined to believe Büsser on this one (note: his rather fantastic allegation about Don Bonner was also later confirmed to me by Don on the telephone). Büsser entrusts me with a photocopy of a book that will prove invaluable: eyewitness accounts by the officers and men who took part in the operation, including descriptions of Giacchino dying in the chicken-run, of Norman calling to him, and the whole grenade business. One (very) sinister note: I asked Büsser whether he was frightened at coming under direct fire, presuming it was his first time. He answered, "No, because I was in the war against the subversives." In other words, this man is a veteran of the Dirty War and no doubt displayed far less chivalry towards female *guerilleras* than he did to Major Norman and his Royal Marines. After spending two very stimulating hours with him I take my leave, asking whether Gilobert had been specially sent back as an undercover man for the invasion. Büsser shrugs and says, "You'll have to ask him that." A very ambiguous answer. And so to the Giloberts (Hector and wife Teresa), quite the most charming people of all the characters whom I have met on the "real" cast list. A good-looking Latin couple, sportively dressed and displaying genuine warmth (rather than Büsser's punctilious civility) they offer tea, biscuits and wonderful reminiscences about the Bakers, the Hunts (especially Mavis), and a truly humanitarian view of the whole conflict. But when presented with the evidence of his spying role Gilobert just smiles and shrugs it off convincingly, on a personal level. His argument is quite sophisticated, in that he suggests perhaps the air force high command used him as a dupe, knowing full well what was going to happen when they sent him in. He suggests they just wanted a reliable bloke on the ground. Anyway, Gilobert maintains he took no uniform or items of uniform with him. No doubt he would explain away the cap (if I confront him with my having seen Büsser's snap) by saying someone gave it to him to help him be identified, since he narrowly avoided being shot during and after the surrender procedures. I must try and get to the bottom of the Gaffoglio/Gilobert uniform puzzle. (Note: in fact I never was able to do so and, in the film, I made the reasonable assumption that Gilobert had a full uniform on under the parka). I had never realised that Gilobert remained in Stanley to the bitter end and was taken prisoner. An amusing last remark from Gilobert, pointedly after I had put the cassette recorder away, concerns the moment when he took his leave of Mavis. She was highly emotional, he says, and threw her arms around him tearfully! The Giloberts, like Büsser, send regards to the Hunts and the Bakers which I shall duly transmit, along with Büsser's regards to counterparts Norman and Noott. The amazing thing is how lacking in animosity the Argentines are about it all. I encounter far less jingoism and petty feeling in Buenos Aires than in Stanley. I round the evening off by meeting my Argentine relatives who insist on taking me for yet another meaty BA meal before I say goodbye.

Monday, 2 December – (After travelling on to New Zealand to prepare the main shoot of the film, I was pulled out with Steve Hardie when co-financing through Portman Entertainment collapsed and the budget escalated. A frantic week of meetings on the way back via Los Angeles had not produced rescue finance. The production seems doomed until ...). There are now two possibilities: firstly that the BBC picks up the entire cost of the film and makes it with its own crew and resources; secondly that Portman bounce back with their partner Jorge Estrada in a co-production to be made in Argentina. Bradley Adams (producer) has flown to Madrid to meet Jorge, who is keen and positive. He knows the script inside out, knows Lieutenant Quiroga and Rear-Admiral Büsser very well and can secure military co-operation for the movie! The big problem would be recreating Stanley and bringing down the British cast. I am told Patagonia looks similar to Falklands terrain but it is a long way down south (opposite the Falklands, in fact). The fact is that we have not found anywhere convincing or feasible on the British Isles to shoot so many exteriors in winter (if we went down the BBC route) and the choice will be between Argentina and the Falklands if Governor Fullerton throws in his full support.

Friday 13 (!) December – Hit another major snag because BBC 2 Controller Alan Yentob feels he must consult with higher powers (John Birt, Director General of the BBC, I believe) about the controversial implications of co-producing this film with Argentina. Their offer is now a substantial one but the problem is that brokers Portman are linking the deal with selling one of their current productions to the BBC at an inflated price and Alan will not horse-trade. The situation goes through another radical change in the afternoon when we go for a crisis meeting to BBC Drama Serials boss Michael Wearing's office. This is the first time I meet the man under whose auspices (together with Alan) the film has moved forward. He is in favour of re-enacting history where it happened (i.e. the Falklands) and prefers the risk of backing the whole film and reaping all the profits (should there be any). We will shoot on Super 16 (widescreen) and the battle scenes on 35mm which still gives a fighting chance of cinema release outside this country. He is energetically working for the film, and we all know that the Falklands would be creatively the most authentic and secure option with a British cast and crew. So, from having my bags packed and ready for four months in Buenos Aires I might now be in England next week and the Falklands soon after (if we can finance the BBC Falklands route) or, should it all go up in smoke, in Zambia with my family and in-laws for a commiserating holiday. But can the BBC, having gone up from £400,000 to £750,000, really commit the entire cost of £1.4 million?

Wednesday 21 January – (Here I was back in the Falklands again doing the recce and titles shoot with a skeleton crew. The production was now ninety percent certain, to be made in the Falklands, Ealing Studios and a few locations in the UK – e.g. HMS *Belfast*). Up at six each morning to make the best use of daylight. Nice to meet Don Bonner again and other favourites. Governor Fullerton is as relaxed, helpful and positive as ever, a source of eternal surprise when dealing with alumni of the Foreign and Commonwealth Office. We swallowed before explaining how we wanted to blow up windows, parts of the lawn, have Marines trample the flower beds etc. – a whole litany of destruction which we would of course rectify at the end of the day... Mr Fullerton took it brilliantly. The MOD are not keen to allow any co-operation because the FO seemed to have leaned on them by reason of a private understanding with Buenos Aires that we would not be dwelling on the tenth anniversary of the British victory. All the more surprising, then, that the Governor should be so happy to assist us, even using his influence to give us the reduced airfares available to service personnel and Islanders. By an extraordinary coincidence the lady of the house, Mrs Fullerton, is the namesake of "Nanny" Fullerton, the servant who is a character in our script! Must be very awkward since there seems to be a degree of upstairs/downstairs tension; one of the female staff pulls a face when Mrs "Governor" Fullerton rings impatiently for service on the old 1930s push-bell from the dining room. We film people are in the kitchen enjoying tea and coffee out of ER mugs. Fortunately for us we completed measuring and photographing in the dining room just before the Governor's wife entered for her boiled egg and toast awaiting her on the table. Perhaps we had kept her from her breakfast and thereby upset her!

Tuesday 3 March – (The first week of shooting at Ealing Studios is complete and the main unit flies down to the Falklands). Here we are merrily trooping down to make the first movie in the Falklands (and almost certainly the last!). Fortunately the aircraft is not a cargo plane like the one Steve Hardie and I flew on first but RAF catering is down to its usual standard and – typically "Crab Air" – the only hot meal is served some seventeen hours into the eighteen-hour flight. Highlight of the journey is spotting none other than Air Vice-Marshal Peter Beer, who is the Commander of British Forces Falkland Islands and has turned down our requests for military co-operation. Brad seizes his chance as the Air Vice-Marshal leaves his VIP seat and queues for the toilet, casually striking up a conversation about who we are and what we are doing. We have been told (and it could be hearsay) that Beer is not pleased that the Governor virtually invited us to the Islands. In any case, he is perfectly pleasant to Brad, but does not volunteer his name or identity (no doubt for reasons of security). Brad, ever the diplomat, tactfully does not reveal that he knows perfectly well whom he is talking to – this would embarrass the Air Vice-Marshal. He merely outlines our case in a roundabout way, and the Air Vice-Marshal wishes us the best of luck on the Islands, saying the project sounded most interesting. (Note: Brad never succeeded in obtaining the face-to-face official meeting with Peter Beer at which he hoped to reveal himself as the man on the aircraft, and we understand a written directive was issued preventing personnel working on our production even unofficially during leave – the subject of quite a few national press articles). We meet Mike Norman and the dozen or so members of the unit who have already been out here for some days preparing. Tonight is Mike's last night after thirty years in the Royal Marine Commandos and we lay on some champagne as a surprise. He is very touched at what must be a difficult time for him without his mates and family, back after ten years in the place he nearly died for.

Thursday 5 March – (extract). Filming the opening Stanley street scene outside a Mrs Betty Ford's house (we also have on the film's payroll A. Nutter and Ron Buckett), we ignite the flame of controversy that will grow to Kuwaiti oil-fire proportions by the end of the shoot. We had noticed in a journalistic reference that signs were put out for the butcher asking for a "Quarter Shepe Please". I thought it was either a local spelling or a misspelling. Either way I thought we should replicate it because I like amusing signs. It was in the background and will scarcely be visible in the film. We also had the Mrs Mozeley character in the street walking a sheep. It so happens that the woman who played her (Anne Reid, whose son was killed on the *Galahad* and who decided to settle near his grave) genuinely takes her pet sheep for walks, and again this was not something invented but can be found in videos of Stanley life. Anyway, people watch us shooting a scene over and over again and, although these are only two out of some 800 images in the film, conclusions are quickly reached. (The Falklanders believe from now on that the film portrays them as complete primitives. Betty Ford, who consented to the sign adorning her gate, was described by radio station manager Patrick Watts a couple of days later as being distraught and having taken to a farm in the hills in order to get over our insult.) A Japanese TV crew who have been doing an item on the Falklands have been stranded by the (typical) non-arrival of the RAF Tristar and so decide to film us. They recount what wonderful co-operation they

191

received from the Mount Pleasant military authorities, including free air-to-air filming facilities aboard helicopters and jets. We are indignant at the way in which they are offered such assistance and we cannot even hire squaddies on their days off. But Air Vice-Marshal Beer is not obliged towards us of course, and is probably "only obeying orders". Tonight is our first action sequence with the gun battle, for beginning, for Government House: three cameras, explosions, pretty well all the local FIDF men who can turn out to re-enact the battle. The real Jim Fairfield, an ex-Marine who is featured in the film, when he volunteers to fight with his former unit, comes to greet us. It is the first time that he has actually returned to the site of the battle. He does not wish to take part in its re-enactment, quite understandably, and I am surprised that as many people who were there do turn up to take part. All goes very well, with the occasional difficulty of trying to yell "cease fire" or "cut" because the assistant director does not believe in megaphones. You begin to understand how ceasefires break down so often, once everyone is wired up and deafened. We will be relying heavily on the FIDF for their invaluable co-operation; they are not happy with some aspects of their depiction within the film, so I am going to take on board what they say and make changes if necessary to the script. Something that surprises me greatly is that very few, if any, residents turn up to watch. Although it is past midnight by the time we get down to action, this is a film about their history, and yet they seem totally ambivalent. This sort of sequence attracts crowds in the UK. But the Islanders are, on the other hand, most sensitive and quick to take offence. I portray them with sympathy as living in a forgotten time, a world of their own unfettered by the conventions we take for granted. Yes, it is comic at times but then every group portrayed in this film comes in periodically for comic treatment. If they call the script condescending then they have misunderstood it. TV companies do not spend *circa* £1.4 million to make fun of the Falkland Islanders.

Friday 6 March – The day begins late for Brad, whose Land Rover gets bogged down when he goes running around Gypsy Cove in an attempt to see penguins. He fails to find the birds and on his return finds his vehicle half-submerged in quicksand. His jog turns into a half-marathon as he reaches the airfield to enlist the help of Gerald Cheek (an FIDF officer who plays himself in the film) and the fire crew, who rescue the vehicle amidst much leg-pulling. Our work continues at a tough and furious pace, up to eight minutes a day including action/effects stuff (for which even in TV you do not reckon on shooting more than three minutes a day). We have to contend with ferocious weather, lack of the most basic local amenities a film crew needs – for example, no white paint for a police car, no letters for an "RN" number plate, etc. Even no nails at one point. Perfect sultry, windy weather when we want it today; normally in film-making you get the opposite of what you want. Patrick Watts, who has hitherto been most helpful to us, appears to be cranking the village pump on the radio. There are reports that we shot a scene of Dennis Middleton and his horse racing through town in which he yells "The Argies are coming!" and that we had young Falklands lasses frolicking naked on a beach with sheep. Wow. Still, the sight of our extras in Argie uniform brought tears to the eyes of one old lady, so we must try and remember the trauma of this community, which accounts for their sensitivity.

Sunday 8 March – One of the hardest filming days I have experienced in eleven years of directing. We are using sixty non-professional extras, working in two languages (some of the people playing Argentines are Peruvian fishermen dragged off squid jiggers), with a minimal crew. The Argentine flag has to get ripped off by the wind at exactly the right moment in the flag-raising during which they are singing. The extras have to perform military drill, sing a national anthem they learned minutes before, and react to commands they cannot hear because I have no megaphone and am the only one who speaks Spanish. Plus we have most of the principal cast in the scene and certain principals get very upset at being made to wait; indeed one principal actor throws a very loud tantrum (though he later apologised). Although we fall two scenes behind, we get some excellent material and a wonderful tracking scene when we assemble the cheering "mass" of Argentine troops on the seafront, chanting "Ar-gen-tina" as Admiral Büsser passes. The scene is scalp-tingling, because we have wonderful emotion in the foreground action, a great spirit among the extras and pretty well every piece of surviving Argentine equipment in it (even though an armoured car is being pushed on a steel bar to make it *seem* mobile). The emotional counterpoint in the foreground is that, despite defeat, Dick Baker in the white flag party is almost weeping with relief at the thought of seeing his children again. Wind and rain tonight for the second phase of the battle. Mike Norman watches Bob Peck relive the moment that he took cover behind one of Government House's ancient cannons, ducking fire and quaking uncontrollably with fear before getting a grip on himself. (He is to tell me later that this was the most difficult moment for him of the shoot.)

Monday 9 March – Another flag-raising day, but this time it is the British flag that is going up for the film's epilogue (the retaking of Stanley). Although it is much easier to recruit Islanders to play Paras and Marines, today is a working day and many of the people playing

Argentines have now left. So we send drivers round in a desperate trawl of the harbour and recruit the crew of a Chilean squid jigger and a Whitbread round-the-world yacht – quite a social mix, but unlike the Islanders the dark ones don't mind playing Argies (though some of the local Chilean *gastarbeitern* have taken a lot of stick for playing the enemy). By getting our Argie POWs to walk round the camera in a circle they look sufficient in number. We are so pressed for time that I have to run two cameras simultaneously throughout – one of them being the apparent "news crew" visible in shot. Although that was a severe compromise, we had the wintry weather we wanted which was perfect. Poor Peter Chapman, the cameraman, kept worrying about image quality (rain on the lens, wobbly shots, etc.) but I'll need it to look awful to match into the rest of the news footage we are using for the nightmare-style end sequence. The rest of the film is shot in a very classical style with no handheld whatsoever, part of the 1950s feel that I am going for (since Stanley in the eighties resembled the fifties elsewhere). In the West Store we had the real Don Bonner play a character greeting his screen *alter ego* on a shopping trip with his mistress. During the unusually calm evening we actually had spectators – two children who watched us shooting some action scenes for a while before trundling off. A crew member asked them if they were bored already but they replied, "No, our mum told us to keep an eye out and report back on what we saw." I think the locals view us with suspicion.

Tuesday 10 March – An early morning meeting is held with the FIDF to accommodate their views on how they should be portrayed. Their written statement on why they did not actually engage the enemy that night is unsigned. Major Norman remains sceptical and unfortunately the man who holds all the answers is now dead (Major Phil Summers of the FIDF). He is alleged to have ordered blanks to be issued on account of cost. I am not including this simply because I do not wish to insult the FIDF. Today it is a very efficient force but in those days even the current commander (Phil's son Brian) admits it was a "bit of a Dad's Army force" and that is, in a lesser degree, how I am going to show it. We arrive at a compromise because there seems to have been some breakdown in their chain of command from the Governor, which would explain why they were not defending the ridge as requested by Major Norman (the ridge from which the handful of Argentine Commandos kept Government House's defenders pinned down until the armoured column encircled them). For our beach scenes today the weather is simply appalling, which is what we wanted; horizontal rain, sixty-knot winds that often blow the boom swinger and other people over. My hat flew straight into the sea, and as I charged across the lovely sand to get it I heard fragmentary yells through the gale. They were reminding me (too late!) that this beach was not proven to be mine-free and the Bomb Disposal team who had agreed to make it safe for us had not done so. Surely this can have nothing to do with the Air Vice-Marshal's directive to his forces not to assist us in any way. Mines sometimes get washed up on the tide. Still, the risks were probably minimal, as locals seem to use the beach without exploding. We continue into a night of equally relentless gales and rain. I pity the three actors who prepared for months to film these scenes, who had modelled performances in the quiet rehearsal rooms of Acton, only to face a tempest from Greek mythology. Not a single complaint from them or the crew, I have to say. Most would have given up and gone home. Morale boost of the evening was when I laid hands on an image intensifier from the FIDF and discovered the normally ever-active producer Brad, fast asleep in a warm dry Land Rover. They all queued up for a good laugh, but in fact this was most unlike Brad. (He never lived it down.) He soon got woken by the gunfire that ensued, when we used the night-scope to direct live tracer bullets out to sea, taking care there were no passing ships and avoiding a cormorant's nest that was near the line of fire. We will put the reverse (i.e. incoming) tracer fire on with optical special effects.

Wednesday 11 March – We film the touching and amusing scene where islanders sing "Auld Lang Syne" as the Governor drives off to exile in his maroon taxi. Our cameraman Peter gets quite overwhelmed and tears come to his eyes. Next stop is the Bakers' house, where we stage the mock execution of the FIDF men which the Argentines put on for some photographers. Mavis Hunt looked down from the window and genuinely thought they were going to be shot, as did two of the people against the wall both on the actual day and, today, Gerald Cheek and Marvin Clark. A bizarre feeling doing this, because we ourselves have to go through the various stages – fear, confusion, and finally laughter as "the joke" manifests itself. Marvin Clark joins us later tonight on the Government House ridge playing one of the Argentines. Horizontal rain in torrents is interspersed with horizontal hail. But somehow, playing one of the Argentines myself, I get really into the whole thing and am able to ignore being soaked. Firing down over those rocks (even if they are blanks), calling on the Governor to surrender (even if he's away on holiday at the moment), one nevertheless has some inkling of what it must have been like. The dreadful weather helps, and the heavy radio on my back. Indeed, I get so stuck into the spirit of things that when we dive for cover in one take, I hit the rocks with such force that I actually crush the metal radio in several places! A great cheer goes up from the crew at my antics. Less heroically, I slip on a rock some time later and an accidental shot from my sub-machine gun nearly hits Peter Chapman in the face. This could have been fatal. Although I knew full well that the gun was not pointing at him, it was nevertheless a deeply unsettling moment, particularly as Peter dropped to the floor yelling with shock. This probably would not have happened if I had done some of the military training which I inflicted on cast members, but in the crazed run-up to filming there had not been the time. At the end of this sodden night of action my feet were squelching in my boots, I was covered in aches, cuts and bruises and was limping (like several others who followed me) from landing heavily with my knee on a particularly sharp rock. And I had nearly shot my cameraman. But I felt fantastic; it is hard to describe the feeling in not only directing but acting out these events behind the bullet-scarred rocks the Argentines fired from (indeed I had to forget directing and concentrate on delivering Spanish in an Argentine accent). Even odder for Marvin Clark who, though playing an Argentine Commando tonight, was an FIDF man on the actual night, pinned down by fire from these very rocks! But we have completed one of our most challenging days in the most dreadful weather. Just tomorrow to go.

Thursday 12 March – Gerald Cheek calls us from the airfield in the morning to say that a Hercules will be taking off shortly. They normally swoop low over Stanley every day but since we arrived they have been conspicuously absent and the airbase knows we want some swooping low-level passes for the scene where the Argentine Air Force buzzes the Marines. Two problems follow: firstly Peter Chapman heads off with his camera to Mount Pleasant (the wrong airport) forty-five miles away; secondly the Hercules inexplicably fails to take off soon after Mount Pleasant is informed that the BBC are waiting to film it. We failed on this occasion, but we did get a marvellous pass of two Chinook helicopters which we very much wanted, while they were practising for Mount Pleasant open day. We begin with a scene on the football field near Government House where Marvin Clark and others were pinned down at various times. Because of the weather and scheduling problems we have had to borrow the goalposts several times from up the hill. For, although this has recently been replanted with grass, it is not actually in use and we have had to keep "moving the goalposts" and releasing them for match kick-offs when we failed to get to the location in time. The real Major Mike Norman makes a wonderful FIDF man in his acting debut, together with excellent first-timer Gary Clement, who also fought in the war as a Marine. Mike has come through with flying colours, displaying commitment, an immediate and profound understanding of the production process, and boundless energy during the difficult night schedules. Our worst day in terms of lack of extras: having milked two hundred of the locals to appear (that's a quarter of the Stanley population) the novelty value is wearing off and rumours continue to abound about the script being unfavourable to the Islanders. We drag some people off an Antarctic survey boat to play Marines only to find (just before we begin the scene with them) that their vessel is about to leave. After a certain amount of begging we discover that it is only their meal-break they will be missing and the problem is resolved by our feeding them later. But "Argentines" remain thin on the ground (I should explain that we could not cast any Argentine actors as I had wanted to because their nationals are banned from the Islands. As enlightened as the Arabs' policy towards Israelis). Pretty well all the crew are dressed up as Argies today, including the girls. The sight of the Argentine flag on the pole finally made the good citizens' patience snap, even though we were filming it being ripped off. We were ordered to take it down by the Council after complaints. We complied, despite the fact that we were entitled to insist on our agreement with the Governor. To add to my woes, the FIDF, having promised to supply the old men who volunteered to fight that night but got turned away, present only a phalanx of very warlike young men. A trawl of pubs fails when the old boys refuse to play ball. And our attempt to arm the FIDF with the kind of primitive weapons which we know some of them had is rebuffed; they claim we are ridiculing them, yet they themselves told us how they lost half of their automatic weapons or magazines to the Marines that night. When designer Steve Hardie produces a flintlock rifle he is told that these do not even exist on the Islands, but he obtained it down the road. We put it away. They were at pains to show how disadvantaged they were that night but are worried about being portrayed as a rabble. We show them neither in a cowardly nor a heroic light but certainly apportion no blame to civilians faced with a massive surprise attack supported by armour and aircraft. Indeed, Major Summers says that the re-enactment of the telephone call, when his late father told Rex Hunt that their HQ was surrounded, touched him and was very much like he imagines it must have been. The FIDF have been very good to us. I have moderated their image in return, for the Marines are very scathing about their performance that night. Anyway, this night we complete our Falklands shoot in the face of so many difficulties. Only one short exterior scene lost, which can easily be recreated in the UK.

Friday 13 March – This is our pack-up day and we venture out to Mount Pleasant to try and sneak some over-flights of aircraft from beyond the perimeter fence, but unfortunately their Open Day (for which pilots have trained for months) is cancelled because of the poor weather. Meanwhile Steve and the design team frantically clean up the destruction at Government House, restoring it to the *status quo ante bellum*. Fortunately the Governor and his wife are slightly late back from holidaying in Chile on the same little Otter that I flew on. We are actually towing the last Argentine prop (an armoured car) out of the back drive as Mr and Mrs Fullerton are driven by Don up the front drive in their official car, GH1. (We learn later how Mrs Fullerton was very distressed at the sight of her flower beds, which of course cannot be restored until next season.) Returning to the penguins at Gypsy Cove, we try to achieve the wide shot where a penguin is mistaken for an Argentine in the dark. It fails, so we resort to Brad's expedient of me dressing in black-peaked cap, white scarf and black clothes, waddling down the tussac grass to the beach, deliberately underexposed. (Note: the shot worked perfectly well in rushes when several people did not even realise it was a trick until the exposure opened up and the penguin metamorphosized into a director chortling with laughter.) It is sad to be leaving the Falklands, which many of us have come to feel very attached to. It is such a unique place and yet I can't imagine I will ever come back here again. Indeed if peace – true peace – ever breaks out then Mount Pleasant, this expensive airbase in the middle of nowhere, will soon get overgrown with weeds and the Islands will revert to their previous state of virtual isolation. But the minefields will probably remain unclearable forever.

Friday 20 March – A day of antics and melodrama. Fortunately all's well that ends well, for this is a production with luck on its side so far. Somehow the MOD directive that we should not be given assistance has failed to reach every unit in the country and we are "somewhere in the UK" at a base whose commander is perfectly willing to assist us. Thank God that these people and the (nameless) regiment that lent us a tank and crew yesterday are willing to help. Meanwhile one of our camera crew acted on a tip-off that some Hercules aircraft would be taking off from a nearby base (Major Mike Norman had been drinking in the hotel with a Yank air crew who just happened to be flying a Herc back to the States). We get one great low-level pass before the cameraman is arrested by the Military Police. But because he is perfectly within his rights, being on public land, they have to let him go. To boost the look of the film, we have hired a former Soviet amphibious Armoured Personnel Carrier at great expense, to come up tonight out of some water which represents the South Atlantic. Unfortunately, the men operating this vehicle leave a valve open and it promptly gets flooded, sinking right in front of the beach which we are using as our location. The novice tank crew are lucky to have got out but will have a lot of explaining to do to the collector who recently acquired and imported this twenty-one foot beast from Czechoslovakia. Thank God we have already filmed the scenes with it shooting up the replica of Government House's yard yesterday afternoon, since the engine compartment is now flooded. If we cannot shift it then not only do we lose the APC from the story but we cannot film at all because we need the beach clear for scenes before the main Argentine landing – the APC's side is still poking bizarrely up above the surface. But God (and the commander of this military unit) is on our side and an engineering tank is sent to the rescue, towing the stricken behemoth from its watery grave and even positioning it nicely for the later scene to make it look as if it has come out onto the beach under its own steam. Thousands of gallons of water pour out from the vehicle for half an hour. The Army boys lend their own APC to come charging out of "the sea" and, hey presto, our armoured vehicle scene has suddenly got double the numbers. Military boats churn up the water to make it as choppy as the South Atlantic just before each take. An exceedingly heavy day but we got, in the end, more than we could have planned or budgeted for!

Wednesday 1 April – Ten years to the day from the start of our film's story. And what could be more fitting than a visit to the set by Sir Rex and Tony Hunt? He professed himself astounded by the precision and eerie familiarity of Steve Hardie's Government House interior. Publicity photographers snapped away, and whereas Rex had been perfectly civil in meeting Fulgencio Saturno (who plays Rear-Admiral Büsser) he refused to shake his hand for the cameras in any kind of reconciliation in this, his reincarnated office. Ian Richardson was rather uncomfortable with the idea of Sir Rex staying around for the climactic surrender scene. Fortunately Rex has to go off for his book launch soon, and will just have time to view the first assembly of some of the scenes at the film's opening. According to Brad it was an absolutely bizarre and even uncomfortable experience showing these scenes to people who actually lived the real thing, particularly because they did not necessarily view it this way or agree with everything we showed. We took many of their points on board. Tony Hunt maintains that he was never quite such a tearaway and therefore we will cut some of these scenes. But that is the point: each person who participated in these events can only recognise their specific role and shape their memories accordingly. I believe that as the only dispassionate observer who has recently met nearly all of them I can arrive at something like an objective truth. Meanwhile I was shooting the surrender scene, in which Fulgencio and Ian were both brilliant as the Rear-Admiral and the Governor. Very difficult for Fulgencio, working in a foreign language, but he was the perfect counterpart to Ian and reminded me a great deal of the real Rear-Admiral Büsser.

Thursday 2 April – The last day of shooting, and no one is more conscious of what was happening ten years ago (almost to the minute in the case of one scene) than Mike Norman. He keeps glancing at his watch as we come up to lunchtime, and it is not because of hunger. "It was now," he says, full of his own thoughts. For this was the precise moment (GMT) of the surrender. A poignant day for Mike and for us, after six action-packed weeks. Lots of horse-play, some of it quite necessary. For example, three Venezuelan lads are playing the Commandos who hid in a servant's bedroom until they were flushed out. An alarm clock goes off, shattering their nerves. Try as they might, they could not master a shocked reaction. I decided drastic methods were necessary and took a leaf out of director John Frankenheimer's diary on *Grand Prix* (when the crowd did not react enough to an imaginary crash off-screen he blew up the canteen truck). As the alarm clock struck, the armourer let off a burst off automatic fire behind their heads, which they had not been expecting. The reaction was utterly convincing, the soundtrack was changed, and they took it in very good spirits. We end the day by firing rocket grenades into archery nets for close-ups of the weapons that will be cut in to the Government House exterior ridge from which Argentine Commandos are bombarding the Marines. Steve has built a fake ridge out of plastic and the result is brilliant for a night sequence. I don my Commando uniform and spout Argentine Spanish for the last time. Ricardo, playing Lieutenant Lugo, has the misfortune of tumbling backwards off the "ridge" just before he is due to deliver a line but fortunately lands safely – the laughter on these occasions comes before it is known if the victim is capable of standing up. So, we come to the end a few minutes before schedule. Some two and a half hours of completed film and not a single scene lost, which is most unusual, but then this was a most unusual crew and cast. They even managed to cram in some extra scenes that I penned as we went along. The very last shot is a surprise. I had written a stage direction – "we see half the Argentine fleet in an aerial view, alternatively, a stock shot". And there, laid before me was half the Argentine fleet, but on something like plastic sheeting, and the fleet looked for all the world like models on plastic sheeting. But what the hell, we wasted some precious film on it. Must find a better shot later. To make the film I have travelled scores of thousands of miles in seven countries; completed some two hundred and twenty scenes – many involving gunfire, explosives and stunts; pulled sailors off round-the-world yachts to play Argentines; sunk an amphibious personnel carrier.... and all with no injuries except for a broken nose sustained by a crew member in a fight and the death of a chicken accidentally crushed by a flying stuntman. Most importantly it was completed on time and (I believe) on (a modest) budget.

More Than 30 Years after the Malvinas:
War in Film and on Television

Sandra Savoini

Introduction

In the field of Argentine post-dictatorship cultural production, the number of audiovisual works on the Malvinas War is far from negligible: since 1982, there have been at least 19 documentaries and 15 fiction films. These include a compilation of short films from various directors entitled *Malvinas – 30 miradas* (2014), as well as whole series – and single episodes within series – delving into the topic, as well as audiovisual teaching initiatives. [1]

---

[1] A brief mapping identifies the following productions.

Documentaries: *Malvinas, historia de traiciones* (J. Denti, 1983), *Malvinas, alerta roja* (A. Rotondo, 1985), *Malvinas, me deben tres* (C. Giordano, A. Marino, I. Matiasich, A. Alfonso, L. Rueda, J. B. Duizeide, 1992), *Hundan el Belgrano* (F. Urieste, 1996), *Malvinas, historias de dos islas* (D. Alhadeff, 1999), *Vamos ganando* (R. Longo, 2001), *El refugio del olvido* (D. Alhadeff, 2002), *Malvinas, 20 años* (R. Lejtman, 2002), *Malvinas, la lucha continúa* (F. Cola, 2003), *Locos de la bandera* (J. Cardoso, 2005), *No tan nuestras* (R. Longo, 2005), *Estamos ganando, periodismo y censura en la guerra de Malvinas* (R. Persano y E. Ciganda, 2005), *Malvinas, tan lejos, tan cerca* (Lanata, 2007), *Malvinas, la historia que pudo ser* (Cuatro cabezas producciones/Discovery Channel, 2007), *Malvinas, 1982. La guerra desde el aire* (Argentina co-production for History Channel, 2008), *Desobediencia debida* (V. Reale, 2008), *Huellas en el viento* (S. di Luca, 2008), *Malvinas, 25 años de silencio* (M. Angueira, 2008), *Malvinas, viajes del Bicentenario* (J. Cardoso, 2010), *Piratas, pastores, inversores* (F. J. Palma, 2010), *14 de junio, lo que nunca se perdió* (D. Circosta, 2011), *1892-1982: dos historias de Malvinas* (P. Walker, 2011), *El héroe del Monte de dos Hermanas* (R. Vila, 2011), *La forma exacta de las islas* (D. Casabé and E. Dieleke, 2012), *Combatientes* (E. Spagniolo, 2013), *Pensar Malvinas* (canal Encuentro), *Malvinas, historia de la usurpación* (canal Encuentro), *Historias debidas IV* (canal Encuentro), *Historias de un país. Argentina siglo XX* (canal Encuentro).

Fictional films: *Los chicos de la guerra* (B. Kamín, 1984), *Los días de junio* (A. Fischerman, 1985), *La deuda interna* (M. Pereira, 1988), *Guarisove, los olvidados* (B. Stagnaro, 1995), *El mismo amor, la misma lluvia* (J. Campanella, 1999), *El visitante* (J. Olivera, 1999), *Pozo de Zorro* (M. Mirra, 1999), *Fuckland* (J. L. Márques, 2000), *1982, estuvimos ahí* (2004), *Iluminados por el fuego* (T. Bauer, 2005), *Palabra por palabra* (E. Cabeza, 2007), *Cartas a Malvinas* (R.

The majority of these works appeared between 2003 and 2015, under a presidency that turned the examination of the dictatorship into government policy. This rekindled and promoted the actions of various civil organizations that had already been working on the pursuit of justice and remembrance. Audiovisual production was a consequence of various measures for the construction of memory closely related to other areas of memory production of the time. Visibility was particularly high in the media around the dates of commemoration – April, when it comes to the Malvinas – when programming on state television channels (Encuentro, INCAA TV and TV Pública) focused on paying homage through various television productions, documentaries and fiction films about the war.

By revisiting conceptions of intertextual and interdiscursive relations between memories from the perspective of semiotics and discourse analysis, we shall identify some veins of meaning that run through these audiovisual works in the context of commemorative television programming. Within this framework, we shall be able to understand the way in which the protagonists of history are construed, depending on the hegemonic discourse of each period (Angenot, 2010).

This essay is based on the proposal by Courtine (1981), among other discourse analysts, for whom relations of meaning bring into play discursive memories, insofar as as they form a bridge that ties the present to the past experience that is being evoked. It is in this context that the representation of the world and of the individuals living in it is developed. In this way, memories can be understood as historical devices of power-knowledge that produce what can be said and shown from the perspective of particular ideologies that permeate different parts of discourse. These memories allow us to understand the way in which the present is built by recovering that which has already been said and seen, given that the production of discourse repeats, transforms or refutes discourses that have already been articulated, contributing to the semiotic construction of reality (Verón, 1993).

Time in Memory
The Malvinas War of 1982 was the only Argentine war of the twentieth century. It took a toll of 649 deaths in the arena of operations and over a

Fernández, 2009), *La campana* (2010), "El último", an episode of *Vindica* (E. Crupnicoff, J. Laplace, M. Ardanaz, N. Parodi, 2011), *Un cuento chino* (2011), *Malvinas – 30 miradas* (30 short films by various directors, 2014), *La asombrosa excursión de Zamba en las Islas Malvinas* (canal PakaPaka).

thousand wounded. Moreover, as estimated by veterans' organizations, it led to the suicide of some 500 soldiers – an estimate, since there are no official data – over the course of the following thirty years. The war was a breaking point not only for foreign policy, but also for domestic policy, as it precipitated the end of the military dictatorship. Malvinas is a proper noun that, after the conflict, became a trope, invoking the concept of war and a particular period in history. It is this traumatic experience, marked by defeat and deception, which has survived over the years as the meaning of the word. This meaning hegemonizes and obstructs other possible ways of understanding that territory.

According to the Real Academia Española, "trauma" comes from the Greek word for "wound". Many of its meanings refer to a wound that persists over time.[2] Certain events that disrupt individual or collective experience can become incidents that inflict serious injuries. However, trauma is not the event itself, but the imprint left on the individual. From an individual's point of view – although it can be co-extensive with a community because certain events that affect a person are partly created out of collective experience – trauma is the result of some sort of violence that goes beyond what is tolerable and persists after the event, especially when it is unresolved because it cannot be seen or articulated. This would be the case for all of those who participated in the war in one way or another, and arguably the case in Argentine society itself.

The process of *de-Malvinization* (which took place, at least, in the first two decades after the conflict) resulted in the general effacement of the event from public memory. The only exception was at anniversaries, when it appeared in the form of highly stereotypical figures and focused on the victimization of the young soldiers, the event being categorized as the consequence of an irrational military adventure. The military government invoked nationalistic stereotypes in order to remain in power, something that proved hard at the time for several reasons, one of them being the serious economic crisis. The paradox is that Malvinas therefore stands at a point of inflection between the dictatorship and democracy. Being a liminal experience, it proved very uncomfortable to think about in the post-dictatorship context.

The film *Los chicos de la guerra*, by Bebe Kamín (1984), is the

---

[2] Trauma: "1. Lasting injury produced by a mechanical agent, generally an external one. 2. Emotional shock that causes permanent damage in the unconscious. 3. Feeling or impression which is negative, strong and persistent" (Real Academia Española, 2001).

epitome of this form of representation. It was the first film to deal with the topic, only two years after the conflict, in the context of the emerging democracy of Raúl Alfonsín. As such, it is an obligatory part of commemorative rituals shown on television every year. In the words of Guber (2001, 88):

> The movie begins with the image of the end of the war, with young soldiers digging the graves to bury their dead (fellow soldiers with whom they shared the same trenches, nationality and generation). This image summarizes the heart of Kamín's message: dead or alive, those kids were victims of the National Reorganization Process, of a war between the armed forces and their countrymen. The British are nothing but the platform on which the Argentine drama was displayed.

This can be seen, for example, in a sequence in which Santiago, one of the protagonists, decides to untie a fellow soldier who has had his arms and legs tied to spikes in the ground by his officers for stealing a sheep (a punishment that became a method of torture). After his offence, the soldier is taken to the commander to justify his actions while the other soldiers declare: "Sí, es cierto, nos están cagando de hambre, nos tratan peor que a los enemigos" ("It's true. They're starving us to death. They treat us worse than they treat the enemy").

This type of representation was pervasive during the 1980s and 1990s, characterized by the predominance of the victimizing narrative that has already been mentioned. This style created consensus because it echoed for many their lived experience of Argentine society, for the reasons stated by Lorenz (2011, 55):

> it corresponded both with the image of the young constructed during the transition back to democracy and with the self-exculpatory view which society was trying to build [...] and this context placed the soldiers in the position of victims of their own officers and of the capriciousness of the highest ranks. The analogy was created by Argentine society, which considered itself a victim of its armed forces. The soldiers in the Malvinas were other, younger victims of the dictatorship.

This interpretative framework tends to depoliticize and to create passive individuals who are part of a discourse infused with altruistic values linked to heroism and commitment. At the same time, it helps to erase the role played by the community before, during and after the armed conflict. This construction is present not only in audiovisual discourses about the war. To a great extent, documentaries and fiction in Argentina in the eighties and nineties on the topic of the dictatorship and the young represent the latter as innocent victims, effacing the ethical and political commitment to processes of collective action and transformation. [3]

In the context of this dominant representation of the armed conflict – or the dismissal of it – Malvinas progressively became a public topic as a result of the demands articulated by certain social actors, such as the veteran or ex-combatant associations (the difference between the terms has political implications and has been the subject of conflicts among the different associations). [4] These groups succeeded in getting their proposals strategically adopted by the governmental discourse in this new social context, which led to new state policies.

As of 2003 the subject, referred to as the "Malvinas question", began to be reframed and became increasingly more prominent as a result of different actions enforced by the government in a variety of cultural (among other) areas. With it came the proliferation of voices and views, which joined the argument about the imposition of meaning relating to the war and post-war, emphasizing the use of testimonies or narratives from the protagonists' perspective. This can be perceived in different fields and discourses, such as in film and television. The changes in the narrative and articulation strategies of the audiovisual productions (documentaries or fiction) used to tell the stories about the Malvinas entail a transformation in the ways of remembering and, consequently, in the ways in which we interpret the recent past. These strategies show an increasing questioning of the role of society and, particularly, of the Argentine state during the post-war period, which are recurrent topics in the discourses heard over the last decade.

The fictional television drama *Combatientes* (2013) – whose title ("Combatants") focuses on Malvinas protagonists – is a prime example of

---

[3] Although they have different styles and epochal characteristics that differentiate them, *La república perdida 2* (Pérez 1986) and *Montoneros, una historia* (Di Tella 1994) are two prime examples of documentaries on the topic.

[4] According to Argentine legislation, a Malvinas ex-combatant is any official, non-commissioned officer or conscript from the Armed and Security Forces who participated in the military actions which took place in the Malvinas theatre of operations (Teatro de Operaciones Malvinas) and in the South Atlantic theatre of operations (Teatro de Operaciones del Atlántico Sur). This statute's accreditation can be issued only by the Force to which each combatant belonged and endorsed by the Ministry of Defence.

this. It was written and directed by Jerónimo Paz Clemente and Tomás de las Heras, and was shown in April 2013 by TV Pública. The drama highlights the traumatic effects which the experience has had on the lives of a soldier and a young serviceman in the post-war period. These characters embody the failure of a social and individual project with which the survivors cannot deal, bringing them close to death. Like many others, this drama deals with one of the issues that marked individuals after the conflict, evidenced by hundreds of suicides that show the difficulties the veterans faced when reintegrating into society during the post-war period.

This television series tells a story that begins in 1982, before the war, introducing five young men drafted to go to the Malvinas – Gustavo, Chapa, Raúl, Facundo and Carlos – who display heterogeneous social features and characteristics. One of them is a factory worker, another is a thief; there is a fearful Jewish singer, a rugby player, a son from a wealthy family and, finally, a designer who dreams of becoming an artist. All these characters, with the exception of Gustavo, show highly stereotypical features and evoke social types of the time, something that seems to be a significant weakness of the show. This may be on account of the fact that much of the information about these (mis)adventurous partners is tinted by Gustavo's perception and memory, Gustavo being one of the two protagonists. The letter informing them that they are subject to the draft is received in different ways by each of them: for some, it means an escape from the life they lead; for others, an obligation they have to accept submissively. They are sent to the Malvinas, to the war front, under the command of Lieutenant Augusto López Cabral, a character whose attributes tear down the typical representations of the military leaders of the time (an innovative characteristic of social discourse which had been missing from the public media scene in previous decades). There, they share their everyday lives in a war situation marked by shortages. Finally, towards the end of the conflict, they have to fight the British hand-to-hand. They are all wounded and four of them die. Gustavo and Lieutenant López Cabral are taken prisoner. On their return, these survivors try to continue with their lives in complete loneliness. On the fifth anniversary of the landing, and in the context of the military coup that took place in Holy Week of 1987 against the democratic government of President Alfonsín, Gustavo tries to contact López Cabral to see if he can help him find his fellow soldiers. Gustavo suffers from memory loss and cannot remember that the other soldiers had died. Although the lieutenant refuses to help him at first, he goes looking for Gustavo as a consequence of his insistence and ends up saving him: suicide is an ever-present possibility, in the same way death was on the Malvinas. So life goes on for them: in this respect, the narrative of *Combatientes* is encouraging.

The discourse of *Combatientes*[AS1] shapes protagonists whose identity is defined, among other things, as being on the border between reason and insanity. One of the formal devices used to achieve this is temporal (con)fusion as a narrative strategy. Temporal disruptions – achieved mainly by means of flashbacks recalling events that happened on the Malvinas during the war – are interspersed with images linked to dreams and fears that allow us to access the individuals' subjective experiences. This framework exacerbates the tension between amnesia and the need to remember in order to know what happened: only accessing the "truth" will allow for the exorcism of the past. Narrative and aesthetic methods are brought together to achieve this purpose.

In this way, the old motif of memory loss, and the difficulty of distinguishing between the true and the false, provide some of the elements that organize the meanings offered to viewers, and with which we are provoked to re-evaluate what we remember, why we remember it and what for, as well as what we forget, why we forget it and what for.

30 Years, 30 Views of the Malvinas

The movie *Malvinas – 30 miradas. Los cortos de nuestras islas* (Malvinas – 30 Views: Short Films on Our Islands), a more recent work released in 2014, is made up of thirty short films created by Argentine and other Latin American filmmakers. The piece proposes to contribute to the construction of audiovisual memory, drawing upon multiple aesthetic, narrative and thematic perspectives. It was made by the Centro de Producción e Investigación Audiovisual (CePIA), part of the Ministry of Culture, together with the Consejo Asesor de la Televisión Digital Terrestre, in cooperation with the National University of Tres de Febrero.

These thirty short films form a mosaic in which differing representations of the Malvinas are outlined and overlap. Many of the narratives are characterized by a parodic style, perhaps because humour – and the distance it creates – is one of the best ways to address fetishes and taboos (Angenot, 2010) in an attempt to escape from nationalistic or victimizing discourses. In this case, we will concentrate on the short film *Entrevista* (Interview), by Sergio Bellotti. As its title indicates, this work shows a meeting between a journalist from an opinion-setting magazine of the time and a general who was part of the dictatorship. The following is a fragment of its dialogue:

Periodista: Para ir cerrando, General, ¿no quiere decir un mensaje a los familiares de los soldados muertos en esta guerra?

General: En todos estos años en los que hemos luchado contra el enemigo interno hemos sido orgullosamente responsables de la tortura, la muerte y desaparición de decenas de miles de argentinos... (Se escuchan balas de fondo) en su gran mayoría jóvenes, incluyendo mujeres embarazadas, casi adolescentes. En comparación, ¿qué son 600 soldados? Incluso algunos de nuestros oficiales los han maltratado y les han hecho pasar hambre, pero siempre hay causas superiores, ¡superiores!

Periodista: ¡Gracias por su testimonio, General!

General: No, por favor, usted se lo merece, y salude de mi parte a su editor. Periodista: ¿Quiere agregar algo más?

General: Mire, si usted quiere un detalle más completo va a tener que esperar un tiempo, unos veinte o treinta años, pero vaya tranquila, su editor va a entender... Veinte, treinta años...

(Risas) Veinte, treinta años...

(Se escucha como banda musical la Marcha de Malvinas)

[Interviewer: To conclude, General, do you want to send a message to the families of those soldiers who died in the war?

General: Throughout the years we spent fighting our internal enemy, we have been proud culprits of the torture, death and disappearance of thousands of Argentines (Bullets can be heard in the background), mainly young ones, including pregnant women who were almost teenagers. In comparison, what are 600 soldiers? Even some of our own officers mistreated them and starved them, but there is always a greater cause, a greater cause!

Interviewer: Thank you for your testimony, General!

General: No at all, you deserve it. Say hi to your editor for me.

Interviewer: Do you want to add anything else?

General: Look, if you want further details, you're gonna have to wait, some twenty or thirty years, but don't worry about it. Your editor will understand. Twenty or thirty years...

(Laughter) Twenty, thirty years...

(The March of the Malvinas is heard)]

As can be seen, the interview highlights the connivance of certain parts of the press during the dictatorship, the lack of recorded testimonies that can be used as proof of "truth", and the arrogance of power.

However, the film's effect lies in its intertextuality. What is said is introduced literally, but from a perspective offered by distance, achieved not only through the passing of time (those necessary thirty years before we can access the details of the events), but also as a consequence of the change in the hegemonic discourse. The latter allows for the development of a knowing addressee who shares the values that are being challenged and is capable of recognizing the utterer's stance. At the same time, this addressee recovers the ideological world to which those characters belonged and perceives their attitudes through signs that tend to ridicule or tone-down the seriousness of those who embody such values: the journalist steps on excrement on her way in, she asks easy questions and does not realize that there is no cassette in the machine; the photographer takes pointless pictures; the serviceman himself seems to overact, and confidently affirms himself to be a "proud culprit" of the torture, disappearances and deaths of Argentine citizens, but is obsessed with unimportant details. In this way, we recover utterances that were supposedly delivered in the past by familiar characters, whose literalism states in a straightforward and brutal manner the logic that organized the actions of certain individuals during that period of our history.

In this respect, the narrative is supported by a widely held view in Argentina nowadays, which equates the victims of state-sponsored terrorism with the soldiers. At the same time, and this is the innovative feature, the fragment quoted above introduces another dimension to this construction of memory, which is the minimization or cancellation of human attributes: "we have been proud culprits of the torture, death and disappearance of thousands of Argentines... In comparison, *what are 600 soldiers?*"

Beyond the struggle over the way in which the subjects are designated and the semantic field which each of them enables for the interpretation of events (together with the performative consequences this entails), the general's question undermines an identity: what are 600 soldiers? The question, addressed to the journalist (a character who symbolizes and shapes public opinion), is really aimed at society in general, thirty years later, by means of metonymy: what are 600 soldiers? The interrogative pronoun "qué" (what) opens a statement about people in an objectifying manner. The statement could be reworded as follows: what *thing* are 600 soldiers (¿qué cosa son 600 soldados?)? Or, more accurately, given that the statement is about fatalities: what are 600 dead soldiers (¿qué cosa son 600 soldados muertos?)? A designation that elides human characteristics is revealed. This enables an understanding of what happened both during and after the dictatorship from a different perspective. The objectification and the emphasis on the low number of victims ("only" 600) when compared to the other ones mentioned in this narrative – these victims are compared here and in numerous other discourses to the young victims of the dictatorship – demean their existence as a group. The narrative highlights the controversial issues of certain post-war discourses on the Malvinas. Are the deaths of these soldiers important?

Which Lives Matter? Which Lives Can Be Remembered?

The emphasis on the inscription of the subjective in the audiovisual production that has been taking place since 2003 is an attempt to answer these questions, heard in public places, by means of a policy of restoring to the Malvinas soldiers their status as subjects. An example of this reconfiguration can be found in President Cristina Fernández de Kirchner's speech during the commemoration ceremony of the thirtieth anniversary of the war:

> Today, before coming here, I read a phrase from one of the (thousands of) young men who fought in the islands and then became a journalist. He might be around here, Edgardo Esteban. And he was saying [...] that the greatest defeat in a war, or in this war at least, is the truth [...]. I also demand justice for those who have not yet been identified, [which is why last Friday] I sent a letter to the head of the International Red Cross so that he may take the necessary measures and intercede with the United Kingdom to identify those men, Argentine and even British, who have not yet been identified, because everyone deserves to have their name written on their tombstone, and every mother has an inalienable right [...] to bury their dead, to get a plaque with their name on it and to cry in front of it. (Fernández, 2012)

Justice, truth and memory permeate an address that, decades before, would have been unspeakable in the Argentine context. The speech recognizes the existence of lives whose disappearance is worth honouring through mourning, which is nothing but an exercise of memory, "because if the end of a life produces no pain, it is not a life, it does not qualify as such and it has no value. It does not constitute something that deserves a burial, but rather that which is impossible to bury" (Butler, 2006, 61). The recognition of these lives' value, as well as of the value of their deaths, gives them a place in history.

In this context, then, the numerous audiovisual productions that have brought back the Malvinas War time and again throughout these three decades could be understood as some sort of collective obituary, honouring the dead and acknowledging the survivors. In the words of Judith Butler (2006, 61), this obituary is "a nation-building action", carrying the marks of the ways in which the past has been remembered in each particular social and historical period.

References

Angenot, M. (2010). *De hegemonía y disidencias*. Córdoba: Universidad Nacional de Córdoba.

Bellotti, S. (2014). Entrevista. *Malvinas – 30 miradas. Los cortos de nuestras islas*.

Butler, J. (2006). *Vida precaria. El poder del duelo y la violencia* (trans. F. Rodríguez). Buenos Aires: Paidós.

Courtine, J. (1981). "Analyse du discours politique. Le discours communiste adressé aux chrétiens", *Langages* 62, 9-128. Available at **www.persee.fr/issue/lgge_0458-726x_1981_num_15_62**.

Fernández, C. (2012). "Acto por el 30° aniversario de la guerra de Malvinas: Palabras de la Presidenta de la Nación". Available at **www.casarosada.gob.ar/informacion/archivo/25789**.

Guber, R. (2001). *¿Por qué Malvinas? De la causa nacional a la guerra absurda*. Buenos Aires: Fondo de Cultura Económica.

Kamín, B. (1984). *Los chicos de la guerra*. Available at **https://www.youtube.com/watch?v=y95uQDBcOyU**.

Lorenz, F. (2011). "El malestar de Krímov: Malvinas, los estudios sobre la guerra y la historia reciente Argentina", *Estudios* 25, 47-65.

Paz Clemente, J. and T. de las Heras. (2013). *Combatientes*. Available at **https://www.youtube.com/watch?v=CQHOlKs_Sl4&list=P Lc5A2QHFlvVIsKzsiItLGTCN9Sxlazool**.

Real Academia Española. (2001). *Diccionario de la lengua española*, 22nd ed.

Verón, E. (1993). *La semiosis social. Fragmentos de una teoría de la discursividad*. Barcelona: Gedisa.

Traumas, Memories and Identity Processes

María Teresa Dalmasso

Within the framework of a culture that, as Tzvetan Todorov points out, appears to be characterized by the cult of memory, semiotics cannot remain indifferent. Being ourselves trapped in the web of signification, and faced with the task of accounting for the mechanisms of construction, reconstruction – and destruction – of the meaning of the past, we propose to shed some light on certain aspects of these semiotic processes, which are inextricably linked to their socio-historical context.

These polemical signifying productions constitute what we call "discourses of memory". Their political dimension grants them a crucial value in understanding the debates that a society wages in order to impose a vision of itself. These are disputes in which all sorts of strategies tending to the (re)axiologization of the past are deployed from a valuation of the present projected onto the future.

An Argentina Built out of Crises and Traumas

Argentina appears, to a large number of its citizens (and particularly to those aged over 50), to be a country in which the succession of political, economic and social crises continues unabated. The continuity of the crises that occurred in the last decades of the twentieth century and in the first of the twenty-first has left a traumatic effect, whose force actualizes and exalts memories in conflict. These recurrent convulsions interrupt the process of mourning and nurture the trauma with cumulative impotence. Throughout these decades, offset by a few moments of apparent recovery, Argentine society has seen its civil rights violated, has suffered political chaos, and has been subject to repressive violence and economic dispossession. The prolonged succession of failures, bitter misunderstandings and violent antagonisms triggered in its citizens a sense of irreversible decline that plunged them into despair. However, given its persistence throughout history, such a state of mind may come to be viewed as a sort of idiosyncratic tic. To explain this apparent constant, perhaps we would have to consider the confluence of historically more distant factors. We might conjecture that some of the reasons may be rooted in the disappointment stemming from the failure to attain the greatness pretentiously foretold by the leaders of our country since the beginning of the twentieth century. In this sense, we might assume, taking our cue from Schwab (2015, 54-55), that this unfulfilled prophecy has triggered a kind of destiny-neurosis.

In a history of virtually constant convulsions, it is imperative to address the passional framework that dominates citizens' behaviour. At first glance, one may observe how these passions encourage – especially in times of instability – a sceptical view of the country's present and future possibilities, render difficult the process of mourning, make the trauma more complex, nurture ghosts and, above all, generate profound cracks in the processes of constructing collective identities.

This assessment throws up questions surrounding certain passional traits that seem to contribute to the generation and establishment of a certain identity image in the doxa. Thus, we are induced to reflect upon the signs of melancholy, a passion that seems to occupy a privileged position in the definition of "Argentineness". Without underestimating the effects left by specific crises, we must ask if our difficulty in abandoning the utopia of a successful and thrusting future is not a factor that hinders the process of mourning, in such a way that, disillusioned and self-deprecating, we are stuck in melancholy. This state goes in hand in hand with a tendency to violent reactions, marked by an agonistic bias that makes us inclined to polemics. That is to say, melancholy and anger[1] would seem to be the visible axes of the passional fabric. Both of them, simultaneously or successively, inflame the discursive flow. These two passions may tentatively be understood as variants of frustration, of the impotence brought about by not-being-able-to-do or not-being-able-to-be, which is channelled agonistically and in a non-exclusive way through aggression and/or self-aggression.

Commemorations

We believe we can see a certain relationship between this difficult work of mourning, recurrently interrupted, and a sort of compulsion to commemorations (resurrected anniversaries, new monuments and changes in their location, or their replacement, new or recovered museums, rooms dedicated to heroes, with some things removed and others newly included) that increases in times when confrontational obfuscation encourages official revisionism and enflames the civic mood. Paraphrasing Pierre Nora (2008, 175), we might say that, at such times, properly national and civic commemoration sinks into the political.

Thus, at the beginning of this century saturated with anniversaries of a mostly unhappy nature – the twenty-fifth and thirtieth anniversaries of the military coup (2001 and 2006), the twenty-fifth and thirtieth

---

[1] See Parret, 1995, 12-27.

anniversaries of the Malvinas War (2007 and 2012), but also the bicentenary of the May Revolution (2010) – dissidences have exploded, because, as Elizabeth Jelin (2002, 248-250) points out:

> at significant public moments, such as the dates of commemorations, not everybody shares the same memories. Memory refers to the ways in which people construct a sense of the past and how they relate that past to the present in the act of recalling or remembering.

This leads on to the question:

> Are the activities carried out a commemoration of past events or vehicles of present political struggle, akin to electoral propaganda or charges brought against political enemies? (Jelin, 2002, 248-250)

Discrepancies become evident in the celebratory modes and accents, in their adherences and in their critical readings, in the moments rescued from oblivion and in those omitted, in the monuments erected and in those moved or suppressed altogether. All these movements prove to be highly revealing of the socio-historical conditions that make them possible.

Memory, Commemorations and the Print Media
Moved by the interest to identify and understand the strategies for the construction of memory/memories deployed in our country over the last decades, as much as their consequences upon the processes of definition of what we would, with due caution, call "national identity", we have embarked upon an exploration of what happens in the intricate discursive web, dwelling with particular interest on moments of commemorative exaltation. This has allowed us to observe trans-formations and displacements whose relation to different social, political and economic circumstances have caught our attention. At the same time, however, we have detected certain behaviours that appear to stem from an unswerving recidivist tendency.

The present research focuses above all on discourses from the print media, especially opinion pieces, testimonies, chronicles and interviews. This emphasis corresponds to the crucial role played by journalistic discourse in the construction of the real (Verón, 1987). These public discourses, characterized by their doxastic and persuasive nature, offer and disseminate interpretations of facts that are made possible by a socio-historically determined discursivity which, at the same time, paves the way for such interpretations to be accepted.

We have concentrated particularly on publications that, even if motivated by the same commemorations – specifically, the twenty-fifth and thirtieth anniversaries of the Malvinas War – are the expression of politically antagonistic newspapers. This has allowed us to appreciate both the continuities and the differences, for although in every society discursive interaction guarantees certain constants in the social production of what is considered probable, debatable, plausible (Angenot, 1989), social discourse does not impose unique interpretants, but rather is characterized by its openness, contradictions and dynamism.

Malvinas, Memory and Identities: a Passional Question

In the previous sections, we have alluded to the passions involved in the creation of memory and memories, and to their intricate relationship with the construction of collective identities. While re-reading the pages of the introduction to *Malvinas. El gran relato,* by the Argentine semiologist Lucrecia Escudero Chauvel, we were particularly struck by a paragraph in which the author recalls the contradictory passions involved in bellicose encounters. Escudero Chauvel refers, in particular, to the feelings of a group of intellectuals who would come together, moved by a passional commitment and by the need not to remain on the margins of an unforeseen event that was shaking every fibre of a "territorial identity" internalized at school. In the face of this tragic adventure, which at the expense of innocent victims hastened the demise of the dictatorship that encouraged it, the aim of these intellectuals – which, in my opinion, was not quite fulfilled [2] – was to shed rational light on what was happening:

> I think this was simply the paradox of the war and the tremendous affective force of the event: the childhood schoolbook where we painted the islands with the national colours and the rationalization of an absurd war which, if won, would perpetuate to infinity the cruel military arrogance. (Escudero Chauvel, 2013, 25)

The scope of the adjective "absurd" applied to the war seems to be restricted to the fact that it favoured the interests of the military, whose power was decaying; but it does not seem to refer to the fact that, given the international context in which the conflict was set, imagining an Argentine victory was equally absurd. This reading calls for a profound reflection upon the need to believe that seemed to dominate society as a

[2] On this subject, see Rozitchner, 2015.

whole, a need that, with all its paradoxes, remains present in the discourses of commemoration, and especially in those related to the Bicentenary (Dalmasso, 2011a, 2011b, 2014). This perception leads us to focus on what we consider a moving effort to uphold the constructions of national identity that have dominated the social imaginary for most of the twentieth century, and which have been progressively eroded at least since the 1960s. During the most critical periods, this process, along with its contradictions, has sunk Argentines into a confusion from which not even the most lucid intellectuals have been able to escape.

This is related, as we previously pointed out, to a resistance properly to elaborate trauma, which has driven us to ignore our own impotence and to resist a reality that is contrary to our longings. In this respect, Carlos Gamerro, in a quotation harvested by Raquel San Martín (2012, 1-3), describes lucidly an Argentine society torn between holding on to the seductions of a promissory image or accepting the one returned to it by the socio-political and economic vicissitudes that inexorably shape daily reality:

> Malvinas is related to an Argentine institutional and everyday discourse of a country that is not where it should be, of a power that declined. Malvinas stands as a symbol of what we lost, of what we imagine we lost or of what we believe we deserve and do not have.

Summarizing what happened in terms of society's mood, Escudero Chauvel (2013, 30) introduces a key element, specifically the role played by the media: "Argentine society constructed a collective actor of desire, which 'did not want not to believe' and granted a level of trust to a specific discursive genre: the news." In this respect, María Seoane (2007) writes:

> with some exceptions, Argentines entered into a patriotic frenzy encouraged by the government, which included a varied and Felliniesque menu: out of fear or convenience, between official censorship and official propaganda, radio stations and television channels bombarded Argentines and incited them to domestic war-mongering, just the climate of support that Galtieri was looking for.

Escudero Chauvel's work delves into the construction of "The Great Narrative" carried out by the media apparatus. In this respect, she posits that the coherence of a narrative that might satisfy the population's passional expectations was preferred to the accuracy of the information provided. This leads her to question the processes of production and recognition that, once assimilated to the doxa, bestowed verisimilitude on the narrative (Escudero Chauvel, 2013, 27-29).

We can imagine that, at that time, the legitimacy granted to the media as informative enunciators afforded the complicity needed by the will to believe. Discourse, underpinned by a doxa nurtured since school and shared by all, constructed a model addressee with whom no actual receiver could not not identify.

Malvinas and their Memories

During the twenty-fifth and thirtieth anniversaries of the war, and above all during the latter, commemorative discourses started to take into account conflicting interpretations of events. In this sense, critical interpretations from certain quarters in respect of the policies pursued by different administrations at different moments started to gain visibility.[3] Reviewing our selection of publications, the most representative of the opposing political positions (*Clarín* and *La Nación* on the one hand, and *Página/12* on the other), we have been able to observe that, on the former anniversary, one of the salient issues is the difficulty Argentines have in thinking about and putting into words the subject of the war. In this regard, Luis Bruschtein (2007) is clear:

> In truth, the war is rarely brought up, because it is a harsh, insidious, disturbing issue. Extreme positions on one side or another are held by those who prefer not to listen, and opinions are fired off according to mood and humour. Malvinas remains on a symbolic plane. It is a symbol of "the homeland", but also of failure, guilt, shame and deceit.

We can see here a clear synthesis of the contradictions that beset a large part of the citizenry when it recalls the events. We see the possibility of considering the existence of two levels of deceit, one supported by the other. Thus, the sustained deceit carried out by the military, and reinforced by the media's narrative, is irrefutable. However, its efficacy seems rooted in the shared conviction of a territorial identity instilled at school. It is around this issue that a group of intellectuals begins to question whether this construction has not been yet another

[3] In 2007 Néstor Kirchner was in office, and in 2012 his wife, Cristina Fernández de Kirchner, succeeded him.

form of deceit. Naturally, this is a destabilizing, provocative interpretation that triggers significant resistance. The state of political tension makes this questioning assume a somewhat virulent tone in the discursivity of 2012, and become one of the axes of confrontation. In this respect, in a certain sense discouraging these doubts and tribulations, Horacio González (2012) summarizes the situation:

> The Malvinas War, in 1982, is an event with dates, a beginning and an end, an arc of time that includes proper names, vituperations, exaltations, many deaths, chronicles and novels [...]. These events are all part of Argentine history, implicated in Argentine history, closely tied to what we recognize as the familiar names of an over-historicized concept of the Nation. I say over-historicized, because the name "Malvinas" makes us contemporaries of a history of *longue durée*, fractured many a time, but traversing, with a rare unity, the periods of Rosas, Roca, Yrigoyen, Perón, the military *juntas* and restored democracy.

This generalized belief, unquestioningly shared throughout our history, this rare unity inspired by the Malvinas, persists over time and might explain – as we have already indicated – the difficulty, even among the most lucid groups of intellectuals, of detaching oneself from the passional relation to the islands. The conviction in our rights over the archipelago, an incontestable presupposition for most Argentines, clouded the capacity to take a critical distance from the events at the very moment the war was unfolding. In this respect, León Rozitchner's (2007) implacable accusation is against the citizenry as a whole:

> Malvinas is a key event in our history, wherein a sinister pact that still holds was sealed: the complicity between the majority of its citizens and state terrorism. This union which terror had tied together has still not been broken. For in the "Reconquest of the Malvinas" the totality of its social forces, both right and left, converged.

Some of the questionings that had started to emerge right after the conflagration exploded around the thirtieth anniversary. While there abound objections born of the contradictions inherent in that unfortunate adventure, others emerge, as we have shown, which focus on the criticism of the presuppositions and arguments upheld by the commemorative and celebratory policies pursued by the government in office. Thus does a group of seventeen ideologically critical intellectuals[4] dare to question the Malvinas issue as a "national cause" and to review the arguments underpinning that position:

> Three decades have passed since the tragic 1982 military adventure, and we still lack a public critique of the support which society gave to the Malvinas War and which mobilized nearly every sector of the country. Among the reasons for such support, not least was the adherence to the Malvinas cause, which proclaims the islands an "unredeemed territory", makes of their "recuperation"[5] a question of identity and puts it at the top of our national priorities and of the country's international agenda.

And they indirectly warn the counter-receiver:

> Let us hope that April 2nd and the year 2012 do not lead to the usual escalation of patriotic claims, but rather provide an opportunity for us Argentines – members of the government, leaders and citizens – to reflect, together and without prejudice, on the relation between our own mistakes and our country's failures. (de Ípola *et al.*, 2012)

This position, which would allow for the possibility that the islanders have a right to voice their opinion as to sovereignty, is opposed not only by those who maintain the deep-rooted position concerning our inalienable rights over the islands, but especially by those who agree with the policies the government adopted on the matter. This seems to offer one of the keys to understanding an issue that pits the dissident sector against, among others, the group of intellectuals gathered under the

---

[4] The group consists of intellectuals, constitutionalists and journalists from Argentina who call for a review of government policy on the Malvinas conflict. Under the title "Malvinas, una visión alternativa" (Malvinas: An Alternative Vision), they issued a document that carries the signature of the intellectuals Beatriz Sarlo, Juan José Sebreli, Santiago Kovadloff, Rafael Filippelli, Emilio de Ípola, Vicente Palermo, Marcos Novaro and Eduardo Antón; of the journalists Jorge Lanata, Gustavo Noriega and Pepe Eliaschev; of the historians Luis Alberto Romero and Hilda Sábato; of the constitutionalists Daniel Sabsay, Roberto Gargarella and José Miguel Onaindia; and of a former member of the National Congress, Fernando Iglesias.

[5] Note the use of quotation marks.

name Carta Abierta [6] (Open Letter) who support the official position. The antagonism shows clearly in the discourses that contest the arguments of the Group of 17. An example of this is found in an article by Edgardo Mocca, who polemically incorporates his counter-receivers' discourse into his own:

> Outraged by the prominence given to the issue in the political arena, the authors, however, have decided to put it at the centre of their own agenda. That is to say that, given the alleged attempt to malvinize politics, they have accepted the challenge and take it upon themselves to demalvinize it [...]. It is very good to take the islanders' rights into consideration, but political sovereignty is not a subjective right: it is exercised or claimed by national states. And, nowadays, the Malvinas territory is not an independent state. Its government is in the hands of an official appointed by the British state. (Mocca, 2012)

Both the difficulty in dealing with this issue, which seems to enforce a conflictive adherence either to nationalism or to anti-nationalism, and the notable direction taken by government policies, are clearly laid out by Raquel San Martín (2012):

> How to join in the claim for sovereignty without being wedded to an extreme nationalism or to the dictatorship that launched the military adventure in 1982? How to review critically the Argentine rights over the islands without being trapped in an anti-nationalist position, now that the government is championing the issue as the new national and popular cause against imperialism?

These questions allow us to glimpse the reasons why, at that specific moment, dissident voices were raised, among which those of the group of seventeen critical intellectuals stand out.

Heroes or Martyrs?
The heading of this section, which rehearses a question that for all its familiarity has lost none of its vibrancy, was suggested to us by Horacio

[6] The members of Espacio Carta Abierta made their first public appearance on 13 May 2008, in the City of Buenos Aires, on a panel that gathered together Horacio Verbitsky, Nicolás Casullo, Ricardo Forster and Jaime Sorín, where they presented their first "open letter". Despite its ideological affinity with the political party Frente para la Victoria, the group defines itself as non-partisan.

González's (2012) statement: "It is not the first time that the subject of who are the heroes and who the martyrs has been discussed in Argentina."

Partly during the twenty-fifth anniversary commemoration, but mostly during the thirtieth, the focus of attention shifted towards the issue of the veterans. We must ask ourselves whether such a shift responds to the intention of avoiding the complexity of a situation doubly contaminated from an ideological standpoint, both by the political circumstances surrounding the war and by the context of the anniversary, or whether it responds, rather, to the will to reinforce the official view of the facts and actors involved in the confrontation. A significant number of the published articles adopt the biographical angle and focus on reconstructing the vicissitudes suffered by ex-combatants of the war, with the additional benefit of inducing the association between the victims of the war and those of the dictatorship. In these chronicles and testimonies, a tragic continuity is traced between the practices deployed by the military during the dictatorship and those used when it came to organizing, conducting and sustaining the war against the United Kingdom. Among the testimonies, we find that of Edgardo Esteban, a veteran, journalist and writer. His narrative provides an insight into the aberrant neglect to which veterans were exposed on their return from the Malvinas, one of whose most dramatic consequences has been the number of post-war victims. The suicides caused by the impossibility of overcoming trauma account for more deaths than those that occurred in combat. The society that had so feverishly encouraged the war now chose denial, perhaps out of guilt or shame. If it was out of shame, we might ask whether it was motivated by its own belligerent impulse, by the deceit to which it was subjected, or by the ridicule of the defeat. Erasing the veterans is a way of erasing the war, a war that should never have happened:

> Besides being defeated, we seemed responsible for the defeat which we arrived at by military decision. From then on, there was a tacit agreement to forget the war; we had to endure being hidden and advised to wipe what had happened from our minds, forcing us to keep it to ourselves. For a long time, remaining silent was the preferred option over doing a mea culpa for a war that was lost, and no one wanted to assume responsibility for the defeat. (Esteban, 2007)

Here, too, society as a whole is the target of the criticism, for once the patriotic impulse faded before the force of a defeat it had refused to imagine, it superficially closed the episode by adding insult to injury, as the veteran César Maliqueo attests in a newspaper article (Savoia, 2012): "In Buenos Aires, when we returned, people were watching the World Cup in Spain." Denial is once again repeated.

As was previously indicated, in the narratives of war references to the mistreatment and unscrupulousness on the part of those of a higher rank dominate, so much so that the comparison between the behaviour displayed by the military during the dictatorship and that displayed towards ordinary soldiers during the war can be found in a significant number of narratives. In them, the ex-combatants are portrayed as the true victims of the conflict. They, however, strive not to be considered mere survivors and claim that what should be highlighted is the extent to which their action was moved by love for their country. Within this framework, opinions are divided in some respects. While some veterans consider that the officers who subjected them to torture during the conflict should be tried, others oppose the idea on the grounds that doing so would be tantamount to making themselves into victims.

During the thirtieth anniversary, many a voice was raised calling for cases to be opened against military personnel who subjected soldiers to torture. Among them was the voice of H.I.J.O.S.:[7]

the heads of the Argentine Armed Forces were practitioners of genocide and took to the islands the criminal practices they had deployed in the 500 or so Clandestine Centres of Detention, Torture and Extermination [the CCDTyE, in Spanish] that functioned in our country. Some of these repressors were convicted at the Trials of the Juntas and at the trials taking place at present [...]. These crimes, committed against Argentine soldiers, are crimes against humanity that must not go unpunished. The cause, thus, must go before the courts. (H.I.J.O.S., 2012)

[7] The name of the group, Hijos e Hijas por la Identidad y la Justicia contra el Olvido y el Silencio (Children for Equality and Justice against Forgetting and Silence), summarizes its main aims as calling for justice, reconstructing personal history, and reasserting the struggles of their parents and of the 30,000 detained-disappeared, as well as calling for the restitution of the identity of their siblings who were kidnapped. Further, they demand the effective lifelong imprisonment of all those responsible for crimes against humanity during the last dictatorship, their accomplices, instigators and beneficiaries.

Nevertheless, the proposal to prosecute this latest version of victimizers engendered by the self-proclaimed National Reorganization Process appears to have gone unheard. It is mainly in *Página/12* that the majority of these protests are registered. Mario Wainfeld (2012), for instance, claims:

> The torture perpetrated by the Argentine military during the Malvinas War is not taken to be a crime against humanity by the courts. So decided a ruling at the Court of Appeal [*Cámara de Casación*], the highest instance that has been issued so far. The Supreme Court should analyze this sentence and eventually revoke it, if it would make room for legal actions brought by the victims.

The claims and frustrations testify to the difficulties of mobilizing a society that seems to have deleted the terrible war and its effects from its agenda. In this respect, Federico Lorenz (2012), making particular reference to progressive sectors and human rights organizations, states:

> The thirtieth anniversary of the Malvinas calls for a deep exercise of introspection on the part of those sectors involved in democracy and Human Rights, a taking of responsibility that allows them to fill the unjust gap which a significant majority built between the young ex-soldiers and them.

Memory('s) Games

In our musings we have paid special attention to certain themes which we considered significant for an understanding of the strategies that play a role in the construction of memory and memories, as well as their conditioning and objectives.

One aspect that has interested us and that deserves to be examined at length concerns the variations produced in the discourses of memory according to the political situation. We think there have been certain thematic shifts, accompanied by a polemical element, apparently linked to the positions commentators adopt in relation to government policies at times of increased conflict. On the twenty-fifth anniversary, the emphasis was put on the war itself, on criticism of military actions and on questions surrounding the reasons for the fervent popular support for the war. However, on the thirtieth anniversary – which happened in times of heightened political confrontation – there emerged, on the one hand, dissident discourses referring to the need to review both the legitimacy of the claims over the islands and the policies pursued by the government (which presuppose such legitimacy), and, on the other, in sectors closer to the official view, there was a proliferation of veterans' narratives that, portraying themselves as victim-heroes, encourage the prosecution of those who victimized them.

It should be noted that those discourses that involve questioning the doxa, such as those of the Group of 17, presuppose a restricted addressee, because they require a kind of competence that is only present in certain sectors of society that question belief in a critical spirit. On the other hand, testimonial narratives, chronicles and interviews, which by virtue of their narrative properties incite compassion towards the protagonists of a drama that reactivates memory and facilitates identification, anticipate an addresse whot shares the doxa rooted in school history; that is to say, those who share a belief that furnishes the bedrock of their adherence. At the same time, the equivalence established between military behaviour allegedly predominant during the war and the military's behaviour during the dictatorship constructs a less restricted receiver because, although preferably orientated towards those progressive sectors committed to human rights, when put together with the veterans' narratives of their suffering, they have the potential to make an impact on those sectors of the population who have shown themselves to be moved by such narratives.

The discursive behaviour of the print media on the occasion of the twenty-fifth and thirtieth anniversaries of the Malvinas War allows us to posit that these memory exercises do not escape the conflicts of the day, but rather make them evident. Thus one sees political conflicts and misunderstandings advanced in the demonstration of argumentative strategies aimed at constructing a plausible, convincing version of the past that agrees ideologically with the current positioning of each of the parties.

To conclude, we borrow Claudio A. Jacqueline's (2012) illuminating definition: "Malvinas evokes and means so many things that it is the synthesis of all Argentine paradoxes."

References

Angenot, M. (1989). *1889. Un état du discours social*. Québec: Éditions du Préambule.

Bruschtein, L. (2007). "Una sociedad presa de los símbolos de Malvinas", *Página/12*. Available at **www.pagina12.com.ar/diario/especiales/ 18-82728-2007-04-02.html**.

Dalmasso, M. T. (2011a). "Semblanzas de la discursividad argentina en épocas del Bicentenario." *Bicentenaire des Indépendances Amérique*

Latine Caraïbes. Paris: IHEAL Institut d'Hautes Etudes de l'Amérique Latine, Institut Français (CD-ROM).

Dalmasso, M. T. (2011b). "El Bicentenario. Discurso social e identidades. La memoria y el presente." *Actas del V Coloquio de Investigadores en Estudios del Discurso y II Jornadas Internacionales sobre Discurso e Interdisciplina.* Villa María: UNVM. Available at **www.unvm.edu.ar/index.php?mod=cmsjornadas**.

Dalmasso, M. T. (2014). "Singularidades del discurso social en torno al Bicentenario" in H. Ponce de la Fuente and M. T. Dalmasso, eds. *Trayectos teóricos en semiótica.* Santiago de Chile: Universidad de Chile, 11-17.

De Ípola, E. *et al.* (2012). "Malvinas: una visión alternativa." Available at **http://lalectoraprovisoria.wordpress.com/2012/02/24/el-grupo-de-los-17-sobre-Malvinas**.

Escudero Chauvel, L. (2013). *Malvinas. El gran relato.* Barcelona: Gedisa.

Esteban, E. (2007). "Sacar nuestro infierno interior y empezar a curar las heridas", *Página/12.* Available at **www.pagina12.com.ar/diario/especiales/18-82726-2007-04-02.html**.

H.I.J.O.S. (2012). "Genocidas: de los centros clandestinos a las Malvinas", *Página/12.* Available at **www.pagina12.com.ar/diario/ elpais/1-190993-2012-04-03.html**.

González, H. (2012). "Malvinas y el liberalismo", *Página/12.* Available at **www.pagina12.com.ar/diario/elpais/1-191005-2012-04-03.html**.

Jacqueline, C. (2012). "Malvinas, la epopeya y el circo", *La Nación, Suplemento Enfoque Especial*, 1 April, 2.

Jelin, E. (2002). "Los sentidos de la conmemoración". In E. Jelin (ed.), *Las conmemoraciones. Las disputas en las fechas "in-felices".* Madrid: Siglo XXI, 245-250.

Lorenz, F. (2012). "Malvinas: prejuicios y deudas", *Página/12.* Available at **www.pagina12.com.ar/diario/elpais/1-190944-2012-04-02.html**.

Mocca, E. (2012). "La alarma por la 'agitación nacionalista'", *Revista Debate.* Available at **www.espacioiniciativa.com.ar/?p=6858**.

Nora, P. (2008). *Pierre Nora en Les lieux de mémoire.* Montevideo: Ediciones Trilce.

Parret, H. (1995). *Las pasiones. Ensayo sobre la puesta en discurso de la subjetividad.* Buenos Aires: Edicial.

Rozitchner, L. (2007). "Una complicidad de muerte que se mantiene en silencio", *Página 12.* Available at **www.pagina12. com.ar/diario/**

especiales/18-82730-2007-04-02.html.

Rozitchner, L. (2015). *Malvinas. De la guerra sucia a la guerra limpia. El punto ciego de la crítica política*. Buenos Aires: Ediciones Biblioteca Nacional.

San Martín, R. (2012). "Malvinas, herida abierta", *La Nación, Suplemento Enfoque Especial*, 1 April, 1-3.

Savoia, C. (2012). "Honra a los caídos en bici por el sur", *Clarín, Suplemento Especial Malvinas 30 años 30 historias*, 1 April, 19.

Schwab, G. (2015). "Escribir contra la memoria y el olvido", in S. Mandolesi and M. Alonso, eds., *Estudios sobre memoria. Perspectivas actuales y nuevos escenarios*. Villa María: Editorial Universitaria Villa María, 53-84.

Seoane, M. (2007). "Los argentinos, entre el fervor y la decepción", *Clarín, Suplemento especial*, 1 April. Available at **edant.clarin. com/diario/2007/04/01/deportes/m-01391499.htm**.

Verón, E. (1987). *Construir el acontecimiento*. Buenos Aires: Editorial Gedisa.

Wainfeld, M. (2012). "Héroes estaqueados", *Página/12*. Available at **www. pagina12.com.ar/diario/elpais/1-190942-2012-04-02.html**.

Returning: The Journey to the Islands
in Contemporary Narratives about the Malvinas

Alicia Vaggione

Owing to its character as a traumatic incident, the Malvinas War[1] remains an historic event to which discourses return time and again to explore, update and negotiate meanings. I choose as my focal point works that consider the journey to the Malvinas as a recurring topic. The accounts of the journey persist both in genres of a more testimonial nature (journals and chronicles), and in fictional literature and film. Through them, we can outline a series of questions about war memories. Answers – which are always hypothetical, plastic and versatile in nature – are offered up by each of the respective pieces.

The journey, associated with movement, enables a return to the past through questions about the present. A particular structure of perspective is put into play: that of the travellers who wander in order to interact with a territory that unsettles them. I am interested in the ability of the journey – linked to the movement that defines and constitutes it – to interact with time. In other words, I am interested in the journey's ability to discontinue meanings about the past that have become more or less stagnant, to give way to a new and very necessary perspective derived from the recording of experience.

In this essay, my concern is to study certain aspects of the journey in relation to memory, focusing on the link between bodies and affects, experience and writing, and past and present, as shown in the documentary *La forma exacta de las islas* [2] (The Exact Shape of the Islands) (2012) by Edgardo Dieleke and Daniel Casabé, as well as in *Fantasmas de Malvinas. Un libro de viajes* (Malvinas Ghosts: A Book of Journeys) (2008) by Federico Lorenz. Both insist on building a memory

---

[1] "The Malvinas War is one of the most controversial and difficult chapters in Argentine history. [...] There are different reasons for its complexity. On the one hand, it was a product of the civilian and military dictatorship which, since 1976, had been relying on state-sponsored terrorism. On the other hand, it had the support of a considerable part of society, including some who opposed the military government. At the same time, it was a demand rooted in the history of Argentine thought, as this country's sovereignty claim over the Malvinas Islands is a longstanding one" (Flachsland *et al.*, 2014, 95).

[2] A film directed by Daniel Casabé and Edgardo Dieleke, scripted by the directors and Julieta Vitullo, with the collaboration of Ricardo Piglia.

made up of multiple ways of reading the war experience and of seeing the island territory located at the end of the world.

La forma exacta de las islas explores the need to get to know the Malvinas by those who write doctoral theses on the topic. The book that emerged from this research, *Islas imaginadas. La guerra de Malvinas en la literatura y el cine argentinos* (Imagined Islands: The Malvinas War in Argentine Literature and Film), was published in 2012, the same year the documentary was released. In the epilogue, we read that Julieta Vitullo (2012, 186), the author, travelled to the islands twice. The aim of the first journey was to write up the conclusions of her research *in situ*: "What guided the first journey was the idea of seeing with my own eyes that place I had read so much about [...]. I wanted the journey to be not only metaphorical but also physical". The second journey was to be the subject-matter of the documentary. *Fantasmas de Malvinas* also narrates the urgent desire to travel, but this time the craving is that of a historian who has focused on investigating the matter in a series of research projects. The book consists of travel chronicles that are largely essayistic in nature.

There seems to be a common concern in these materials. A literary critic and an historian who have investigated the matter of the Malvinas reveal the importance of accessing the islands and recording that experience. What is being narrated in this space "between" the research practice, the writing of it and the experiences of the journey? What meanings does the insular (*lo insular*) acquire? What memories of the territory are updated? What memories of war are drawn upon?

By means of unique paths which I am interested in defining, I consider that these materials – diverging from the canonical traits of the genres of documentary and chronicle[3] – play a role in creating new ways of reading an event whose meanings are never finite. This essay is divided into two parts, one for each piece, and its aim is to assess their features and the questions they raise.

On *La forma exacta de las islas*

The Islands: "The Place Where Everything Happened"
The film *La forma exacta de las islas* is about the journey to the

---

[3] Current critical opinion challenges the presumption of veracity as a rule specific to these genres. New variations are reflected in order to show hybrids and markers of subjectivity that redefine and invent an event rather than mirror it.

Malvinas, creating journeys within journeys. The film aims to grasp the way in which certain lives are scarred by a particular experience or place. Recording a variety of stories, *La forma exacta* builds multiple ways of viewing the island territory.

The movie offers both images of the islands as they stand now and accounts of the way in which they were seen by travellers and castaways who reached their harbours. It creates an archive of images and sounds: in many scenes, if we focus on listening, it is hard to differentiate the sound of the sea from that of the wind. Be that as it may, we cannot remain indifferent to those physical and perceptible records.

It could be said that the documentary alternates between two times, representing the two journeys of Julieta Vitullo, the protagonist of the film and researcher on fiction in literature and films about the Malvinas. One of the trips took place in 2006, when Julieta's desire to travel to the islands arose. The objective of this impulse to travel is to access the reality of that imagined territory that is part of the fiction she writes about and researches on. The initial proposal, "I am finally on Malvinas. I'm coming to Malvinas to finish my dissertation", was altered by an unexpected event that disrupted the proposed plan. During that week in December 2006 (generally, trips to the Malvinas are long), Julieta met two Argentine veterans and, instead of writing the end of her thesis, began the production of a film following the travellers' footsteps.

In this material recorded by Julieta's camera, as well as in the veterans' introduction of themselves, they first tell us their names, Dacio and Carlos, immediately followed by an unforgettable fact of their lives: they were born in 1963. This first fact marks out those young men as being eighteen years old at the time of the war. They went back to explore the conflict area, in the words of the film "the place where it all happened".

Returning seems to rest on the connection between the ways of assigning meaning to experience, a connection that has never been entirely resolved. Although they outline the possibility that the journey might have beneficial effects and help them "move on", these hopes involve a perception of time that is neither linear nor chronological, but rather intensive and purely emotional. On this emotional plane, reinforced by the contact with the territory, a meeting with that which is new is established:

> I don't know. When I come back I'll continue with my stuff, but perhaps with a new perspective and thinking about helping our comrades who want to come back.

I can tell you that I can analyze this trip because I already did it before I came. In the sense that I knew I was going to look at this with different eyes, with greater life-experience behind me.

Perhaps the only thing I found that I wasn't expecting was the beauty. (Casabé and Dieleke, 2012)

The beauty that moves Dacio, the hills beneath the sun which he never got to see during the war, is wonderfully captured by the camera countless times during the movie. It captures footage of the beaches, the hills, the streets, the lit homes of Stanley. It captures images of roads that crisscross the islands, accompanied by the sound of the wind. [4]

Carlos, the other veteran, also shares the way in which the trip allows him to see things differently, to shake off a way of thinking about the islands that has remained frozen since the time of the war, in order to appreciate that life went on here as well. The perception of movement is such that, several times during the film, Carlos fantasizes about the idea of staying and settling down there.

The recording carried out by Julieta follows the travellers closely and joins them on their visits, which somehow resemble the typical journeys of veterans exploring the islands: visiting the Darwin Cemetery; finding and identifying the places where they fought, where they lost fellow soldiers or took shelter from the cold and hunger. Julieta's camera records their unsettling, winding, yet precise search to recognize the places and pay tribute to unforgettable dead comrades with fragile wooden crosses.

Rupture

It is fragments of this film – which registers the unexpected encounter, in 2006, with the veterans and follows their footsteps – that were taken up in November 2010, when Julieta returned, accompanied by the two filmmakers who directed the documentary, Daniel Casabé and Edgardo Dieleke. She returned driven by the need to go back to that territory which had marked her life beyond the writing. Well into the film, the viewer finds out that Julieta fell pregnant during the first trip, that she

[4] Paola Cortés Rocca's reading pauses to concentrate on images. Critics believe *La forma exacta* steers away from a word-based representation to "offer a visual and perceptive experience of the islands", where the landscape "is not something one thinks of as decoration, but rather as geography that incorporates very different overlapping layers: that of war, love, history, national identities, friendship, eroticism, mourning" (Cortés Rocca, 2014).

decided to keep the child after she returned to Buenos Aires, and that her son, Eliseo, died a few hours after he was born.

This narrative, which revolves around maternity and loss, is reflected in the restrained and frugal gestures of Julieta's face, and introduces an emotional plane on which the feminine is highlighted, a turning point in fiction towards an awareness in which, read in the context of war narratives, the masculine figure and homosociality prevail.

It would be possible to read something encoded in Julieta's pain that seems to be related to that of other mothers in its inimitable uniqueness. Linear time disappears once again. One of the images shows Julieta walking around a cemetery while the voice-over narrates how she found a book documenting a plague that ravaged the islands in the nineteenth century, taking mainly children's lives. The book shows a picture of a mother with her dead son in her arms.

Other images of Julieta in Darwin Cemetery are tinged by a tone evoking loss, as the camera shoots the tombstones on the field, slowly going from one cross to the other so that the viewer can read the names of those killed or notice the names of those missing.

At this point, the documentary establishes a strong connection in which the individual experience of loss is related to others. The plague in the nineteenth century and the Malvinas War seem to outline a common background where death is featured as an interruption of lives that had their entire future ahead of them.

In this cancellation of the future, the Mothers of the Plaza de Mayo are called upon through metonymy and as a result of the echo produced by the intensity of the images in the film. As stated by Nora Domínguez (2007, 283), the Mothers barge into the public arena and displace "the representation of a unique mother with one singular son [...] in order to show that the greatest accomplishment of motherhood is reaching out to the group of sons with one embrace or motherly voice, when the place of the mother becomes plural".

A quotation from the writer Carlos Gamerro – part of the theatre version of the novel *Las islas* – gives the documentary its name and, at the same time, acts as an encapsulation of the recorded experience outlined by the movie, focused on the figure of rupture: "Does anyone know how many days the war lasted? Nobody? It isn't true there were survivors. There are two bites torn out of the hearts of every one of us."

Based on the experience of rupture, of something that breaks/cracks and cannot return to its former shape, but rather mutates, acquiring new contours, the movie constructs – with its combination of accounts and experiences – meanings that, time and again, go beyond the personal sphere.

Released thirty years after the Malvinas War, *La forma exacta* gives an account of multiple possible perspectives, this time through images captured by those who were children during the war: the directors and Julieta herself.

On *Fantasmas de Malvinas. Un libro de viajes*

Writing, Travelling and Memory

The book *Fantasmas de Malvinas* is a chronicle that narrates the journey of a historian who travelled to the islands. A disturbing question is posed on the first page: "Can we return to somewhere we have never been before?" Even though it is the first one, the trip is conceptualized as a return and, from page one, invokes a temporality that is not subject to linear chronology, but is connected to that which comes back as a ghost, that which cannot be overridden by memory.

The chronicles open and close with chapters entitled "Luggage". They are entries, similar to those one finds in a personal diary, about the aim of the trip. The first chapter lists a series of elements to be used when recording the experience in writing, as well as garments that will be useful on the trip:

> I have a blank notebook [...], a tentative schedule and a list of questions I have accumulated over the years [...]. I am taking a considerable number of warm garments that are easy to put on and take off because the weather in the Malvinas, like that in the provinces down south, changes all the time. (Lorenz, 2008, 27-29)

The comparison between the weather or the landscape on the islands and Patagonia (the province of Tierra del Fuego, mainly) is a consistent characteristic of the text, creating a sense of proximity and even familiarity between the islands and the closest parts of the continent.

Regarding the writing, there is an initial scene that is recalled: that of the child writing letters to soldiers during the war. This scene,[5] almost

[5] The narration of this initial writing scene and our interest in reading it as a beginning is related to Sylvia Molloy's study of autobiography in Spanish America. Critics concentrate on a central episode in the lives of the autobiographers they study: the encounter between the self and the book, which highlights the importance the act of reading itself acquires. This central position can be observed in Lorenz's chronicle of his journey, transferred to the act of writing.

elliptically developed – "I who wrote them letters every day" (Lorenz, 2008, 31) – acts as the beginning of the writing persistence that continued and is now present in the practice of the historian. At the same time, it encodes and encapsulates some central issues: the role of schools during the months of the war (where thousands of letters from children to soldiers were written) and the markers of the generation to which the writer belongs.

The journey, as an experience that allows for the encounter with the other and the foreign, results in multiple ways of seeing and looking. The chronicles constitute a chorus of perceptions about the landscapes and the meetings with the islanders and veterans visiting the islands. They incorporate other voices. Those of the veterans have a central place. They are sometimes mentioned directly ("I don't know what force brought me here, and which now that it brings me here, won't let me go back"), as well as being introduced by the chronicler ("They want to keep promises, close wounds, settle debts and spend a night in their old place. Time stopped for them when the war marked them forever, even though they went on living" [Lorenz, 2008, 87]). The chronicle records the marks left by war, written on the lives and memories of the subjects as well as on the materials that are still spread around the islands as footprints of the battles. Examples of this are the parts of a Pucará plane and multiple other objects:

> The islanders dragged it from the place where it crashed in 1982 to the place where it is now. However, more than a vexation, it looked as if someone had delicately arranged it for the purpose of studying it: the wings were spread out, the fuselage was broken [...], the tail was resting on a side, the wounds left by the shots could be seen in different parts of the structure. (Lorenz, 2008, 85)

> Scattered all over the floor there are remnants that represent the life of those men in the pits: wood, blankets, ponchos, rusty irons and telephone cables. (Lorenz, 2008, 88)

The objects that can be found all over the island, which the chronicler records and photographs, are also footprints or fragments of memory.[6] They are outdoors, worn and preserved at the same time by the cold

---

[6] In *Fantasmas de Malvinas*, there are no pictures of the journey. These can be found in other books by the author, as well as in *Pensar Malvinas*.

weather of the islands. [7] They are there, questioning those who find them and are capable of reading them.

I mentioned at the beginning that the chronicles create a non-linear temporality. This means that they build a memory that, far from linear in form, is designed in tiers: "To me, the islands are *successive layers* of locations, places and memories" (my emphasis).

Those Who Stayed

A tone of mourning is present throughout the chronicle. This tone and its meaning are strengthened when visits are made to the places where the dead are buried. The visit to Darwin Cemetery, where the bodies of the fallen Argentine soldiers lie, is the first stop on the historian's trip to the island:

> There is something desolate about Darwin. It might be the wind. [...] There is a cross at each grave, white and glistening due to the rain. At their feet, some of the black plaques display a name, others simply state "Argentine soldier known only to God". There are paths between the crosses, and the grey and black gravel crunches under our feet, as if it was necessary to assert every step. (Lorenz, 2008, 35)

The graves of the unknown soldiers are part of a pending debt, waiting for memory to be repaired by history. In his study *Epitafios. El derecho a la muerte escrita* (Epitaphs: The Right to a Written Death), Luis Gusmán (2005, 18) highlights the way in which funerary writing in ancient Greece was regulated by strict legislation that took two rights into account: the right to a written death – knowing who the dead are and where their grave is – and the right to tears as an expression of the sorrow of the bereaved. This is still a pending matter in the politics of memory in

---

[7] These objects that are still part of the landscape, probably preserved by the cold weather, invoke the documentary *Nostalgia de la luz* (Nostalgia for Light) by Patricio Guzmán, who took advantage of the Atacama Desert's lack of humidity (which maintains everything unaffected) to search for and read history's footprints: "What *Nostalgia* [...] seems to be highlighting is how there are many pasts within the past. When the connection (between land and sky) is achieved, when the pasts of galaxy time intersect with cave paintings, the signs of nomadic populations and indigenous peoples, the history of nineteenth-century miners, and the history of the prisoners and missing persons of the dictatorship, the documentary turns the desert into a place of revelations" (Boero and Vaggione, 2014, 125).

Argentina.

A different chapter states that the cenotaph that commemorates the dead is located in the city of Buenos Aires, in Retiro, across from the Torre gifted by the British community in 1910. Inaugurated in 1990, it includes twenty-five black plaques with the names of fallen soldiers. To Lorenz (2008, 176), the pressures caused by this war are all over this monument, where the only thing that matters is the fact that these men died for their country: [8]

> on the monument, it doesn't matter if the dead were officers who cared about their men or evil beings who meted out the same punishment to their subordinates as they did to the missing [*chupados*] in detention centres. It doesn't matter if the young men who are being commemorated were proud of sacrificing their lives or if they did so cursing.

As we mentioned, Lorenz's book closes with a chapter entitled "Luggage". This takes us to the last scene, in the customs room at the airport, where the travellers have to let go of some objects they will not be able to take with them. Yet memory can be that which we carry, that which we take with us:

> Acting as memory smugglers, those who return take with them objects that bring us closer to the islands, which are remote even when we are standing on them.
> The land of positions and of the cemetery.
> Small loafs of peat.
> Rocks in the hills.
> Sand on the beaches.
> Shards, large or small, oxidized and coarse. Outsoles of combat boots, waterbottles.
> The ladies in Customs are polite but categorical:
> – Nothing that can be used to recall the war can leave these

[8] As we have said, the Malvinas War is a complex episode in recent Argentine history. In her book, Julieta Vitullo (2012, 12), the protagonist of *La forma exacta de las islas*, states the following: "The fact that it was initially supported by the majority of society while the regime behind it was going through its greatest legitimacy crisis, together with the fact that the defeat led to victory (because it opened the path towards the return to democracy), turns this word into something of a blind spot in national history."

islands. [...] It's funny: in that case, we shouldn't be allowed out either. (Lorenz, 2008, 18)

To conclude, it is important to highlight that the materials addressed reveal the view of those who were children during the Argentine dictatorship. These children were two, three and four years old in the case of Vitullo and the directors of the documentary. Lorenz was finishing primary school when the war took place and he remembers writing letters to the soldiers.

In this sense, both pieces of work show the need of this generation to investigate what happened on the Malvinas through the language of literature, film and history, as well as emotionally, in their relationship to what they show and tell us. Maybe that is the reason behind the journey. Ricardo Piglia (2005, 114) considers that "the journey is a way of creating the experience, in order to write about it later". Both *La forma exacta de las islas* and *Fantasmas* support writing from experience, a type of writing that dives into the complexity of history, producing multiple ways of interpreting an event about which we need to keep on thinking.

References

Boero, M. S. and A. Vaggione. (2015). "Pasados materiales: Notas sobre el documental *Nostalgia de la luz* de Patricio Guzmán", *Revista digital: Artes, letras y humanidades* 8, 123-130. Available at **http://fh.mdp.edu.ar/ revistas/index.php/etl/issue/view/72**.

Cortés Rocca, P. (2014). Unpublished text read at the presentation of the film *La forma exacta de las islas*, The Rojas Museum, Buenos Aires.

Casabé, D. and E. Dieleke. (2012). *La forma exacta de las islas* (audiovisual production).

Domínguez, N. (2007). *De dónde vienen los niños. Maternidad y escritura en la cultura argentina*. Rosario: Beatriz Viterbo.

Flachsland, C. *et al.* (2014). *Pensar Malvinas. Una selección de fuentes documentales, testimoniales, ficcionales y fotográficas para trabajar en el aula*, 3rd ed. Buenos Aires: Ministerio de Educación de la Nación (audiovisual production).

Gamerro, C. (1998). *Las islas*. Buenos Aires: Simurg.

Gamerro, C. (2011). *Las islas*. Theatrical production, unpublished directed by Alejandro Tantanian.

Gusmán, L. (2005). *Epitafios. El derecho a la muerte escrita*. Buenos Aires: Norma.

Lorenz, F. (2008). *Fantasmas de Malvinas. Un libro de viajes*. Buenos Aires: Eterna Cadencia.

Molloy, S. (1996). *Acto de presencia. La escritura autobiográfica en Hispanoamérica*. Mexico: Fondo de Cultura Económica.

Piglia, R. (2005). *El último lector*. Barcelona: Anagrama.

Vitullo, J. (2012*). Islas imaginadas. La guerra de Malvinas en la literatura y el cine argentinos*. Buenos Aires: Corregidor.

Dancing with Death
Lyric Poetry in and out of Conflict

Bernard McGuirk

Poetry of war, in parallel to, or meandering alongside, the walks in the fictional woods plotted by combat and post-conflict fiction, might be said to dance with death. The analogy draws on, in order to depart from, a classical if ever-problematic distinction drawn between the genres of prose and poetry. Paul Valéry's assertion that "one should guard against reasoning about poetry as one does about prose" assumes that the "walking" performed by narrative fiction reaches "the place, the book, the fruit, the object of desire" and "at once entirely annuls the whole act; the effect swallows up the cause, the end absorbs the means and, whatever the act, only the result remains". Poignantly, in the context of any analysis of the literature of war, Valéry's counterclaim for poetry is phrased as follows: "The poem, on the other hand, does not die for having lived: it is expressly designed to be born again from its ashes and to become endlessly what it has just been. Poetry can be recognized by this property; that it tends to get itself reproduced in its own form: it stimulates us to reproduce it identically" (Valéry, 1939, in Lodge, 1972, 261).

In analysing poems that address the 1982 South Atlantic conflict and its complex historical and cultural contexts, it will be necessary to resist the ever-lurking danger of a phoenix image of war poetry that would tend to render all wars one, or bury the particular trauma in expression of a general or anaesthetized pain. For the spectre of the transcendental might be seen to haunt the poetry of war more insistently and insidiously than is the case in narrative or dramatic revisitations of the scene of action. Whenever the lyrical enters into confrontation with the unspeakably real, the *danse macabre* that traditionally ensues might serve to expiate theologically. Out of such ashes, however, it is not always the phoenix of cyclical destruction that may be seen to rise. For poetry can also plead, or scream, ideologically, can prompt political engagement and urge social change.

Transcendental echoes

If the Falkland Islands and their whereabouts had been something of a mystery, at best, or nothing at all for most, in the British social imaginary until the outbreak of the crisis, the Islas Malvinas had been the inspiration, in Argentina, of many a patriotic poet or, as is often the case with nationalisms worldwide, poetasters. Anthologies of verses evoking the mists and the myths of the history-shrouded Isles can be found throughout a nation where the topic of the loss and the will to recuperate the territory had penetrated not only the political discourse of successive eras and governments but also the literary exercises of generation after generation of school children. The first poem by an author of renown to deal with the Malvinas-Falklands conflict was the initially untitled "Juan López y John Ward", published in Buenos Aires in *Clarín* on 26 August and, in a by no means unproblematic translation, in *The Times* of London on 18 September 1982. [1] The poem has been dissected variously and multiply, as part of the Borges critical industry, but it is still pertinent to situate it in the context of the genre of war poetry:

Juan López y John Ward

Les tocó en suerte una época extraña
El planeta había sido parcelado en distintos países, cada uno provisto
de lealtades, de queridas memorias, de un pasado sin duda heroico,
de derechos, de agravios, de una mitología peculiar, de próceres de bronce,
de aniversarios, de demagogos y de símbolos.
Esa división, cara a los cartógrafos, auspiciaba las guerras.

López había nacido en la ciudad junto al río inmóvil.
Ward, en las afueras de la ciudad por la que caminó Father Brown.
Había estudiado castellano para leer el Quijote.
El otro profesaba el amor de Conrad, que le había sido revelado
en un aula de la calle Viamonte.
Hubieran sido amigos, pero se vieron una sola vez cara a cara, en unas
islas demasiado famosas, y cada uno de los dos fue Caín, y cada uno, Abel.
Los enterraron juntos. La nieve y la corrupción los conocen.

El hecho que refiero pasó en un tiempo que no podemos entender.

(Borges, 1982a)

Juan López and John Ward

It was their fate to live in a strange time.
The planet had been carved into different countries,
each one provided with loyalties, with loved memories,
with a past which doubtless had been heroic, with

---

[1] The poem was reprinted in Borges, 1989, 500.

ancient and recent traditions, with rights, with grievances,
with its own mythology, with
forebears in bronze, with anniversaries, with demagogues and
with symbols. Such an arbitrary division was favourable to war.

López had been born in the city next to the motionless
river; Ward in the outskirts of the city
through which
Father Brown had walked. He had studied Spanish
so as to read the *Quixote*.
The other professed a love of Conrad, revealed
to him in a class in Viamonte Street.
They might have been friends, but they saw each other just once,
face to face, in islands only too well known, and each one was Cain and each
    one, Abel.
They buried them together. Snow and corruption
know them.

The story I tell happened in a time we cannot understand.

(Borges, 1982b)

So be it? Amen? The construction of an opening gambit of Olympian distance, impersonality, objectivity, disinterest, a refusal to take sides, a mere "naming of parts"; thus might the word "fate" be seen to operate, reiterating a classical trope of juxtaposing destiny with the "strangeness" of time, as if history were always in excess not only of its writing but also of our understanding of it. The apparent predetermination implicit in the division of the planet into potentially martial factions would make it appear that, not for the first time, here is a Borges going transcendental; opting for the difference between countries as predestined, unavoidable point of departure on a road to cyclically repeated wars. According to the terms of such an irresistible binary, the only predictable construct would be that of Nationalisms, Histories writ large, official versions, "loyalties" to be tested, and attested, by checklists of "past", "heroic", "cherished memories", "anniversaries". The writing implements of such a polarized reading of history are meticulously mapped: "rights" and "wrongs".

Thereby a mythology has been produced and, in Borges's representation of it, is shown to be inseparable from proprietary rights and ownership. The reality effects of such strong myths are the hammered bronze echoes of anniversaries, the resonance of demagoguery and the unequivocality of symbols. Only once in the opening sequence of the poem has a "doubtless" crept in, near-casual prefiguration, its ironizing

240

frame easily missable, of an overt, a sententious and, thus far, it might seem, a dangerously unopposed, omniscient voicing: "Esa división [...] auspiciaba las guerras" (less meticulously mapped – without, indeed, any cartographers at all – in translator Terragno's "Such an arbitrary division was favourable to war").

As in the case of all closed meanings, the planet-wide carve-up into differing Nationalisms, into different signifieds, might indeed have been for too long read as ordained by fate and agreed by men... agreed but arbitrary, and with no positive terms. Read retrospectively, however, the "different countries" of the opening sequence might be said to require a re-writing of their respective histories in excess of the confining terminology, the straitjacket of those nationalizing ideologies which endow countries with auguries, auspicious or ill, both of, and for, war. It is in this light, therefore, that the wording "was favourable" might be said to point to an over-dominant metaphysics, the supposedly unavoidable (and historically repeated) resolution of conflicting mythologies of nation through military confrontation.

As the Juan López and John Ward of Borges's text are schooled in the respective cities of their differential fates, the private and public strands of their lives (their perusal of Cervantes, or Conrad, their perambulations along the River Plate or through Chesterton's suburbs) are interwoven only to lead them to the particular circumstance of their signifying encounter. This particularity is not just constructed on difference. The specificity of the brief attributions to Buenos Aires (inherited, displaced, and impoverished locus of an *hidalgo* tilter at dreams) and London (misplaced scene of an Edwardian, rose-tinted, and bumbling detective theology) is complemented by a prolonged disclosure of, and an openness to, reciprocity and its potential. An encountering without othering is tentatively approached via Juan and John as nostalgic, ingenuous, *literati*, through their readerly preparing for, their conceiving of, the translatability of a mediated other – that Other filtered through literatures, through traditions, through superannuated societies, and which consists of cultural difference. The hypothetical status of such *un*reality effects is however confined, consigned, to but a short sentence, "They might have been friends", before the onset, the onrush, of a more divisive outcome... the inter-bayonetry of that form of cultural transfer which will always set its face against negotiated settlement (of differences). War-war, not jaw-jaw.

In a "just once", in sheer instantaneity, the Borges text confronts the meeting of faces though not of eyes. The only available sphere of action is the double actant space where each is Cain and each is Abel. For the absolute narrative, transcendent History, can cope with, and will apportion, no blame, no fault, no right, no wrong. In such an ironized story, the Juan/John "fate" is, inevitably, both to live and to die in "a strange time", buried together under the cover not of darkness but of a more pervasive, chilling, snowy blankness, and the corruption of a shared, a *same* death, which, macabre aspiration, abolishes the difference of self and other, self in other. A same death which permits no story, no history of their difference, their common particularity, resolved or dissolved in the illusory coming together of the time and its telling. But is "a time we cannot understand" merely a conclusive note of resignation to fate, to strangeness, to incomprehensibility? Or an invitation to read back through the poem, attempting to listen not to what "*we*" cannot understand but rather to the fact "*I* tell"?

The excessive relation of the individual's voicing to simultaneous histories-become-History constitutes an invitation to listen again, whether to the Borges poem or to the official spokesmen of the Thatcher Government, the Ian MacDonalds, the John Notts. What we are asked to hear is a counterpoint to the clipped, flat, matter-of-fact intoning, cultivatedly understating, the course, and the discourse, of a history of the excessively famous, the notorious. Thus the Borges poem subverts, even as it broaches, the construction of dangerous *clichés* of *in*difference; will not allow Juan and John an infamous loss of private identities whereby they are turned into "The Unknown Soldier", become transfused by, confused with, a sentimentalizing *dulce et decorum est pro patria mori*... Particular differences between Juan and John should be no less legible now than is that cryptic distinction at play within *Juan López* and John *War*d; the projected inscription of Jorge Luis's own initials into a (warred) relationship with the (linguistic) Other overtly inscribed by both trace and excess of intra-textual conflicts.

Counterpoint and excess also serve to characterize the relation of the Borges poem to its Wilfred Owen precursor, "Strange Meeting" (written 1918, first published 1919). Direct echoes are muted but an overt interpellation in Borges's opening line, "strange", convokes both title and the ghosts from Owen's face-to-face encounter in Hell in order to prefigure his own protagonists' entrenched inseparability in an all too similar "profound dull tunnel". Owen's first-person – "out of battle I escaped" only to confront his also dead adversary of but yesterday's jab and parry – is allowed a point of view:

> "Strange friend," I said, "here is no cause to mourn."
> "None," said that other, "save the undone years,

242

The hopelessness. Whatever hope is yours,
Was my life also".

(Owen, in Silkin, 1981, 197)

Borges, however, ethically refraining from any identifying relation with the combatant Owen's option for eerie dramatic dialogue, borrows only the hypothetical. "They might have been friends" performs the defamiliarization necessary to his own respectful visit to the grave of the predecessor's poem, and his strategic retreat from it. If Borges's Juan and John are not permitted to enter such an exchange as "I am the enemy you killed, my friend. I knew you in this dark" (Owen, in Silkin, 1981, 198) it is because of an updating swerve. In appropriating but requiring to go beyond Wilfred Owen's "Strange Meeting", the later poem reminds us too that it is written after the era of *La Grande Illusion*: "but they saw each other just once, face to face". Concomitantly, Owen's "Let us sleep now..." finds in Borges's "Los enterraron juntos" a counterpart but without hint of consolation. "My hands were loath and cold" derives from a personal voice not available in the Argentine's bleaker rendering of the icy effect of war: "Snow and corruption know them". Thus is the final line of the Borges poem calculatedly prepared for. Facts? History? Such events as have rendered *too* famous mere outcrops of the South Atlantic must exceed understanding; must confound nationalistic apportionings of roles of right and wrong; must allow for no making capital out of *History*; must refuse the writing of *Myth*. [2]

The "Falklands Conflict" came to represent a particularly dominant metaphysics of presence in the strife-torn early 'eighties. Amongst the scandalously repressed absences of that period of burning UK inner cities, of strikes and counter-strikes – Brit *versus* grit – was the term *Malvinas,* itself repressing another by now faint imperial echo, less of Britain's "naming of parts" than of Brittany's parting with names – St Malo, whence *Les Iles Maloïnes*. Now, out of France, in a late twentieth-century rivalry of post-imperial but never post-economic colonizing powers, was cast the shadow not of Breton exiles but of bolt-on Exocets. The creation of a meta-geography (and a metal market) favourable to war suggests that the ever-bullish economy of Nationalism emerged, in April

---

[2] The Borges strategy, here, as I read it, confirms Simon Featherstone's view that "To treat wartime as a parenthesis of history is to depoliticize it, blur the social and cultural complexities of its literature and thought and ultimately make it mythical rather than historical" (Featherstone, 1995, 23).

1982, as a fragmentary narrative of half-locatable places where, with stunning rapidity, all too recognizable visages of power chose to come face-to-face. Perhaps not apocryphally, the Galtieri-Thacher struggle over southern (dis)comfort on the rocks is said to have been described by Borges as that of "two bald men fighting over a comb".

On choreographed *intra*-colonialism

A powerful representation of history as repetition yet of translation as betrayal occurs in a poem from her 1987 collection *Ova completa* by the Argentine writer Susana Thénon. If the somewhat less than celebratory pre-quincentenary gift of Prime Minister Thatcher to the Galtieri regime came ten years too early, at least the unseemly rush across the South Atlantic, again to see and sack new worlds, allowed Thénon the time (she died in 1990) to situate the translatability of inseparably monarchic, ecclesiastical and military post-colonialism as not only a commonplace North-South, English-Spanish, relation but also as an effect shown to be operative between Spanish and Spanish, between Spanish American and Spanish Americans. Here, Thénon shows up the virtual taboo subject of *intra*-colonialism. Within the political-ideological frontiers of Spanish America, there would appear to be a need not (only) for translation of the message of resistance against cyclical colonizing aggression into the language (English) of its latest perpetrators but (also) for its repetition, in difference, to the often indifferent (Spanish American) other:

Poema con traducción simultánea Español-Español	Poem with Simultaneous Translation Spanish to Spanish
Para ir hacia lo venidero para hacer, si no el paraíso, la casa feliz del obrero en la plenitud ciudadana, vínculo íntimo eslabona e ímpetu exterior hermana a la raza anglosajona con la latinoamericana. 　　Rubén Darío, *Canto a la Argentina*	To move towards what is still to come, to construct, if not paradise, the happy house of the worker in the plenitude of the city, intimate bond ties and outer strength unites in brotherhood the Anglo-Saxon race with the Latin American. 　　Rubén Darío, *Song to the Argentine*
Cristóforo 　(el Portador de Cristo) hijo de un humilde cardador de lana 　(hijo de uno que iba por lana sin cardar) zarpó del puerto de Palos 　(palo en zarpa dejó el puerto)	Cristóforo 　(the Bearer of Christ) son of a humble carder of wool 　(son of one who got wool without carding) cast anchor from the port of Palos 　(stick in his grasp he left the port)

no sin antes persuadir	not without first persuading
a Su Majestad la Reina	Her Majesty the Queen
Isabel la Católica de las bondades de la empresa	Isabel the Catholic of the bounties of the enterprise
por él concebida	by him conceived
(no sin antes persuadir	(not without first persuading
a Her Royal Highness	Her Royal Highness
die Königen Chabela la Logística	die Königen Chabela of the Logistics
de empeñar	of pawning the
la corona en el figón de Blumenthal	crown in the eating-house of Blumenthal
con-verso)	con-vert)
así se vertiesen litros y litros de	even if spilling litres and litres of
genuina sangre vieja factor RH negativo	genuine old blood factor RH negative
(así costase sangre sudor y lágrimas	(even if they cost blood sweat and tears
antípodas)	antipodean)
se hicieron a la mar	they made out to sea
(se hicieron alamares)	(they made decorative fastenings)
y tras meses y meses de yantar solo	and after months and months of vitt'ling alone
oxímoron en busca de la esquiva redondez	oxymoron in search of the elusive roundness
(y tras días y días de mascar	(after days on end of chewing
Yorkshire pudding	Yorkshire pudding
y un pingüino de añadidura los domingos)	and a penguin in addition on Sundays)
alguno exclamó tierra	one of them cried land
(ninguno exclamó thálassa)	(none of them cried thálassa)
desembarcaron	they disembarked
en 1492 a. D.	in 1492 AD
(pisaron	(they trod
en 1982 a.D	in 1982 AD)
jefes esperaban	chiefs were waiting
en pelota	stark naked
genuflexos	genuflecting
(mandamases aguardaban	(bosses waited
desnudos	stripped
de rodillas)	kneeling)
Cristóforo gatilló el misal	Cristóforo triggered the missal
(Christopher disparó el misil)	(Christopher fired the missile)
dijo a sus pares	said to his peers
(murmuró a sus secuaces)	(whispered to his followers)
coño	coño
(fuck)	(fuck)
ved aquí nuevos mundos	see here new worlds
(ved aquí estos inmundos)	(see here these unwashed)
quedáoslos	keep them
(saqueadlos)	(sack them)
por Dios y Nuestra Reina	for God and our Queen

(por Dios y Nuestra Reina)
AMÉN
(OMEN)

(for God and our Queen)
AMEN
(OMEN)

(Thénon, 1987, 27-28)

The very title of Thénon's poem broaches humorously the problematic issue of difference *within* as opposed to the more conventional difference *between* languages. However many millions the United Nations might spend on the provision of simultaneous translation, its peace-making or peace-keeping services will always founder amidst the kind of pious idealism or melting pot Utopianism encapsulated by, but not restricted to, the Rubén Darío epigraph. Seldom will a rhyme be so ironized as when *eslabona/anglosajona [links/Anglo-Saxon]*, read retrospectively and *after* Thénon's text, rattle out, in (un)chained melodrama, the bond(age) of brotherhood links. Here, the South-to-North "chain" metaphor is no less prone to a solution-cum-pollution, cure-cum-poison reading than is any *pharmakon*. For Thénon's poem undoes many a familiar metaphysics. Not least a time-honoured adoptive practice whereby the Nicaraguan Darío is appropriated as honorary Argentine; whereby over-awareness of cultural difference struggles with under-bewareness of dependency; wherein a high-serious tradition of Buenos Aires *literati* resistance to the condescendingly deemed "facile" word-play of such as *Ova completa* is contestatorily pastiched by Thénon's intervention. [3] The sacrosanct territory of Borges's own meditation on *non*-simultaneous Spanish-to-Spanish translation, in "Pierre Menard, Author of the Quixote", is revisited. Here, in what effectively operates as "Margaret Thatcher, Author of The Conquest", the precursor Columbus cannot be (agonically) engaged with... without excess. An excess of history and an excess of language. The official version will ever be shadowed by a parenthetic (trace of) supplementarity.

A *traduttore/traditore* view of translating as traducing need not be confined to language; the question of history as repetition, as action replay, is posed only to be deposed; "source" is mined only to be undermined; "target" will be gauged by missal *and* missile... intertextuality cum infra-red brutality. Playing the translation game, Thénon's poem indulges an illusory binary of past *versus* present, 1492 *versus* 1982, (West-seeking) aetiology *versus* (heat-seeking) teleology. It is as if the brackets which represent, visually, the simultaneous

[3] *Ova completa* is Thénon's spoof on the necessary incompleteness of any and all *Obra completa* or *Complete Works*. Or of any and all translation.

246

translator's version were, auditively, earphones conveying the message of a constant, and sardonic, interference.

"Cristóforo", linguistically and culturally foreign to the Spanish ear – Genoese commoner in spite of the Greek grandeur of his name's etymology – might retrospectively be interpreted as the Bearer of Christ to the New World though, to the pretentious contemporaries of the court of Ferdinand and Isabel, the *Reyes Católicos*, he was but the importunately supplicant son of a wool-weaver... only much later to be Agnus-deified. (Crackling through the earphones come the interfering obscenities: on the make via "lana"/"lucre"; but not scoring via "sin cardar"/ "without *screwing*"?) The historic casting of the anchor of Discovery from the southern Spanish port of Palos de Moguer echoes excessively (clenched in the fist is the sword-cross staff of the Conquistador). Lest we forget Enterprise Culture, the bonds no less of 1492 than of 1982, and should the near-equivalent Isabeline/Elizabethan (II) coincidences not suffice, the Christ-bearer impresario must serve Her Catholic Majesty with both goodness and bounty... never forgetting a courtier's syntax. The *logos* of persuasion in the Windsor-once-Saxe-Coburg Gothic transference is multiply scrambled. H. R. H. The Princess Lilibet is infantilized, in echo of the Infanta Chabela (=diminutive of Isabel), persuaded to pledge the seal of Royal Appointment, the Crown-pawned conversion of HM fleet at the diktat of the all-consuming military Logistics of the Falklands War Effort. A monetarist's bargain struck over a cheap me(t)al in a "figón"/"eating-house"? By smooth tonguing (con-verso/with-verse)? Conversely, background noise might be un-jammed... Blumenthal, persecuted, exterminated by fifteenth-century Spaniards and twentieth-century Germans (or Argentines) alike, but never wholly expellable, or silenced. Is *con-verso* the Jew trans-ported, rather than integrally converted?... And, by the way, was Colombus himself a New Christian? The propaganda "pure blooded" line(age) of *limpieza de sangre* – genuine dynasty or not – intermingles RHesus/Royal Highness with the negative factor guaranteed to spill New World blood or, in a Churchillian rhetoric revamped for the Task Force of Albion's Expedition to the South Atlantic, the "blood, sweat and tears" of an Antipodean adventurism. Shall "we" always fight them on the beaches... whatever the cost?

And so, to sea (and sew to see the officers' braid? Press-studded by the press-ganged?). Old time-spans of months on board and the archaism "yantar", "to dine", recall the first voyage of Colombus, some ten weeks of unrelenting flat(Earth)ness with nothing to ingest but solitude and air. The proximity of oxymoron to oxygen – in echo of the expression "comer aire"/"to starve" – encapsulates the sharp-dull ache of the epic (but, for the near mutinous hungry sailors, the unrelenting) failure to reach the Indies by sailing West. For the "Brits", nearly five centuries on, the speedier expeditionary rhythm cannot disguise the chewing monotony. For them, separation from home means no (trace of) Sunday roast with the Yorkshire pudding, let alone the (difference of) beefing about Mrs Thatcher's "enemy within", the Yorkshire miners – only *The Sun*-style (supplement of) penguin-stereotyping... "10 Things You Didn't Know About the Argies".

The operation of worrying linguistic excess, up to this point in Thénon's poem, has made any repeat-call "to get back to history" but a reminder that the discourse of history, too, comes laden with between-the-lines reading possibilities. For the textualizing of the climactic event of the *annus mirabilis* is framed thus: "one of them cried land/(none of them cried thálassa)". What access can there be to tone, other than through the supplementarity of a saturated translation? The dry relief of arrival at the *terra incognita* of the Other finds expression always against the intertext of linguistic and, here, of historico-literary difference. Before the encounter with, fear of, the Other can turn into xenophobia, Xenophon-through-earphone intrudes in a (quasi-)simultaneous trans-lation. *Thálassa!* – cry of blissful return homewards, from Mesopotamia to "civilization" of war-weary Greeks – is the crafty classicist Susana Thénon's own oxymoronic landfall-seaview reminiscence of *Anabasis* (401BC) – inverted pre-figuration of the poem's doubled "a.D." basis.

Written dates now perform in excessive relation one to the other, highlighting the limitations of the frame of history. *Un*repeatability, *un*translatability, allows particular perceptions of political events to resist such blanket rallying calls to imperial adventurism as that of a Churchill-echoing Iron Lady of 1982. The "a.D." repetition has acquired, via the covert classical B.C. precursor text, not only a historical comparison but also, with renewed emphasis, a religious difference. An Athenian nationalism under reconstruction was the backcloth to the expedition of Xenophon, "one of the 'Ten Thousand Greeks' who went to Asia to seek their fortune, unaware till it was too late to withdraw that Cyrus meant to win the Persian empire by a blow directed deep into its heart". [4] Any "unawareness" on the part of the *conquistadores* is no less open to interrogation as "disembarked" becomes "trod". Four hundred

---

[4] Thénon held a Chair of Classics at the University of Buenos Aires. For a fuller understanding of her play with *Anabasis*, see *Encyclopaedia Britannica*, 1963, vol. 23, 836.

and ninety years on, the effect of historical accuracy and objectivity in the representation of Discovery is undermined by the echoing tread of Christendom's inseparably colonizing-proselytizing mission. For lurking in the background is "la Católica"/"la Logística", the Church Militant, ever-crushing underfoot the serpent of an eternally sinful Edenic barbarism. Thénon's poem also feeds on oxymoron.

The archetypal primal scene of North-South/East-West encounter is re-enacted in rapid-fire rhythms as the tread-mark of post-Freudian as well as of post-colonial imprinting is trans-scribed. Christopher Colombus, Bernal Díaz del Castillo, Pero Vaz da Caminha, scriptors all, shadow the official résumé: hierarchy in suspense, raw nakedness, religious submission (belatedly: Argentine guv'nors on tenterhooks, stripped, on their knees). And the phantom-scribes in the translation from Santo Domingo to Port Stanley? "Our" own correspondents. Un-author-ized versions. An excess of history, too, is revealed in the surplus moral (re-)armament of the missal (missile). Christ is borne on the trace(r)-bullet-points of binary bearers, preached (hissed) to peers (or followers)... apostles all. And who are these disciples to punish? The expletive, somewhat unusually in the documenting of history, remains *un*deleted in official and unofficial versions. Translation intervenes only as an intensifier. Force, contempt, sex, obscenity... transgression. Behold new worlds/Go forth and multiply possession. (Behold these unwashed "Argies"/*Gotcha!*).

The intonation would appear to be univocal as the text approaches its Vespers. For the only time, the earphone parentheses apparently contain the self-same locution in the translation as in the original: "for God and Our Queen" (encore). Faithful? Where linguistic and historical diff-erences disappear is in *cliché*, language emptied of particularity, the imprecation which carries us once more onto the breach of all nations at war. Fateful? Or avoidable as soon as differential reading is allowed? For the boomed imperative of faith-*full* resignation "AMÉN" faces faith-*less* future when translated with the inclusion of a supplementarity borrowed, perhaps, from the opening line of the epigraph: "to move towards what is still to come". If the *question* of history, if the *question* of language, if all *questions* of representation are, indeed, always already excessive with respect to histories, languages, and representations, then the "So be it" of Church and State conformity will always be the least digestible of imperatives. The slippage from "AMÉN" to "(OMEN)" supplements South-to-North vassalage with a warning of resistance to all unquestioned assumptions regarding translation and translatability. In the politicization of reading practices, the necessary supplementarities, in any case, are to be traced not only between the lines and between the cultures, but also *within*. The claim that Susana Thénon's poem confronts *intra*-colonialism inseparably from its uncompounded progenitor needs be re-addressed now only by re-posing the question of the repeatability of "AMÉN" within Latin America. So be it?

To any and every Latin American who has said, since 1982, "What *we* need is a Margaret Thatcher", the poem pleads "coño" (and only in brackets "(fuck)" for the Anglo-Saxons who never listen until it suits them). For in the wings, always opportunist, are the listeners – on the inside as well as on the outside – who will (mis)interpret the plea, hear differently the same words. For those Latin Americans who still regard their own history and language as subordinate to their *empresa* – Cristóforos? – prayer will easily be (mis)read as imprecation, invitation... "(see here these unwashed)" [...] "(sack them)" [...] "(OMEN)". From *within*, too, comes the subversion, the ominous call for outside intervention by those who have always (ever ready) been poised to pounce, and to sack – "(fuck)".

A discredited counterpoint of West-East effects will now have already been represented by scenes chosen from that England conceived of as "back home" in the roast-beef-and-Yorkshire-pudding imaginary of the 1982 Task Force. For the wounded deprived of a place in the front ranks of triumphalism at the October Falklands Victory Parade held in central London, being hidden away as the "negative factor" surplus to representation of the Nation, here was perhaps an unintended opportunity. A chance to ponder their exclusion from the (national) front-row as being strangely in keeping with the relegated role of millions of other Britons? One function of this coda might be to extend a belated but open invitation to all, to reflect again, if not always, on the internal differences at work *within* the "United" Kingdom just before and, after, intensified, the so-called external Malvinas conflict was over. For those in Britain who ask why so little poetry of war has derived from the Falklands-Malvinas conflict, the present analysis can provide only indirect answers. When we find an early counterpart in English to both the texts of the Argentine poets and to literary representations of the plight of "los chicos de la guerra", the voice comes from a site and from a history of very particular enunciation. "Back home" is neither England nor, ostensibly, is it at one with, or even in, a "united" realm.

A dis-United Kingdom

In his "'Shaman of shifting form': Tony Conran and Welsh *barddas*", the poet M. Wynne Thomas suggests that "Conran's greatest success in this 'freer' mode [...] is probably his elegy (or synthetic *awdl*) for the Welsh soldiers who died at Bluff Cove". [5] He concludes:

> The Welsh are appropriately among the last to fall victim to that vision of British Empire to which they have so eagerly subscribed ever since Tudor times, suppressing in the process all memory of their own separate history, that stretches back to the period of the *Gododdin* [...] Conran's own unremittingly dark elegy brings Aneirin's ancient poem tangentially to bear on the Welsh present, to powerful tragic effect. The young soldiers (addressed as "Gentlemen all", in a quint-essentially English turn of phrase used here with a combination of irony and sincerity) are represented as the victims not only of Margaret Thatcher's aggressive chauvinism but also of a Welsh "nation" culpably besotted with the Britishness that has left it economically devastated [...] fertile ground for military recruitment. (Wynne Thomas, 1995, 98-9)

In the poem in question, Tony Conran's exploiting of the ironies of the sixth-century epigraph from an epic precedent is both more harshly focused and structurally elaborated than was Thénon's scathing mockery of Rubén Darío's ingenuous pan-Americanism:

Elegy for the Welsh Dead, in the Falkland Islands, 1982

> *Gwyr a aeth Gatraeth oedd ffraeth eu ilu.*
> *Glasfedd eu hancwyn, a gwenwyn fu.*
> *— Y Gododdin (6th century)*

(Men went to Catraeth, keen was their company.
They were fed on fresh mead, and it proved poison.)

[5] To be precise, forty-eight men died aboard the Landing Ship Logistics RFA *Sir Galahad* when it was bombed at 17.10Z hours on 8 June 1982 by three Skyhawk 4B fighter aircraft from the Argentine Air Force's 5th Fighter Group based at mainland Río Gallegos. Nearby *Sir Galahad* her sister ship, the RFA *Sir Tristram*, was also bombed by another two Skyhawks. This caused another two fatalities. Included in the dead on *Sir Galahad* were thirty-two Guardsmen and non-commissioned officers of 1st Battalion, Welsh Guards. A total of 135 wounded were treated in three hours by twenty-seven men of 16 Field Ambulance's Advanced Dressing Station at Fitzroy. The two vessels were not at Bluff Cove, but anchored five kilometres due south in Port Pleasant near Fitzroy settlement.

Men went to Catraeth. The luxury liner
For three weeks feasted them.

They remembered easy ovations,
Our boys, splendid in courage.
For three weeks the albatross roads,
Passwords of dolphin and petrel,
Practised their obedience
Where the killer whales gathered,
Where the monotonous seas yelped.
Though they went to church with their standards
Raw death has them garnished.

Men went to Catraeth. The Malvinas
Of their destiny greeted them strangely,
Instead of affection there was coldness,
Splintering iron and the icy sea,
Mud and the wind's malevolent satire.
They stood nonplussed in the bomb's indictment.

Malcolm Wigley of Connah's Quay. Did his helm
Ride high in the war-line?
Did he drink enough mead for that journey?
The desolated shores of Tegeingl,
Did they pig this steel that destroyed him?
The Dee runs silent beside empty foundries.
The way of the wind and the rain is adamant.

Clifford Elley of Pontypridd. Doubtless he feasted.
He went to Catraeth with a bold heart.
He was used to valleys. The shadow held him.
The staff and the fasces of tribunes betrayed him.
With the oil of our virtue we have anointed
His head, in the presence of foes.

Phillip Sweet of Cwmback. Was he shy before girls?
He exposes himself now to the hags, the glance
Of the loose-fleshed whores, the deaths
That congregate like gulls on garbage.
His sword flashed in the wastes of nightmare.

Russell Carlisle of Rhuthun. Men of the North
Mourn Rhegd's son in the castellated vale.
His nodding charger neighed for the battle.
Uplifted hooves pawed at the lightning.
Now he lies down. Under the air he is dead.

Men went to Catraeth. Of the forty-three
Certainly Tony Jones of Carmarthen was brave.
What did it matter, steel in the heart?
Shrapnel is faithful now. His shroud is frost.

With the dawn men went. Those forty-three,
Gentlemen all, from the streets and byways of Wales,
Dragons of Aberdare, Denbigh and Neath –
Figment of empire, whore's honour, held them.
Forty-three at Catraeth died for our dregs.

(Conran, in Abse, 1997, 155-6)

The threads of difference within, on the British side, are unwoven and re-knitted in a grim tapestry of wars separated less by kind than by the centuries and by vernaculars. If there is any, however rickety, unifying frame, it can only derive from a Welshness in-the-making... and, plaintively, in simultaneous destruction. For what keeps on coming, and coming, is that cyclical move from valley and mountain and quayside and cawl; to poisoned mead and to Catraeth – or, in this case, Port Pleasant – as carrion. The modern poem comes in English to its Welsh precursor of Aneirin's *Y Gododdin* much as Borges's text in Spanish revisited that of Wilfred Owen's English. Always and already at work is resistance to any hegemony of language or of history, or of dominance imposed on a cultural expression ever-struggling to remind the present of its betrayed but still differential past. The poem's text does not render explicit the political dilemma of the many in Wales who, in 1982, could but show reluctance to enter military conflict against an Argentina which, still, and famously, harboured the Welsh settlements, and Welsh-speaking communities, of Patagonia. [6]

The carding and weaving of the Thénon and Conran texts, and the dye of Borges and of Owen with which they are tinted, are but coincidental, never accidental effects. In his archiving of First World War poetry's resources, Jon Silkin catalogues patriotic cant; angry prophecy; compassion; desire for change (Silkin, 1981, 30-34). Parallels beckon; notes of triumphalism, celebration, feasting. Whether the reference to

---

[6] Tony Conran wrote in a letter to me: "I'm quite excited at the idea of people reading me in Argentina. My grandfather was an engineer there and my father was born, I think, in Mendoza. So it really is the land of my Fathers! It's difficult to know whether that has anything to do with the poem, but probably it gave an added feeling to the mix."

the incited euphoria of war preparations be sixth-century Welsh, fifteenth-century Spanish, or early *and* late twentieth-century British, it is the "easy ovations" that are most facilely remembered. Conran's juxtaposition of "luxury" and "feast" with the chill reality of a South Atlantic "raw death" as "garnish" is (strange meeting!) close to Thénon's discursive fauna. For her parodic "penguins", read Conran's subversive shift from Romantic albatross routes – "The Rime of the Ancient Mariner" – via all too transparent military coding ("Passwords of dolphin and petrel") to the most realistic metaphor of the danger of the South Atlantic for the obedient men who, again, went to Catraeth: the near-homonym echoes starkly... "killer W(h)ales". Again, as in Thénon's "missal"/"missile" play, the formidable alliance of Church and Military both raises and sets the (ethical?) "standards". If one function of religion is to prepare men for it, neither garb nor garnish can ever disguise the most "raw" of death's realities.

A recurring feature of the Owen, the Borges and now the Conran treatment of war in poetry is their keynote: "strange"; "extraña"; "strangely". The unavoidable sense of bewilderment encapsulated most explicitly by Borges's line "The story I tell happened in a time we cannot understand" has been shown, already, to be but one, perhaps the simplest, mode of defamiliarization, or literature's "making strange". Thénon, by dinningly repeating consecutive translations of political and cultural untranslatabilities, and by juxtaposing Hispanic and Anglo-Saxon inherited imperial paradigms, made a mockery of the very notion of simultaneity, of shared perceptions, of any common humanity in such *un*strange meetings as the coming together of imperial *clichés*. The strategy of Conran is almost identical to that of Borges, the naming not of parts, but of names. The "making strange", in both cases, becomes inseparable from a "making familiar". For Borges, emblematic Juan and John, for Conran, plural reality effects akin to the cenotaph's, the memorial's, naming of the dead, and of the home and circumstance, the place and time of each. To Silkin's catalogue might be added a perhaps too obvious resource of any poetry of war: testimony.

At the funeral of Pablo Neruda, in September 1973, only days after the murder of his friend and colleague, the Chilean President Salvador Allende, the people turned out – facing great danger in the guise of police brutality, military detention and torture, the "raw" reality of instant disappearance. No less raw was the chant they voiced in dialogic unison. As some shouted out the name "Pablo Neruda" yet others chorused: "Presente, presente". Death not as absence but, in the rejoicing over a name, names, as a forcefully reconstituted presence. Nothing new, hardly original, and certainly a resource drawn upon by the Argentine Mothers of the Plaza de Mayo, but a technique that the Conran poem exploits so that the named *and* numbered Welsh dead ("forty three" of them)[7] can never be wholly excluded from history; need not be relegated as "excessive" to the needs of another Nation's capital Victory Parade... as was to be the lot of their surviving, wounded, or disfigured fellow combatants.

Malcolm Wigley of Connah's Quay. Present. Clifford Elley of Pontypridd. Present. Phillip Sweet of Cwmback. Present. Russell Carlisle of Ruthun. Present. Tony Jones of Carmarthen. Present... Yet it is also the past that is reconstructed by Conran's poem. For the naming function stretches back: "Men of the North/Mourn Rhegd's son in the castellated vale" re-broaches, before the return to a refrained "Men went to Catraeth", the historic legacy of betrayal with which the poem began. *Y Goddodin*'s epic Welsh language is borne elegiacally in echo through the place names of Tegeingl, Pontypridd, Cwmback, Ruthun, Carmarthen, Aberdare, Denbigh, and Neath, until transferred to "The Malvinas [note Conran's chosen version of the Islands' name] of their destiny" by "Those forty-three/Gentlemen all" – dragons caught up in, and out, by that deadly myth, "Figment of empire". Borges bridled. Thénon lampooned. Conran sneers. The excessive relationship of myth to history can be seen to operate in a further, perhaps more complex process of naming. The Conran poem does not leap from the sixth to the twentieth century in an undifferentiated scream of patriotism. National difference and cultural identities are explored in complex social layers whereby the politics that spawned the Falklands War effort are deemed to be inseparable from the names of men and of communities so fatally affected: "The desolated shores of Tegeingl,/Did they pig this steel that destroyed him?/The Dee runs silent beside empty foundries./The way of the wind and the rain is adamant."

As adamant as Maggie and "not for turning"; either in the de-industrialization of North Wales (and much of the rest of a dis-United Kingdom) or in the steadfast dispatching of the British Task Force. In the political economy of the poem, an infrastructure of elegy (in clear echo of the Scottish precursor Hamish Henderson's *Elegies for the Dead in Cyrenaica*, written 1942-7, published 1948)[8] can but defer explorations

---

[7] In addition to the thirty-two Welshmen who died on board RFA *Sir Galahad* another eleven were killed elsewhere in the war.

[8] I am indebted to Macdonald Daly for this observation.

of such bases as the close economic ties which have long, and tightly, bound Argentina to the UK. An exchange market of import and export is not to be confined to transferrable currencies of gold and silver, bank notes and coinage. The baser metals shuttle back and forth, too, whether in the form of railway lines or bullets. "But what did it matter?" Steel in the heart (of Argentina). Or shrapnel?

Any unlayering of the Conran poem can be no less indicting in terms of ideologies. "Doubtless he [Clifford Elley of Pontypridd] feasted" – but, when he is snatched from the valleys, into "the presence of foes", "the shadow [which] held him" was all too identifiable. Insignia of "the staff and the fasces of tribunes" refer not only, directly, to the Roman imperial legacy of ever-westward conquest but also, obliquely, to the General Staff and the Galtieri Fascism in which "our virtue" has embroiled him. He, no less than the "Phillip Sweet of Cwmback [...] shy before girls", has been afforded little time to pass from a dance-hall dilatoriness of late adolescence to the rapid-fire reel with the strumpets of death who now swoop over him and "congregate like gulls on garbage". No hint here of "once more onto the breach", rather, as ever, onto the dump, unburied, dishonoured – "under the air he is dead". No Borges decorum of sleeping, eternally, with the enemy, beneath the snow, is given to these "Gentlemen, all, from the streets and byways of Wales". Their "shroud is frost". Snow, frost... "the wind and the rain". Will the poem come to rest elementally, leaving history to languish in the mists, and the myth, of inexplicable, unresolved time? Not so for Conran. A configuration of "loose-fleshed whores", of "Gentlemen", of "honour", of "steel in the heart", is denounced as but a figment. "Empire/whore"... the signature is become singular; and, legible, the hand is that of the Iron Lady. The "mead" of 1982 is the poisoned chalice of "our [late imperialist] dregs". Yet, however adamant, elemental, no regime survives forever. The Conran poem *performs* the song of the wind and the rain, not as "my Lady's fool". For, like the Shakespearean precursor it echoes, it is still the song of Feste, "the wisest fool of all".

It breaks two to tangle

Performing a song of the River Plate, one of Borges's last poems braves the iciest winter of a discontent, a prescience of death which invades even sleep, turning dream into nightmare. No decorum now, only certitude; and an immediacy which starkly identifies the bookish dreamer, through a subjective correlative, with the man-of-action. A younger Borges had often poeticized the ambivalent relation of literature to history in mock-heroic associations of writer-fighter. In the twilight of this late *milonga*, an aged Borges engages directly, in the first person, with "glacial isles" unnamed though unmistakable:

Milonga del muerto	Milonga of the Dead Man
Lo he soñado en esta casa entre paredes y puertas. Dios les permite a los hombres soñar cosas que son ciertas.	I have dreamed him in this house amidst walls and doors. God permits men to dream things which are true.
Lo he soñado mar afuera en unas islas glaciales. Que nos digan lo demás la tumba y los hospitales.	I dreamed him out at sea on some glacial isles. Let the tomb and hospitals tell us the rest.
Una de tantas provincias del interior fue su tierra. (No conviene que se sepa que muere gente en la guerra.)	One of so many provinces of the interior was his land. (It is better not to know that people die in war.)
Lo sacaron del cuartel, le pusieron en las manos las armas y lo mandaron a morir con sus hermanos. Se obró con suma prudencia, se habló de un modo prolijo. Les entregaron a un tiempo el rifle y el crucifijo. Oyó las vanas arengas de los vanos generales. Vio lo que nunca había visto, la sangre en los arenales.	They took him out of the barracks, they put in his hands the weapons and they ordered him to die with his brothers. It was done with consummate prudence, it was spoken with due propriety. They gave him at the same time the rifle and the crucifix. He heard the vain harangues of the vain generals. He saw what he had never seen, blood on the sands.
Oyó vivas y oyó mueras, oyó el clamor de la gente. El sólo quería saber si era o si no era valiente.	He heard shouts of "Long live!" and "Die!", he heard the people's clamour. He only wanted to know if he was or wasn't brave.
Lo supo en aquel momento en que le entraba la herida. Se dijo *No tuve miedo* cuando lo dejó la vida.	He knew it the moment the wound pierced him. He said to himself *I wasn't afraid* when life left him.
Su muerte fue una secreta	His death was a secret

victoria. Nadie se asombre	victory. Let no one wonder
de que me dé envidia y pena	that I feel envy and pity
el destino de aquel hombre.	at the fate of that man.

(Borges, 1989, 497-98)

The tactic Borges indulges is that of rendering explicit, exemplifying, and then subverting, the conventionality of the genre of war poetry. By inserting into the *milonga* form what will emerge as a detailed narrative of a young soldier's rapid-fire translation from barracks to tomb via battlefield and hospital, his strategy is one of localizing in an apparently sentimental style an easily performable song of regret. "Milonga del muerto" assumes the simplest of popular song forms (in this case the even-verse assonanced octosyllabic quatrains of the traditional Buenos Aires or *porteño* lament with guitar accompaniment) whilst indulging both the generic protest and a rather more unusual formal ploy. As a poem (but not as a song) Borges's *milonga* can be seen (but not heard) to be constructed around a bracketed statement of the socially (im)permissible. The political expediency and the historical recording of wars in the late-twentieth century were calculably informed by statistics of the number of body bags likely to be used in a given conflict. The impossibility of keeping the reality of death from the public has been highlighted in the Vietnam and, in hi-tech vividness, the Gulf and Iraq Wars. "Calculated acceptable losses" do not form part of what is disclosable in public or in private in this instance: "(It is better not to know/that people die in war.)"

A political convention of keeping apart the military reality and the broadcast representations of heroic soldiering is paralleled by a poetic distancing effect. The opening insertion into a personal dream of an archetypal story of bravery and eventual death under fire is double-edged. The dream which is not a dream functions as a mode of indirection whereby the social convention or a political expediency of discretion in the reporting of war is almost at once to be blown apart, not least by the ironically immediate *deus ex machina* dispensation which the poem's third and fourth lines permit in a Supreme Commander's "lifting", as it were, of reporting restrictions. What follows the crafty avoidance-of-censorship manoeuvre could hardly be a starker, a less restrained, account of the cynical incompetence of "the vain generals" of Argentina's misadventure in "some glacial isles". For six quatrains, any niceties, any fuller hospital reports, or tomb-stone inscriptions – let alone official versions – are set aside in favour of documented facts, preterite in tense and, in effect, getting over and done with that narrative which had entered the national imaginary and those necessary desires of the collective psyche. Worrying excess in the getting back to history is carefully reduced to a minimum, but that very minimum operates strongly as a supplement to dream. The poem ends by turning to effect the excess of yet another, always inadequate, narration of an individual's violent death, a catalogue of barracks-to-trench action familiar from Owen to Conran.

It will be recalled that Juan López and John Ward were not allowed what I termed an infamous loss of personal identity whereby they are turned into "The Unknown Soldier". In the case of the *milonga*'s soldier, too, though he is unnamed, a relation of encounter without othering is subtly constructed. At the level of historical verisimilitude, the circumstances of his military service and premature death come to constitute a reality effect. But "I have dreamed him" is an opening and, it should now be stressed, a closing device which situates the (inter)action on a psychic as much as on any specifically glacial, insular, or other battlefield. The ethical restraint which informed Borges's technical distancing from Wilfred Owen's first-hand experience of combat is here dropped. In the circular ruins of his first-person dream-narrative, the poetic effect of self-other projection and identification is poignantly advanced in the last ten lines of the *milonga*. Up to this point, the dreamed conscript has been granted no attributes to distinguish him from other young provincial soldiers caught up in and brought down by vainglorious and pious discourses of "the rifle and the crucifix". The device whereby he is given individuality is both ethical and literary, because recognition of his valour derives from the dreamer's projected desire and from an acclamation: "and shall *I* face death without cowardice?"... *moriturus te saluto*? Many times, Borges has revisited Argentine national identity in-the-making, whether linguistically, literarily, or culturally, ever as an open, incomplete process. [9] The borrowing of characteristics from *porteño*, pampa, or provincial differential histories might indeed have prepared his readers for the imprecation of the final quartet of "Milonga del muerto": "Let no one wonder that I feel envy and pity at the fate of that man."

Insertion of a first-person voice operates as a reversion to a strategy which Borges had used in the early years of his poetic production. Here

[9] See especially Borges's short collection *Para las seis cuerdas/For the Six Strings* of 1965. The first of the ten milongas, "Milonga de los hermanos"/"Milonga of the two Brothers", ends on the Cain *versus* Abel note which "Juan López y John Ward" carefully inverts.

the process involves a prefiguration of the subject's own death whereby in sleep, on the vehicle of dream, the persona travels with the recruit to the glacial isles. The potentially excessive metaphor of a shared mortality is counter-balanced by the inseparability of "pity"/"envy", offering a particular re-reading of such a standard response to war (poetry). Here, heroism is embraced... but with sad compassion. I would suggest that the creative voice of the indelibly Argentine *milonga* seeks – not at all paradoxically – to break free of the limiting terms of the framing of national and personal identities. The dialogic relation of writer to fighter, revisited at the very end of Borges's life in the context of the recent Malvinas conflict, again challenges too easy assumptions regarding the interface of the making of history and the writing of its representation. There need be no wonderment at the treatment of the complex interplay of "envy and pity" if we recall the strategic mode whereby the poem of the two Johns dealt with the (un)translatability of a *mediated* self-other relationship. Again, in this *milonga*, the writing operates in excess of a soulful lament, in excess of both self-identification with and difference from the other. Again, a poem resists making capital... in this instance, out of *N*ation.

Returning to questions of cultural difference and of excess, the seemingly restrained discourse of Jorge Luis Borges, responding both to such a European precursor as Wilfred Owen and to certain Argentine canons of literariness, can be said to construe the particularity of any national culture as indissociable from a capacity to read; to read the other as a function of the ability resistantly to read the self. The Susana Thénon and Tony Conran poems are differently excessive. Thénon's rhetoric affronts conservative Argentine good taste. Conran's might just do the same in the United Kingdom, were little Englanders ever to read him. But strange meetings do, occasionally, occur. It is often necessary to translate not only *between* but also *within* cultures; to wage war *in* poetry. But what kind of rhetoric would such poetry be?

Explaining what Gramsci calls a "war of position", but from inside a United Kingdom still striving to come to terms and to texts with the multi-cultural but by no means simultaneous *trans*nation within, Stuart Hall elaborates:

A "war of position" is where you advance on a number of different positions at once [....] The real break comes not from inverting the model but from breaking free of its limiting terms, changing the frame. (Hall, 1983, 56-85)

Whether it is possible to find in poetry of, on, or inspired by the Falklands-Malvinas conflict instances of effective response to the challenge posed by Hall would appear to hinge not so much on the *dulce* as on the *decorum* of the question posed. Referring specifically to the 1982 conflict and its ramifications, Simon Featherstone, in *War Poetry: An Introductory Reader*, confronts the genre's demands and shibboleths head on:

> Of all twentieth-century literatures, war poetry seems in many ways the least open to the intrusion of any kind of literary theory. The direction of much contemporary theory [...] has been towards the divorce of literature and life, and the sign and its referents. But war poems seem to insist on the closeness of writing to often appalling personal experience and confront readers with what the critic Paul Fussell has termed "actual and terrible moral challenges" [...] To do anything other than acknowledge that experience and those challenges can seem recklessly improper [...] Whilst it is clearly true that a reading of war poetry which followed [such as] Baudrillard's approach and did not acknowledge an experimental base would damage the writing and its purposes, the view of war poetry as the expression of extreme experience alone is also limiting. In this reading war poetry is largely separated from the literary and intellectual cultures of the society which produced it and seems to come from what Keith Douglas terms "another place", unaffected by the historical and social forces of peacetime. Its authors then become icons of suffering rather than participants in the complex and changing cultures that preceded, affected and were affected by the wars [...] But in recent years, the political context for reading war poetry and interpreting the popular culture of war has changed, particularly after the Falklands War of 1982. The political shift to the Right after 1979 caused a revelation and revival of nationalist feelings and rhetorics in England, and these found a popular focus in the war with Argentina [...] The triumphalist rhetoric of much of the tabloid press was one obvious manifestation of a reversion to pre-First World-War jingoism. (Featherstone, 1995, 1-2).

Naked "truths"

A comparison of the work of two women, one in Britain, the other, again Thénon, in Argentina, both writing in the mid-'eighties, is enlightening. In a notable poem from her 1985 collection *Standing Female Nude*, Carol Ann Duffy wryly captures both involvement in and distance from the absurd game of a risky war:

Poker in the Falklands with Henry and Jim

We three play poker while outside *the real world*
shrinks to a joker. So. Someone
deals me a queen, face up, and the bets roll.
I keep a straight face up my sleeve and peep
at the ace in the hole. Opposite me

the bearded poet raises on two kings. *In my country*
we do this. But my country sends giant
underwater tanks to massacre and I have
another queen. The queens are in love
with each other and spurn kings, diamonds
or not. A quiet man coughs and deals. Wheels

within wheels within worlds without words.
I get a second ace and raise
my eyebrows imperceptibly. A submarine drones on
amongst dolphins. Fifty and raise you fifty
for *the final card*. The cat is nervous as

Henry tells me any second the room could explode
and we would not know. Jim has three jacks
but I have three queens, two aces and a full house.
Perhaps any moment my full house might explode
though I will not know. Remember
one of us is just about to win. God.
God this is an awful game.

(Duffy, 1985, 54)

The calculated use of italics constitutes an invitation to the reader to
indulge another ploy, another gambit, the construction of a matrix
formed by joining together elements of a micro-poem within the poem:

the real world
In my country
we do this
the final card
God this is an awful game

Performing palimpsestically upon the text of the whole poem, the
emphasized or highlighted words draw attention to the double game
evoked in the title. The condensed, domestic, intimate space of the three
card players is invaded by a dual tension as concentration on the game,
with its raised stakes and the emergence of a potentially winning hand,

also allows the mind to wander towards a parallel reality. At first, the shrinkage of *"the real world"* to the level of "a joker" conveys the lack of seriousness with which a population is able to take an event in a place even the name of which was but vaguely known – shades of Adrian Mole's, "At tea-time I was looking at our world map, but I couldn't see the Falkland Islands anywhere. My mother found them; they were hidden under a crumb of fruitcake" (Townsend, 1982, 189).

The vision of "a queen, face up", however, triggers an expansion of double awareness, of the card and of the sovereign; the game is on. Poker-faced nationalism. As "the bets roll" an image of the mobilized Task Force plumbs the consciousness of a gambler already struggling to retain concentration, floundering amidst mixed metaphors, zeugmas, and emotions in the face of a stake-raising adversary. In repetition, "my country" acquires not strength but prompts incredulity, at the disproportion of "giant" and potential "massacre". As the machinations of the players intensify, as tactics are pondered, the coming together of two realms is captured in "Wheels/within wheels within worlds without words." The queens are not for turning... spurning other powers, whatever the cost.

The compression chamber of the poem takes on the claustrophobia of a submarine prior to engagement with the enemy. The play with "fifty", "fifty" serves both to raise stakes and to suggest the closeness of the outcome anticipated, before *"the final card"* is dealt. Tension is pervasive and nervousness explicit; a cat may look at a Queen and men alike. The realization that "my full house might explode/though I will not know" brings together the multivalent references to game, sovereign space and "underwater tanks" in a textual play that seeks an ironic release. There can only be one winner. Providence? The exclamation, or expletive, "God" leads to nothing more transcendental that the resolution of an explicit admission: *"God this is an awful game"* – explosion of the tension between italics and romans, between worlds one no less real than the other. There is no escape from politics in play. Even for those for whom war seems but a game of words.

Or a game of worlds? Or Poles. For Duffy's sly echo of a long-absorbed (failed but deemed heroic) expedition to Antarctic regions plays with the brinkmanship of facing down the adversary in a risky game of politics. Someone else got there first, but I still want to trump the usurper, have the winning suit, lay down my colours, plant my flag. [10]

---

[10] An echo of Scott's discovery that Roald Amundsen had already planted the flag of Norway.

Captain Scott's 1912 diary entry, "Great God! this is an awful place", had not stopped his adventurism turning him into a national hero; a headline maker.

By 1990, in her collection *The Other Country*, the total absorption of the Falklands conflict, and of the tabloid rhetoric surrounding it, into the political consciousness and, indeed, unconscious of the United Kingdom, is picked up by Duffy in another of her generational markers:

Poet for our Times

I write the headlines for a Daily Paper.
    It's just a knack one's born with all-right-Squire.
    You do not have to be an educator,
    just bang the words down like they're screaming Fire!
    [....]
Cheers. Thing is, you've got to grab attention
    with just one phrase as punters rush on by.
    I've made mistakes too numerous to mention,
    so now we print the buggers inches high.
    [....]
I like to think that I'm a sort of poet
    for our times. My shout. Know what I mean?
    I've got a special talent and I show it
    in punchy haikus featuring the Queen.
    [....]
Of course, these days, there's not the sense of panic
    you got a few years back. What with the box
    et cet. I wish I'd been around when the Titanic
    sank. To headline that, mate, would've been the tops.
    SEE PAGE 3 TODAY GENTS THEY'RE GIGANTIC.
    KINNOCK-BASHER MAGGIE PULLS OUT STOPS.
    [....]
And, yes, I have a dream – make that a scotch, ta –
    that kids will know my headlines off by heart.
    [....]
The poems of the decade . . . Stuff 'em! Gotcha!
    The instant tits and bottom line of art.

(Duffy, 1990, 40)

The enduring poems of the populist 'eighties decade just completed are tongue-in-cheekedly supplanted by the catch-phrases that British kids know off by heart. Before being smothered by page-three titillation ("they're gigantic"), they might just have paused but briefly over the news, on the front page of *The Sun* of Tuesday 4 May 1982, there to glimpse the death notice for three hundred and twenty-three Argentine sailors aboard the cruiser ARA *General Belgrano*: "Gotcha!"[11] Theirs, and Carol Ann Duffy's, were times no longer of their parents', or Sinatra's, nostalgic mock-discretions ("too few to mention") but, brazenly ("mistakes too numerous"), of Kelvin McKenzie's instant reporting, the smash-and-grab journalism of heat-seeking headlines, or an (Exoc) "et cet" (era) of puns in poor taste.[12]

Duffy, in this instance, and in contrast to the integrated preoccupation with the war and personal conflict of her earlier poem, can be seen to be flirting again with the Falklands moment but in very different social circumstances from those, say, of Susana Thénon. The passing reference here gauges the superficial pressure exerted on British culture by the Falklands factor whereas the immediacy of Thénon's reaction, to both the particular Malvinas moment and the general *proceso* effects of the Dirty War, inscribes conflict into the very fabric of her text. Her poetics, too, is a confrontation with a politics of the now: it demands that "a poet for *our* times" be alert also to periods and rhythms past, or very recent, in order to pursue, find, reveal and accuse the guilty. Such poetry, certainly confronting what Fussell termed "actual and terrible moral challenges", and in accordance with Featherstone's reminder of the urgent "closeness of writing to often appalling personal experience", will be not final but phonal: loud; screaming out for justice; baying against impunity:

PUNTO FONAL	PHONAL POINT
(TANGO CON VECTOR CRÍTICO)	(TANGO WITH CRITICAL SLANT)
"la picana en el ropero	"the prod in the wardrobe

[11] The total fatalities from the torpedo attack on the *General Belgrano* by the Royal Navy's nuclear-powered submarine HMS *Conqueror* amounted to thirty percent of the 1,091 ship's company. This total accounted for fifty percent of all Argentine casualties in the Falklands-Malvinas War. Of these, thirty per cent of the fatalities aboard the cruiser were eighteen-year-old conscripts, whilst eighty-four percent died as a direct result of the two torpedoes detonating inside the ship. There were sixty-nine survivors who suffered from hypothermia in their life rafts after abandoning ship, and eighteen died from this condition. One method employed by survivors in an attempt to keep warm in the freezing cold was to urinate on each other. A few hours later, on the same day as the appearance of *The Sun*'s iconic single-word headline, an air-launched AM-39 Exocet missile slammed into the starboard hull of the frigate HMS *Sheffield* to kill twenty of her ship's company and ignite huge internal fires that led to her eventual sinking.
[12] Kelvin McKenzie was editor of *The Sun* newspaper from 1981 to 1993.

todavía está colgada	is still hanging there
nadie en ella amputa nada	no one amputates anything on it
ni hace sus voltios vibrar"	or makes its volts vibrate"

¡ESO ES DECLAMACIÓN!	THAT IS DECLAMATION!

(Thénon, 1987, 47)

President Raúl Alfonsín's first law, a guillotine to prevent military personnel "acting under orders" from having to face due legal processes, was designated *Punto Final*. Amen? Full Stop? Are the instruments of torture, and the memories of torturers, to be hidden away, in the Argentine psyche, as easily as the sadly dormant guitar of the popular tango, "Mi Noche Triste"? [13]

la guitarra en el ropero	the guitar in the wardrobe
todavía está colgada	is still hanging there
nadie en ella canta nada	no one sings anything on it
ni hace sus cuerdas vibrar	or makes its strings vibrate

The play "final"/"fonal" occurs at the intersection of politics and of art, and of the direct ideological and intertextual echo of tango with an unquestioningly conservative and unquestioning society, all-too-readily sucked back into a sentimental but violent solitude of yesteryear and the story of its sad night of the soul. While it can be argued that her word games disrupt masculinist metaphysics, narrow erotics and linear temporality, not least in the very title of the collection *Ova completa*, Thénon's poetry also foregrounds a heightened awareness of the danger inherent in any writing, or any reading, too dependent on the ludics of language. [14] As was the case with Duffy's card-sharp language games in "Poker in the Falklands with Henry and Jim", Thénon is ever prepared to subvert her own practice in order to achieve an effect that is politically the more subversive. [15]

---

[13] From Pascual Contursi's "Mi Noche Triste" of 1915. Carlos Gardel first sang it in 1917.

[14] *Ova completa* plays with the impossibility of plenitude in the very moment that it echoes *Obra completa/Complete works*. The feminist eggs of *Ova* are broken, of necessity, in order to make yet another *hommelette* of self-contained and satisfied man; "Exposing what is mortal and unsure/To all that fortune, death and danger dare/Even for an egg-shell". *Pace*, Hamlet.

[15] Cf. "Women writers are similarly excluded from a canon predicated upon a

Other frontiers, other fronts

Gabriela Nouzeilles and Graciela Montaldo, in a chapter on "State Violence" in *The Argentina Reader: History, Culture, Politics*, look back judiciously, and with no reduced incredulity, twenty years after the Malvinas conflict, at the climate against which Susana Thénon's poetry rails:

> The persecution of political dissidents – which began at least two years before the coup – was institutionalized and expanded to create a systematic killing machine. Scholars have found no easy explanation for the degree of cruelty and indifference to human life shown by the military and its supporters [....] During the eight years of the dictatorship, thousands of people mysteriously "disappeared" at the hands of death squads, which, acting with total impunity, kidnapped union leaders, writers, journalists, students, and political activists. Cultural life was meticulously screened by a censorship committee, and all universities and unions came under government control. Efforts to maintain a repressive security state were complicated by an economic model that generated unemployment, corruption, and inflation [....] The art and literature produced under the dictatorship bear the scars of political brutality. Although some artists openly denounced state violence, others cloaked their opposition in hidden messages of muffled despair [....] In 1982, after six devastating years of dictatorship, the poet Néstor Perlongher catalogued in "Corpses" what remained of a society that had become utterly suffused with death. Just as art provided the tools for protest, it also created a locus of resistance. (Nouzeilles and Montaldo, 2002, 395-6).[16]

When it comes to changing the frame, indeed to declamation, few have confronted that other notorious instrument of torture, homophobia, with the polemical poetic power of Perlongher. His is an overtly critical slant on the repressive consequences of a homophobic Argentina for the psyche both of individual victims or scapegoats and of the nation. Perlongher's position is spelled out in several of his short essays: "All power to Lady Di: Militarism and Anticolonialism in the Malvinas

canon of 'major writers' whose moral and literary development is dependent upon the pressure of war experience on literary sensibility" (Featherstone, 1995, 20).

[16] William Rowe's meticulous rendering into English of "Cadáveres" is reproduced in Nouzeilles and Montaldo, 2002, pp.455-64.

Question" (1982); "The Illusion of Certain Islands" (1983); and "The Desire for Certain Islands" (1985), summarized thus: [17]

> The mere fact that handsome adolescents, in the flower of their youth, may be sacrificed [...] in the name of certain insalubrious islands is reason enough to denounce this sad farce. (Perlongher, 1997a, 179)[18]

Such profound critiques of the way the nation had sought to constitute, project, and protect itself may be seen to be closely related to issues broached thus far. Benjamin Bollig encapsulates the attack Perlongher carries to the repressive demarcators of the national territory as follows:

> Perlongher can be seen therefore in the early 1980s proposing an alternative approach to territory – soldiers as lovers, mobile communities based on desire, porous borders – not only to the *proceso* dictatorship, but also the left-wing opposition to the dictatorship. The key difference, again, is that Perlongher's writing focuses on desire and the social. In his poems and essays, Perlongher uses the concept of nationality to discuss communities united by specific interests, in this case desire, and the social organisations that challenge or oppose them. Furthermore, he uses the concept of territory to present and discuss the places or sites where such a community, perhaps only briefly or as a possibility, may find its very marginalised space. These sites, once acknowledged or recognised in Perlongher's poems, can question the rules for the construction of the nation-state that combat the development of new forms of political communities. (Bollig, 2008, 57)[19]

---

[17] "Todo el poder a Lady Di: Militarismo y anticolonialismo en la cuestión de las Malvinas" (1982); "La ilusión de unas islas" (1983); and "El deseo de unas islas" (1985).

[18] "El solo hecho de que guapos adolescentes, en la flor de edad, sean sacrificados [...] en nombre de unos insalubres islotes, es una razón de sobra para denunciar este triste sainete."

[19] Bollig adds, in his indispensable analysis of the writings of Perlongher: "In 1981, after the publication of *Austria-Hungría* and another of Perlongher's many arrests, this time accompanied by a beating from the Mendoza police, Perlongher went into exile in São Paulo [....] I use the term 'exile' with caution. Perlongher's exit from Argentina was entirely voluntary; he returned on several occasions even before the fall of the military. However, Perlongher's life in Argentina, both as a

In an emblematic poem, "Las tías"/"Aunts" (1985), Perlongher takes up a stance and a point of view wholly different from but complementary to the treatment of sexuality in the poems analysed thus far:

> Yet in the process of ritually dishonouring the Argentinians, did the British raise some uncomfortable questions about their own honour, the credibility of their own claims to (hetero)sexual legitimacy? The homosexual imagery which dominated the popular rhetoric of power and abjection, however ritualised or redundant, brought with it some unsettling truths about the military's own ambivalent relations with and attitudes towards inversion over the ages. Despite its current hostility towards overt homosexuality within its ranks, throughout history the composition of the effective fighting unit has been founded on the military's tolerance, if not active encouragement, of unusually intimate bonds among its members [....] Nor have the military's links with homosexuality been solely confined to the efficient organisation of the combat unit. Among active British pederasts prior to the First World War, "we find soldiers specifically the focus of desire. The Other Ranks of H. M. Brigade of Guards had of course been notoriously employable as sexual objects since early in the nineteenth century, and the first German edition of Symond's *Sexual Inversion* (Leipzig, 1896) contained an appendix, '*Soldatenliebe und Verwandtes*' (The Love of Soldiers and Related Matters), examining the pursuit of soldiers as a well-known special taste". (Fussell, 1975, 279, in Foster, 1999, 139).

Whereas such writers generally deal with homosexuality from the point of view of looking in and looking at the homoerotics and the homophobia of their societies, Perlongher looks back from within a discourse. His framing of conflict occurs at the frontiers of war and sexuality:

Las tías

> y esa mitología de tías solteronas que intercambian los peines grasientos del sobrino en la guerra en la frontera tías que peinan tías

gay man and as a socialist, had been made impossible and untenable by the activities of the police and military in the country [....] The criticism that Perlongher received for his critique of Argentine intellectuals from exile is recounted by Patiño" (Bollig, 2008, 58).

que sin objeto ni destino babas como lamé laxas se oxidan y así "flotan" flotan así, como esos peines que las tías de los muchachos en las guerras limpian desengrasan, depilan sin objeto en los escapularios ese pubis enrollado de un niño que murió en la frontera, con el quepis torcido; y en las fotos las muecas de los niños en el pozo de la frontera entre las balas de la guerra y la mustia mirada de las tías en los peines engrasados y tiesos así las babas que las tías desovan sobre el peine del muchacho que parte hacia la guerra y retoca su jopo y ellas piensan que ese peine engrasado por los pelos del pubis de ese muchacho muerto por las balas de un amor fronterizo guarda incluso los pelos de las manos del muchacho que muerto en la frontera de esa guerra amorosa se tocaba ese jopo; y que los pelos, sucios, de ese muchacho, como un pubis caracoleante en los escapularios, recogidos del baño por la rauda partera, cogidos del bidet, en el momento en que ellos, solitarios, que recuerdan sus tías que murieron en los campos cruzados de la guerra, se retocan los jopos; y las tías que mueren con el peine del muchacho que fue muerto en las garras del vicio fronterizo entre los dientes muerden degustan desdentadas la gomina de los pelos del peine de los chicos que parten a la muerte en la frontera, el vello despeinado.

(Perlongher, 1997b, 82)

Aunts

and that mythology of maiden aunts who interchange the grease-laden combs of the nephew in the war at the frontier aunts who comb aunts who without object or destiny dribbles lax like lamé grow rusty and thus "float" float thus, like those combs that the aunts of the boys in the wars clean take the grease out of, pluck without object on the scapularies that coiled pubis of a boy that died at the frontier, with his kepi askew; and in the photos the grimaces of the boys in the pit of the frontier between the bullets of the war and the musty gaze of the aunts on the greased and stiff combs thus the dribbles that the aunts lay like eggs on the comb of the boy who heads off for the war and again touches his forelock and they think that that comb greased by the pubic hairs of that boy killed by the bullets of a border love even holds the hairs from the hands of the boy who dead at the frontier of that loving war touched that forelock; and that the hairs, dirty, of that boy, like a pubis curling on the scapularies, gathered from the bath by the rushing midwife, taken from the bidet, in the very moment that they, solitary, that their aunts remember that they died in the fields crossed by the war, adjust their forelocks; and the aunts who die with the comb of the boy who was killed in the claws of the border vice between the teeth bite taste toothless the lotion of the hairs of the comb of the boys who set off for death at the border, fuzz unkempt.

The opening words, rendered without an initial capital, suggest a continuum, an intervention into an already existing mythology, rendered pejorative by the dismissive demonstrative "ese"/"that" but echoing, putatively, the "mitologías" of the two precursor war poems by Borges. Whereas Borges had flirted with going transcendental, Perlongher at once goes down; in register, linguistic and social, and in getting quickly to the point.

Like any other mythology, the repository of "Las tías" is there to be exposed, to be penetrated, to have the elements of its social construction identified, isolated, analyzed. And the vehicle of this prose poem in such a process is an unusual confrontation of the elegiac and the abject. The form and the rhythms of a funeral dirge combine with a shuttle treatment of doubled abjection wherein the frontier is both the site of death of young men in war and the locus of lingering attachment to vivid memory of older homosexuals left behind in another border zone.

Perlongher's lyricizing of the "place of aporia [...] at the border [...] the threshold line, or the approach of the other as such" brings his writing into communion with Derrida's seminal meditations on mourning. For "Las tías" says, too, that "there is no singular memory"; that "Ego=ghost"; that "'I am' would mean that 'I am haunted'"; that "wherever there is Ego, *es spukt*, 'it spooks'" (Derrida, 1994, 133). The spectres of war of Perlongher's poem are the *revenants* of an in-betweenness that dare not speak its name amidst the trumpeted grand narrative of intensively processed nationalism. The text whispers its ambivalences in numerous word-plays that an Argentine reader might miss if not attuned to the jargon of a proscribed and perforce closeted world of "floating" shadows; of *tías* "without object or destiny". Deprived of any straight-line logophony of their own, in a society of predominantly monological attachment to a project of war, the "aunts" seek to avoid the literal labelling of their *ego* through repeated if futile attempts to return to where *id* was.

If there is abjection in the act of return, it is characterized not by self-pity but by a transference onto objects spooked and spooking: grease-laden combs, a scapulary, and curled pubic hair, the war photographs that capture the image and the grimace of boys dying at a frontier of the battle but also in the pit of an *entrelugar*, a no-man's land, of "balas" or bullets and the "mustia mirada" or "faded gaze" that fixes on the twisted cap of the legendarily depicted "sleeper in the valley", or "mummy's little boy" inherited through the genre of war poetry. Echoes of Arthur Rimbaud's "Le Dormeur du val" and Fernando Pessoa's "O menino da sua mãe", perhaps, but with a difference; for "menino" read "sobrino", the loaded circumlocution of "nephew" used by the older man when introducing the young soldier-companion in, but not to, a society prepared to pitch boys into trenches if into no other, risky, conflictual, or unsettling position. Especially not the "amor fronterizo" which, when the poem ends, will have been so strongly re-classified as the "vicio fronterizo" as to bring down, too, the *tías* who clutch but the combs of the dead boys. "Frontier" has operated as a transferred epithet in a dual conflict; the Malvinas moment and the claws of an unrelenting anguish, the private struggle of the "campos cruzados" – "crossed" but also cross-over "fields" of battle, zones of lost contact.

A deadly game of solitaire is played out on multiple fronts. Indignities of trench or of bidet are transformed into an unsentimental but affectionate intimacy of a fate shared. Again, Perlongher's is a rare case of poetry into which conflict has entered in the very construction, rather than the mere representation, of war. Internal transformations, such as "un amor fronterizo guarda incluso los pelos de las manos del muchacho"/"a border love even holds the hairs from the hands of the boy", allow memory to re-trigger and perform arousal – always respectfully, tenderly, as "en la frontera de esa guerra amorosa se tocaba ese jopo"/"at the frontier of that loving war touched that forelock". Turning on the play of meaning on the word *jopo*, the forelock, or quiff, or bang, of the hair of the young man's head, in common parlance, another memory is roused. For, in *argot*, as in the Teddy-boy cum Elvis-era equivalent of the D.A., the duck's-arse hairdo, the term evokes, too, the naked buttocks of the young lover lost. [20]

The shifting point of view, the gaze, and the recollection of both the *tías* and the *sobrino*, interchanged, and intermingled, operate in a prolepsis-analepsis relation of intensifying effect. The "vello", the soft hair, the down, of youth, and of affective memory, remains "despeinado",

[20] Cf. the expression "alborotar o explotar el jopo" which plays on and with the multiple connotations of the verbs to excite or to work, to exploit or to explode. Exploding genres, exploding gender roles... The play on "pe[i]ne" and "balas" requires no such elucidation. So come on, coxcombs. You make the balls, I'll fire them.

uncombed, at the poem's end. The force of Perlongher's radical intervention finds no "arbitrary division" in the multivalent conflict. All is left unkempt, dishevelled, loose, undone... and, still, forever, in contrast with the panopticon order of things, seductively, entangled. Rising to whatever challenge, left over or behind, "Las tías" is an equivalent to Susana Thénon's intellectual but no less visceral play; it is Néstor Perlongher's *desova incompleta*.

Ending the patriot game

Writing often from a self-imposed exile in Brazil, Perlongher had sought and, who knows, freed from censorship, found that other, conflictual, or unsettling position patently unavailable at home to the *sobrino argentino* of "Las tías". In contrast, it is less the radical other than the radical othering of the Malvinas War that is taken up, back home, and in the post-conflict. In a traumatized Argentina, a no less haunted voice utters, emblematically, in a 1985 song by Alberto Cortez, lyrics that have endured for a post-conflict generation, and beyond:

A Daniel... un chico de la guerra	To Daniel... a kid of war
A mí los dieciocho	My own eighteen years
me pasaron de largo,	passed me by,
estrenando opiniones,	as I ventured my opinions,
intenciones y cantos.	intentions and songs.
Como todos los chicos,	At that age, like the rest,
con el puño cerrado	with clenched fist
y en las puertas abiertas	I waited at the open doors
el futuro esperando.	of the future.
Al tuyo, bruscamente	Your future was brusquely
te lo desamarraron	set adrift from you
y te hiciste a la niebla	and you set off in the mist
en el mar del espanto.	in the sea of fright.
Encallaron tus sueños... Daniel	They ran your dreams aground... Daniel
en la turba y el barro.	in turf and mud.
Fue la muerte bandera...	Death was a flag...
y la vida un milagro.	and life a miracle.
Lo mío fue distinto... Daniel	My lot was different... Daniel
lo mío no fue nada.	my lot was nothing at all.
Yo no tengo esa sombra...	I do not have the shadow...
que vaga en tu mirada.	that wanders in your gaze.

Mi batalla fue el riesgo
de un machete escondido
y mi pozo de zorro,
un amor y un olvido.
Mi fusil, las pintadas
en los muros vacíos
y el morir por la Patria,
un discurso florido.

Tu excusa de ser hombre:
algo más que el motivo
de la barba y el porte
y el salir con los amigos,
fue volverte habitante... Daniel
de la lluvia y el frío;
asumir el naufragio
con los cinco sentidos.

Mi asunto fue un asunto
de madre preocupada
que no fuera muy tarde
el regreso a la casa.
De domingo a domingo
me peinaba las alas,
sin andar cada jueves
reclamando su alma.

La tuya, sin embargo,
agotaba hasta el alba
las escasas noticias
de las islas lejanas.
Un indicio cualquiera... Daniel
un rumor que saltara,
por pequeño que fuera...
era ya la esperanza.

El tiempo irá trayendo
la amnesia inexorable.
Habrá muchas condenas
y pocos responsables.
Dirán que fue preciso,
dirán, "inevitable",
y al final como siempre
será Dios el culpable.

My battle was the risk
of a hidden exam crib
and my fox-hole
was a love and getting over it.
My rifle was the paintings
on empty walls
and to die for my Country,
meant a flowery speech.

Your excuse for being a man
was more than to show
off your beard, or the adult walk,
or going out with friends,
it was to go and inhabit... Daniel
the rain and the cold;
to embrace shipwreck
with all five of your senses.

For me it was just a case
of a mother worried
that I should get home
not too late.
From Sunday to Sunday
she would smooth my wings,
without spending every Thursday
demanding her soul.

Yet your mother
'til dawn drew on
the scant news
from the distant islands.
Even if it were just a hint... Daniel
any rumour that came,
even if it were small...
for her was still hope.

Time will go on bringing
its inexorable amnesia.
There'll be many condemnations
and few held to account.
They'll say it was essential,
"inevitable", they'll say,
and in the end, as ever,
God will get the blame.

La historia necesita	History needs
en sus escaparates,	to hide in its shopfronts
ocultar el trasfondo	the background
de tanto disparate.	to so much nonsense.
No es tuya la derrota... Daniel	Defeat is not yours... Daniel
no cabe en tu equipaje,	it doesn't fit into your luggage,
¿Acaso las gaviotas...	Are the seagulls perhaps...
otra vez en el aire?	in the air again?
Lo mío fue distinto... Daniel	My lot was different... Daniel
lo mío no fue nada.	my lot was nothing at all.
Yo no tengo esa sombra...	I do not have the shadow
que vaga en tu mirada.	that wanders in your gaze.

(Cortez, 1985)

The label, "the kids of war", used pervasively throughout Argentina in the immediate aftermath of conflict – notably after the 1982 Daniel Kon book of interviews with returning veterans and its sequel, the 1984 Bebe Kamín film *Los chicos de la Guerra* – is individualized and contrastively re-inscribed here. For the one left with nothing is not the dead Daniel but the harrowed and guilt-ridden subject that is his posthumous interlocutor. For Kon, the war had been "the final suicide act of a generation of Argentines. The conscripts who went to the islands were only just coming out of childhood when the 1976 coup took place. From that moment on, they never experienced anything other than social and political repression" (Kon in Burns, 1986, 142).

In the Cortez lyrics, the violent disruption of a teenage humdrum rhythm of posturing, indignation, bravado, and gestural defiance – albeit under the watchful eye of a grooming, ever-protective matriarch – is occasioned not so much or directly by the sudden outbreak of war as by the snatched theft of a future never now to be lived. Literally, in death, for the lost combatant Daniel; no less viscerally, in life, for the out-of-arms companion. "Brusquely" operates on two temporal planes, the immediate and the violently prolonged. The commonplace ciphers of "mist and sea", "turf and mud" locate, as in the case of "Juan López y John Ward", the desolate theatre of the Malvinas as fateful and final resting place. What has no particular place but a ready-made space for habitation is the ghostly shade that wanders in the still present gaze, the final glance exchanged with the surviving friend, of the absent Daniel. That *revenant* accompanies the subject left behind in a piece-by-piece reconstruction of his own battle, his own dysfunctional weaponry, his own engagement with the nauseating "discurso florido" of manipulative politicians then and yet to come, with their sloganizing game of "Patria", all both an echo of the harangue of Borges's *milonga* and an anthem to current emptiness.

Yet guilt knows no vacuum, and flooding in come memories and re-evaluations. Mother's world was religiously ordained, Sunday to Sunday, and timetabled. Not for her that more urgent regime, obliquely but sharply encoded in the "Thursday" reference to those other Argentine mothers of a tortured and absented generation, "las Madres de la Plaza de Mayo", whose weekly march and vigil sought, indeed seeks, long after the moment of individual losses and murders, to "demand the soul" of their loved ones, of their undead but emptied selves and of a haunted nation. Problematically, for the speaker, the "scant news", the "hint", the "rumour", however small, that once held out some hope to every Daniel's mother, are unavailable or, worse, meaningless in the silent, often officially silenced, post-conflict.

In the song's verses, the very concept of future has undergone a transformation from doomed youth to the entombed prospects of a surviving generation. No illusion, grand or otherwise, narrative or lyrical, is left over, barely even conceivable. The fate of the nation is not, and cannot be, consigned to mourning and some vague investment in the nostrum that time heals. A wedge is driven between the window-dressing ("escaparate") demanded by a certain brand of history, or of history-making, and the drivel ("disparate") that hides behind any such posturing or self-re-affirming nationalistic discourse.

Coda: *des-re-rere malvinización*

A *danse macabre* of the early post-conflict yesteryear had cast its phantoms long across the stage of a traumatized Argentina. Some four decades on, it is instructive to take stock of the legacies of what over-simplifying discourses of history, but certainly no poetry of substance, have dubiously dubbed winners and losers of a futile if deadly war. While in other genres, of fiction, theatre, cinema and memoir, the Malvinas-Falklands *topos* has been relentlessly revisited, the lyric it would seem has paused, even in the form of song, exhausted perhaps, or sated, in the intensity of the immediate and subsequent moment.

If prose, fictional or otherwise, has continued to walk towards some "object of desire", some resolution or further controversy, ever at the risk of, say, indulging a locally termed and ardently debated (rackety) Malvinization or, its putative if paradoxical counterpart, the (rickety) Brexiteering adventurism of its posturing former adversary, the poetry addressing the 1982 discordance has come to rest; or "become endlessly what it has just been". Yet it "does not die for having lived". Its lingering, elegiac, rhythms prevail.

...A double spectre is haunting Argentina; and, Albion, too? It took two: "Daniel y yo"... Daniel and I.

References

Abse, Dannie, ed. (1997). *Twentieth Century Anglo-Welsh Poetry.* Bridgend: Seren Books.

Bollig, Benjamin. (2008). *Néstor Perlongher: the Poetic Search for an Argentine Marginal Voice*, Cardiff: University of Wales Press.

Borges, Jorge Luis. (1982a). "Juan López y John Ward". *Clarín*, 26 August.

Borges, Jorge Luis. (1982b). "Juan López and John Ward", translated by Rodolfo Terragno. *The Times*, 18 September.

Borges, Jorge Luis. (1989). "Milonga del muerto". *Los conjurados, Obras completas*. Buenos Aires: Emecé.

Burns, Jimmy. (1986). *The Land that Lost its Heroes: the Falklands, the Post-War and Alfonsín.* London: Bloomsbury.

Cortez, Alberto. (1985). "A Daniel... un chico de la guerra". *Entre líneas.* Available at **www.albertocortez.com/canciones/detail.asp?id =1.**

Derrida, Jacques. (1994). *Specters of Marx: The State of the Debt, the Work of Mourning, and the New International*, trans. Peggy Kamuf. New York: Routledge.

Duffy, Carol Ann. (1985). *Standing Female Nude.* London: Anvil Press.

Duffy, Carol Ann. (1990). *The Other Country.* London: Anvil Press.

Encyclopaedia Britannica. (1963). London: Encyclopedia Britannica.

Featherstone, Simon. (1995). *War Poetry: An Introductory Reader.* London: Routledge.

Foster, Kevin. (1999). *Fighting Fictions: War, Narrative and National Identity.* London: Pluto.

Fussell, Paul. (1975). *The Great War and Modern Memory.* Oxford: Oxford University Press.

Fussell, Paul. (1990). *Killing in Verse and Prose.* London: Bellew Publishing.

Hall, Stuart. (1983). "The Problem of Ideology: Marxism Without Guarantees", in *Marx: A Hundred Years On*, ed. B. Matthews. London: Lawrence and Wishart, 56-85.

Lodge, David, ed. (1972). *Twentieth Century Literary Criticism: a Reader.* Harlow: Longman.

Nouzeilles, Gabriela and Graciela Montaldo, eds. (2002). *The Argentina Reader: History, Culture, Politics*. Durham, N.C.: Duke University Press.

Perlongher, Néstor. (1997a). "Todo el poder a Lady Di: Militarismo y anticolonialismo en la cuestión de las Malvinas" (1982), "La ilusión de unas islas" (1983), and "El deseo de unas islas" (1985). *Prosa plebeya*. Buenos Aires: Ediciones Coluihue.

Perlongher, Néstor. (1997b). "Las tías", *Alambres, Poemas completos 1980-1992*. Barcelona: Seix Barral.

Silkin, Jon, ed. (1981). *The Penguin Book of First World War Poetry*. 2nd ed. Harmondsworth: Penguin.

Thénon, Susana. (1987). *Ova completa*, Buenos Aires: Sudamericana.

Townsend, Sue. (1982). *The Secret Diary of Adrian Mole Aged 13¾*. London: Methuen.

Wynne Thomas, M. (1995). "'Shaman of shifting form': Tony Conran and Welsh *barddas*". *Thirteen Ways of Looking at Tony Conran*, ed. Nigel Jenkins. Cardiff: Welsh Union of Writers, 78-102.

Notes on Contributors and Sources

María Teresa Dalmasso is a Professor and researcher at the National University of Córdoba, Argentina. Her research, conducted from a semiotic perspective, has focused on the study of Argentine social discourse during the period beginning with the return to democracy (1983) and continuing until today. Her works have been based primarily on the analysis of films, journalistic discourses and political discourses and essays. Some of them have been collected in books and other national and international journals. She is director of the Doctorado en Semiótica at the National University of Córdoba. Her "More Than 30 Years after the Malvinas: War in Film and on Television" is taken from *MemoSur/MemoSouth: Memory, Commemoration and Trauma in Post-Dictatorship Argentina and Chile* (London: CCC Press, 2017).

Macdonald Daly was Lecturer in Modern Literature and then Associate Professor in Culture, Film and Media at the University of Nottingham, from which he retired in 2016. He has edited works by H. G. Wells, Elizabeth Gaskell, D. H. Lawrence, Lewis Grassic Gibbon and Ellis Sharp, and co-edited books as various as *Karl Marx and Frederick Engels on Literature and Art* (2006), *The Genres of Post-Conflict Testimonies* (2010) and *"Black and Whites" and Other New Short Stories from Malaysia* (2012). His most recent books are *Reading Radio 4* (Palgrave Macmillan, 2016) and *Politics and the Scottish Language* (New Ventures, 2020).

Uriel Erlich was a sociologist specialising in public policy who taught at the University of Buenos Aires. He was a consultant in the Secretariat for the Malvinas, the Antarctic and the South Atlantic, and advisor to the Commission on Overseas Relations of the Argentine National Chamber of Deputies. He wrote the monograph *Malvinas: soberanía y vida cotidiana* (Villa Maria: Editorial Universitaria de Villa María, 2015) and died in untimely youth shortly after the publication of its English translation, *The Malvinas Question* (London: SPLASH Editions, 2021). "1965-1982: The Negotiations" is taken from that translation.

Lucrecia Escudero Chauvel is an Argentine critic and semiotician, Professor of Theory of Communication at the Université de Lille, France. She has been Chief Editor of *deSignis*, the Journal of the Latin-American Semiotics Federation. Author of *Malvinas, el gran relato: Fuentes y rumores en la información de guerra* (Barcelona: Gedisa, 1996) and

Media Truth: Fiction and Rumors in War News (Toronto: Toronto Semiotic Circle, 1996), she has pioneered research on and analysis of the media and the Falklands-Malvinas conflict. "The Life, Passion and Death of a Rumour" is a chapter from her book *Media Stories in the Falklands-Malvinas Conflict* (Nottingham: CCC Press, 2014).

María Fra Amador Argentine academic and researcher who has taught at the University of Bologna in Buenos Aires, she is a political scientist specializing in anthropology and psychology. She has also worked at national and international level in government affairs and in the development of social guidelines and the organization of indigenous and peasant communities. Her "Malvinas-Falklands Revisited: Prelude, War and Aftermath" was first published in *Post-Conflict Cultures: Rituals of Representation* (London: Zoilus Press, 2006).

Diego García Quiroga is a former Argentine naval officer. In 1982, as a young lieutenant, he took part in the first Argentine landing in Port Stanley. Seriously wounded in the attack on the Governor's House, he was flown back to the mainland and did not recover until many months after the conflict. In 2000, after fulfilling his wish to command the unit with which he had served during the war, he resigned from the Navy with the rank of Commander and left his native country to start a new life. He now lives in Oslo, Norway. He co-edited, with Mike Seear, *Hors de Combat: The Falklands-Malvinas Conflict in Retrospect* (Nottingham: CCC Press, 2009), from which "First In, First Out: A Casualty of War and Life after the Conflict" (here slightly re-titled) has been taken. In this anthology it has been synthesized with most of the later Introduction to his *Letting Go: Stories of the Falkands-Malvinas War* (London: Jetstone, 2016).

Eduardo C. Gerding, MD served in the Argentine Navy, where, amongst other appointments, he was the Chief of the Medical Department of the Batallón de Infantería de Marina de Comando y Apoyo Logístico (Marine Corps Logistic Battalion) and then the 5th Marine Infantry Battalion (1987-1990). Retiring with the rank of Lieutenant-Commander, he became the Medical Coordinator of the Malvinas War Veterans at the Instituto Nacional de Servicios Sociales para Jubilados y Pensionados (INSSJP) and also wrote research articles on naval history for *The Buenos Aires Herald*, *The Southern Cross* and medical articles for the *International Review of the Armed Forces Medical Services*. His "The Anglo-Argentine Post-Conflict Common

Ground: the Combat Veterans' Aftermath" is reprinted from *Hors de Combat: The Falklands-Malvinas Conflict in Retrospect* (Nottingham: CCC Press, 2009).

Bernard McGuirk Emeritus Professor of Romance Literatures and Literary Theory and Director of the Centre for the Study of Post-Conflict Cultures, University of Nottingham, author of many books, including *Falklands-Malvinas: An Unfinished Business* (Seattle: New Ventures, 2007), a groundbreaking study of cultural representations of the 1982 War. This book contains his essay on war poetry reproduced here, to which he has added a new postscript.

Jeremy McTeague served in the Falklands War as 10 Platoon Commander, D Company, 1st Battalion, 7th Duke of Edinburgh's Own Gurkha Rifles. He retired from the Army in 1985 with the rank of Captain, spending the next three years with Barclays Bank International in the UK and South Africa. He then became a lobbyist working for UNITA to bring about an end to the civil war in Angola, and continued to work in the communications field until 2005, when he joined a philanthropic foundation in Geneva. His "Who Cares About the Enemy?" is taken from *Hors de Combat: The Falklands-Malvinas Conflict in Retrospect* (Nottingham: CCC Press, 2009).

José María Ruda (1924-1994) was an Argentine politician and diplomat. His presentation to the United Nations of September 1964 was instrumental in securing resolution 2065 of the United Nations General Assembly (December 1965), which formally recognised a sovereignty dispute between the UK and Argentina concerning the Falklands-Malvinas. His "Statement to the Special Committee on the Situation with regard to the Implementation of the Declaration on the Granting of Independence to Colonial Countries and Peoples, 9 September 1964" has therefore since become a foundational text of modern Argentine diplomacy and negotiation with respect to the Islands. It is reproduced in full (with corrections) from the UN documents archive.

Sandra Savoini holds a Ph.D. in Literature (2009) from the National University of Córdoba, Argentina. She is Professor of Semiotics in the Department of Film and Television, School of Arts, as well as in the Department of Semiotics, the Centre for Advanced Studies, School of Social Sciences, at the National University of Córdoba. The focus of her investigations and publications is the discourse analysis of the media, as well as constructions of social identities through discourse. She has published many chapters and articles in books and journals. Her "Traumas, Memories and Identity Processes" was first published in *MemoSur/MemoSouth: Memory, Commemoration and Trauma in Post-Dictatorship Argentina and Chile* (London: CCC Press, 2017).

Mike Seear Originally commissioned into the Royal Corps of Transport, he transferred to the Light Infantry in 1971. He served in numerous emergency tours of duty in Northern Ireland counter-terrorist operations during that decade and, having been seconded to 1st Battalion, 7th Duke of Edinburgh's Own Gurkha Rifles in March 1982, was Operations and Training Officer in the Falklands War. Serving also in other parts of the UK, Malaysia, Hong Kong, Canada, Germany, USA and Norway, he retired from the British Army in 1988 with the rank of Major to join Scandinavian Airlines in Norway as Head of Security and Emergency Response. Since 1996 he has been a crisis management consultant, and is the author of *With the Gurkhas in the Falklands: A War Journal* (Barnsley: Pen and Sword, 2003) and *Return to Tumbledown: The Falklands-Malvinas War Revisited* (revised ed., Nottingham: CCC Press, 2014). His "First In, First Out" is taken from the latter volume, while his "Seeking 'The Other' in the Post-Conflict, 1982-2006" is reprinted from *Hors de Combat: The Falklands-Malvinas Conflict in Retrospect* (Nottingham: CCC Press, 2009).

Sophie Thonon-Wesfreid French Barrister at the Paris Bar, she has been responsible for bringing to court the case of the disappearance and torture of French citizens during the Argentine and Chilean dictatorships. Her "'Saving the Nation': Post-Conflict from the Point of View of the 'Guilty'" first appeared in *Hors de Combat: The Falklands-Malvinas Conflict in Retrospect* (Nottingham: CCC Press, 2009).

Stuart Urban since 1982 has made highly regarded, award-winning popular TV drama and movies that have sold around the world, winning him two BAFTAS (for *Our Friends in the North* and *An Ungentlemanly Act*). In 1997 he established Cyclops Vision Ltd, producing and directing successful feature and documentary films including cult comedy *Preaching to the Perverted, Against the War* (a collaboration with Harold Pinter), the thriller *Revelation* starring Terence Stamp and Udo Kier and the feature documentary *Tovarisch I Am Not Dead*, released in UK cinemas, winner of several international awards and shortlisted for Britain's Grierson Award. His "On the Making of the film *An*

Ungentlemanly Act" (here slightly retitled) is taken from *Hors de Combat: The Falklands-Malvinas Conflict in Retrospect* (Nottingham: CCC Press, 2009).

Alicia Vaggione is Professor and researcher at the National University of Córdoba, Argentina. Her research focuses mainly on the relationship between culture, body and illness. She has published the book *Literatura/enfermedad. Escrituras sobre SIDA en América Latina* (2014) and a number of journal articles. Her "Returning: The Journey to the Islands in Contemporary Narratives about the Malvinas" is reprinted from *MemoSur/MemoSouth: Memory, Commemoration and Trauma in Post-Dictatorship Argentina and Chile* (London: CCC Press, 2017).

Alan Warsap BM BCh FRCGP Serving in the Royal Army Medical Corps from 1962-1995, his previous appointments included Senior Lecturer in General Practice, Royal Army Medical College, Senior Medical Officer, Royal Military Academy Sandhurst, Director, Army General Practice, and President, 5 Division Permanent Standing Medical Board from 1995-2004. He was the Regimental Medical Officer of 2nd Battalion, the Scots Guards from 1980-84, which included service in the Falklands War and at the Battle of Tumbledown. He retired from the British Army in 1995 with the rank of Brigadier. His "2nd Battalion, the Scots Guards: The Tumbledown Legacy" is reprinted from *Hors de Combat: The Falklands-Malvinas Conflict in Retrospect* (Nottingham: CCC Press, 2009).

Index

14 de junio, lo que nunca se perdió, 201

1892-1982: dos historias de Malvinas, 201

1982, estuvimos ahí, 201

A

Abel, 239-41, 259
aesthetics, 207
Afghanistan, 46
AFP (press agency), 120, 122, 124-25, 127-28, 131-32
Agrupación de Buzos Tácticos, 69, 73, 78-83, 85-86, 100, 102
Agrupación de Comandos Anfibios, 69, 79-83, 85-86, 88, 91, 97
alcoholism, 107
Alfonsín, Raúl, 175-77, 204, 206, 266
Algiers, 68
Allende, Salvador, 254
Amundsen, Roald, 263
An Ungentlemanly Act, 179-200
Anaya, Jorge, 69, 128, 176
Angola, 56, 67
ANSA (press agency), 122, 127, 131-32
Antarctic Treaty, 54
Antarctica, 53-54, 78-79, 143-45, 197, 263
anxiety, 116, 157
AP (press agency), 122, 125, 127, 131
ARA General Belgrano, 20, 137, 154, 176, 201, 265
Argentine Chamber of Commerce, 174
Argentine Chancery, 121
Argentine Federal Court of Justice, 176
Argentine Ministry of Culture, 207
Argentine Ministry of Defence, 123, 205
Argentine Ministry of Foreign Affairs, 144
Argentine National Congress, 168, 177, 219
Army Medical Services, 109
Ascension Island, 105, 131, 136
Astiz, Alfredo, 175-76
Ayr, 157

B

Bahía Blanca, 83
Baker, Dick, 181-82, 188, 193
Baker, Mike, 195
Bandung Conference, 44
Barbados, 47
Battle of the Somme, 108-109
battle stress, 104, 107
Beagle Channel, 78, 83
Beer, Peter, 190-92, 195
Birt, John, 189
blockade, 45, 125, 127, 129-31, 138
Bluff Cove, 21-22, 251
Bolivia, 36, 46, 67
Bonner, Don, 185, 187-90, 194, 198
Borges, Jorge Luis, 179, 239-44, 246, 253-60, 271, 276
Brazil, 36, 46, 132, 273
British Broadcasting Corporation (BBC), 76, 179, 184, 189-90, 196
British Forces Falkland Islands, 190
British Guyana, 45
British Honduras, 45, 52
British Legion, 109
Büsser, Carlos, 98, 187-89, 193, 199

C

Cabo Belgrano, 56

Cain, 240-41, 259
Callaghan, James, 13
Cámpora, Héctor, 45, 47
Carapintadas, 177
Carrington, Peter (Lord), 19, 140
Cartas a Malvinas, 201
cartography, 26
Casa Rosada, 170
Casabé, Daniel, 227
Cavandoli, Carlos, 58
censorship, 216, 258, 267, 273
Centre for Policy Research, 159
*Centro de Producción e
    Investigación Audiovisual*
    (CePIA), 207
Cervantes, Miguel de, 110, 241
Chaga's disease, 160
Cheek, Gerald, 192, 195-96
Chesterton, G. K., 241
Children for Equality and Justice
    against Forgetting and Silence
    (H.I.J.O.S.), 222
Chile, 20, 46, 83, 165, 175, 186, 194,
    198, 254
China, 45, 66
Chomsky, Noam, 147, 149
Chronic Fatigue Syndrome, 158, 166
Churchill, Winston, 149, 247-48
CIA, 68
Clarín, 120-33, 135, 138-39, 168,
    170, 217, 239
Clark, Marvin, 195-96
Clausewitz, Carl von, 71, 82
Clement, Gary, 196
Cognitive Behaviour Therapy, 157
Cold War, 15, 44-45, 66
colonialism, 12, 25, 34-36, 38-43,
    47-53, 55, 142, 148, 174-75, 181,
    183, 244, 249
Columbus, Christopher, 246, 249
Combat Stress, 104, 157
Combatientes, 201, 205, 207
commemoration, 172, 202, 204,
    210, 213-18, 221
Communications Agreement (UK-

Argentina), 54-55, 142
Communism, 45, 66, 147
Comodoro Rivadavia, 19, 70, 73,
    100
comorbid diagnoses, 153, 159
compensation, 108
Conrad, Joseph, 239-41
Conran, Tony, 250-51, 253-56, 259-
    60
conscripts, 153, 155, 168, 205, 259,
    265, 275
*Consejo Asesor de la Televisión
    Digital Terrestre*, 207
Contursi, Pascual, 266
corruption, 66, 173, 178, 240, 242-
    43, 267
Cortez , Alberto, 273
Costa Méndez, Nicanor, 53, 59, 128
Craiglockhart, 107-108
Cuba, 45, 56, 66, 83
Cyprus, 109
Czechoslovakia, 198

D

Daily Record, 133
Daily Telegraph, 76, 122
DAN (press agency), 126
Darío, Rubén, 244, 246, 251
Darwin, 21, 146, 153, 230-31, 234
de Bruno, María Isabel Clausen,
    168-72
de Ipola, Emilio, 219
decolonization, 39, 41, 44, 47, 49-
    50, 142, 146
defence expenditure, 14
Defence White Paper, 143
de-industrialization, 46
democracy, 14, 45, 47, 58, 65-66,
    68, 149, 178, 203-204, 206, 218,
    223, 235
depression, 107, 157, 159-60, 165,
    167
Derrida, Jacques, 271

detention centres, 235

Dhofar, 149

Díaz del Castillo, Bernal, 249

dictatorship, 14, 16, 46-47, 57, 148-
49, 173-78, 180, 187, 201-205,
207-209, 215, 220-22, 224, 227,
234, 236, 267-68

Dieleke, Edgardo, 227

diplomacy, 12-13, 16, 19, 26-29, 34-
35, 38, 45, 48, 50, 53, 57, 59, 71,
121, 127-28, 130, 138, 143-44,
147-49, 185

"Dirty War", 13, 188, 265

disappeared, the, 176, 206, 208-
209, 222, 231, 234-35

discourse, 9-10, 124-26, 133, 139-
40, 202, 204-207, 209-10, 212-
18, 220, 223-24, 227, 239, 242,
248, 254, 259-60, 269, 276

documentary, 201-202, 205, 227-
31, 234, 236

Douglas, 21

Dozo, Lami, 21, 128, 176

"Due Obedience" law, 177

Duffy, Carol Ann, 261, 265

Dunkirk, 179

E

Ealing comedy, 180

Ealing Studios, 190

East Falkland, 20-22, 165, 169

Eastern Malvinas, 28, 33, 35

Eco, Umberto, 121-22, 125, 128-29

education, 54-56

EFE (press agency), 120, 122, 125,
127-28, 131

El Boletín del Centro Naval, 135

El Diario, 126

*El héroe del Monte de dos
Hermanas*, 201

El mismo amor, la misma lluvia,
201

El Palomar, 19

El refugio del olvido, 201

El Rincón, 83

El visitante, 201

Espacio Carta Abierta, 220

esprit de corps, 110

*Estamos ganando, periodismo y
censura en la guerra de
Malvinas*, 201

Etchecolatz, Miguel, 177

European Economic Community
(EEC), 47, 147

ex-combatants, 9, 15, 205, 221-22

existential authority, 153, 158, 160,
167, 172

Exocet missiles, 20-21, 84, 176, 243,
265

Ex-Servicemen's Mental Health
Society, 104

Eye Moving Desensitisation and
Reprocessing (EMDR), 157

F

Fairfield, Jim, 186, 192

Falkand Islands Journal, 8

Falkland Island (*sic*), 29

Falkland Islands Committee, 142

Falkland Islands Company, 42, 45,
54, 56

Falkland Islands Council, 59, 144

Falkland Islands Defence Force, 85,
185, 192, 194-97

Falkland's Island (*sic*), 30

Falklands Museum, 184

*Fantasmas de Malvinas. Un libro
de viajes*, 227-28, 232-33

fascism, 15, 256

Faslane, 133

fear, 11, 67, 106, 110, 113, 115-16,
123, 136, 157, 180, 185, 193, 195,
216, 248

Fearn, Robin, 59

film, 11, 15, 98, 129, 164-65, 179-
200, 203-205, 207-208, 227-31,

236, 275
"Final Point" law, 177
First World War, 107-108, 129, 155, 253, 269
fishing, 55-56, 58
Fitzroy, 22, 105-106, 109, 251
flashbacks, 107, 207
Ford, Betty, 191
"Fortress Falklands", 181
Fox Bay, 117
France, 28-29, 37, 120, 127, 243
Frankenheimer, John, 200
Franks Report, 140
Freedman, Lawrence, 57
Frente para la Victoria, 220
Fuckland, 201
Fullerton, William, 185-86, 189-91, 198

G

Galtieri, Leopoldo Fortunato, 59, 69, 128, 145, 146, 149, 169, 174, 175, 176, 216, 244, 256
Gamerro, Carlos, 216, 231
Gardel, Carlos, 266
GCHQ, 182
Geneva, 166, 167
Geneva Convention, 42
genocide, 177, 222
Georgia Islands, 39, 79, 133, 137, 140
Gerding, Eduardo, 155, 171
Giacchino, Delicia Rearte de, 103
Giacchino, Pedro, 69-70, 72, 80-99, 101, 103, 185-188
Gibraltar, 44, 48, 51, 120, 122, 127-29, 135
Gilobert, Hector, 184, 187-88
globalisation, 16
Goat Ridge, 22, 105, 112
Goose Green, 19, 21, 146, 153, 164-65
Government House (Stanley), 69,

76, 84, 86-87, 90-92, 97, 99, 101-103, 179-80, 183, 185-86, 192-96, 198-200
Graf Spee, 129
Gramsci, Antonio, 260
Gran Malvina, 56
Graves, Robert, 108
Grytviken, 19-20, 175
Guarisove, los olvidados, 201
Guatemala, 45
guerrilla movements, 57, 66
Guevara, Che, 66
guilt, 107, 154, 157, 217, 221, 275-76
Guinea, 56
Gulf of Santa Catarina, 132
Gulf Wars, 104, 132, 157, 160, 258
Gurkhas, 21-22, 106, 111, 164-66, 168
Guzmán, Patricio, 234
Gypsy Cove, 192, 198

H

Haig, Alexander, 19, 127-29, 131-32, 138, 145, 147, 149, 175
Hall, Stuart, 260
heart disease, 160
Heath, Edward, 13
Henderson, Hamish, 255
Historias de un país. Argentina siglo XX, 201
Historias debidas IV, 201
HMS Endurance, 143-45
HMS Sheffield, 20, 84, 176, 265
Hong Kong, 52, 57, 166
House of Commons, 54, 125, 127, 148
House of Lords, 165
housing, 56
Hoz, Martínez de, 46
Huellas en el viento, 201
human rights, 50, 177, 223-24
Hundan el Belgrano, 201
Hunt, Mavis, 76, 181-82, 188, 195

Hunt, Rex, 76, 87, 92, 179-82, 185-88, 195, 197, 199
Hunt, Tony, 185, 199
Hunter-Killer submarines, 122, 128, 131-32
Husvik, 144
hydrocarbons, 14, 55-57
hypothermia, 153-55, 265

I

identity, 207, 209, 213-17, 219, 222
illegal detention, 176
Illia, Arturo, 44, 51
Iluminados por el fuego, 201
Imperial War Museum, 75, 102
imperialism, 180, 220, 248, 251, 253, 255, 256
industry, 46, 56
insomnia, 157
Institute of Naval Medicine, 156
Instituto Nacional de Estadísticas y Censo, 160
Instituto Nacional de Servicios Sociales Para Jubilados Y Pensionados, 153, 161
International Institute for Strategic Studies, 122
intertextuality, 121-22, 129, 202, 266
intra-colonialism, 244, 250
Iraq War, 258
irritability, 157
Israel, 147, 197
Italy, 122
ITV, 120

J

Jagan, Cheddi, 149
Jamaica, 47
John Fitzgerald Kennedy University, 161
Johnson, Samuel, 142

journalism, 101, 120, 123, 133, 135-36, 191, 214, 219, 265, 267

K

Kenya, 47
Khartoum, 179
kidnapping, 57, 67
Kipling, Rudyard, 71, 89
Kirchner, Cristina Fernández de, 210, 217
Kirchner, Néstor, 217
Kirkpatrick, Jeane, 142, 147
Kirschbaum, Ricardo, 135
Kosovo, 118

L

La asombrosa excursión de Zamba en las Islas Malvinas, 202
La campana, 202
La deuda interna, 201
La forma exacta de las islas, 201, 227-28, 235, 236
La Grande Illusion, 243
La Nación, 130, 146, 158, 217
La Prensa, 144
La república perdida 2, 205
LADE (Argentine State Air Lines), 55, 184
landscape, 230, 232, 234
Larrey, Dominique Jean (Baron), 155
Le Monde, 127
leadership, 53, 118
leaseback, 13, 16, 142-43
Leatherhead, 157
Lebanon, 147
Leith, 19, 144
Libya, 67
Limbu, Budhaparsad, 164
literature, 15, 78, 228-29, 236, 238-78
Locos de la bandera, 201

López Rega, José, 45, 57

Lorenz, Federico, 204, 223, 227, 232-36

Los chicos de la guerra, 201, 203

Los días de junio, 201

Luce, Richard, 59

Lugo, Gustavo Adolfo, 83-84, 86, 91, 97, 200

M

Macdonald, Ian, 242

Madres de la Plaza de Mayo, 175, 231, 255, 276

Malvinas – 30 miradas, 201-202, 207

Malvinas Day, 170, 172

Malvinas, 1982. La guerra desde el aire, 201

Malvinas, 20 años, 201

Malvinas, 25 años de silencio, 201

Malvinas, alerta roja, 201

Malvinas, historia de la usurpación, 201

Malvinas, historia de traiciones, 201

Malvinas, historias de dos islas, 201

Malvinas, la historia que pudo ser, 201

Malvinas, la lucha continúa, 201

Malvinas, me deben tres, 201

Malvinas, tan lejos, tan cerca, 201

Malvinas, viajes del Bicentenario, 201

Malvinas-Falklands Theatre Operations Command, 126

Mar del Plata, 78-79, 81, 83, 102, 124-27

McGuirk, Bernard, 9, 11, 15

McKenzie, Kelvin, 265

media, 9, 11, 51, 120-40, 170, 202, 206, 216-17

memory, 72, 74, 77, 85, 92, 96, 102, 115, 199, 202-203, 206-207, 209-10, 212-226, 227-37, 239-40, 266, 276

Menem, Carlos, 177

mental health, 106-109

mental ill-health, 104-105, 107-109

MI6, 182

Middleton, Dennis, 184, 193

Military Junta, 11, 13, 67-69, 128, 138, 143, 145-46, 148-49, 173-76, 178, 222

military occupation, 57

milonga, 256, 258-60, 276

minefields, 117, 181, 195, 198

mining, 55, 56

Montaldo, Graciela, 267

Monte Caseros, 20, 165

Montevideo, 54, 129

Montoneros, una historia, 205

mood disorders, 158

Moody Brook, 84, 89, 91, 97, 170

Moody Valley, 170

Moore, Jeremy, 21, 76-77, 146, 176

Mount Challenger, 19

Mount Harriet, 21-22, 164, 169

Mount Longdon, 19, 22, 153, 170

Mount Pleasant, 192, 196-97

Mount Tumbledown, 19, 22, 104, 109, 112, 146, 153, 156, 167, 171, 184

Mount William, 19, 22, 106, 113-14, 156

mourning, 210, 212-13, 230, 234, 271, 276

Movement of Non-Aligned Countries, 44

Mozambique, 56

Mullet Creek, 69, 84, 88

murder, 176, 254

N

Namibia, 56

National Health Service, 119

National Security Doctrine, 45, 173
National University of Tres de Febrero, 207
nationalism, 248, 263, 271
Neruda, Pablo, 254
neurasthaenia, 108
New Zealand, 184, 186, 189
Newport, 157
news, 15, 80, 120-40, 169, 194, 216, 264, 274, 276
newspapers, 32, 101, 120-40, 144, 168, 215, 222, 265
nightmares, 107
Nixon, Richard, 173
No tan nuestras, 201
Nootka Sound Convention, 31
Norman, Mike, 76, 102-103, 180-182, 188, 191, 193-94, 196, 198, 200
North Atlantic Treaty Organisation (NATO), 135, 166, 182
Northern Ireland, 43, 49, 180
Norway, 77, 166, 168, 263
Nott, John, 123-25, 134, 242
Nouzeilles, Gabriela, 267
nuclear submarines, 120-24, 127-28, 133, 140, 176

O

oil companies, 14
oil crisis, 45, 55, 57
Onganía, General Juan Carlos, 45, 52
Operation Black Buck, 20
Operation Blue, 71, 79
Operation Condor, 46
Operation Corporate, 19
Operation Paraquet, 20, 175
Operation Rosario, 19, 69, 71, 79-80, 187
Operation Sutton, 20-21
Oracle (submarine), 127
Organization of the Petroleum Exporting Countries (OPEC), 55
Oslo, 166, 168
Owen, Wilfred, 108, 242-43, 253-54, 259-60

P

Página/12, 136, 217, 223
Palabra por palabra, 201
Palestine, 56, 67
Palestine Liberation Organization, 56
Paraguay, 46
Parkinson, Cecil, 146
Patagonia, 20, 32, 42, 86, 156, 168, 189, 232, 253
patriotism, 70, 80, 216, 219, 221, 238, 253
Peck, Bob, 193
peer support, 16, 157, 171-72
Pensar Malvinas, 201, 233
Pepys Islands, 27
Pérez de Cuéllar, Javier, 20, 147, 149
Pérez Grandi, Jorge, 170-72
Perlongher, Néstor, 267-73
Perón, Isabel, 13, 47, 66-68, 173
Perón, Juan, 45, 47, 56-57, 66, 68, 173, 218
Perónism, 45, 68
Peru, 20
Petrella, Fernando, 56
Piglia, Ricardo, 227
Pinochet, Augusto, 175
Piratas, pastores, inversores, 201
Plaza de Mayo, 68, 169, 174-75, 231, 255, 276
Poland, 155
politics, 205, 212-224, 234
Pony's Pass, 97
Port de la Croisade, 28
Port Egmont, 26, 28-32, 34, 37-38
Port Harriet, 88
Port Howard, 19, 105

Port Louis, 28
Port Pleasant, 22, 251, 253
Port Soledad, 28-30, 33-36, 38
Port Stanley, 20-21, 65, 70, 76, 84,
    86-87, 90, 92, 94, 97-98, 105,
    123, 145-46, 180, 183-84, 188-89,
    191, 193-94, 196-97, 230, 249
Port William, 84
Portsmouth, 19-20, 126, 129
Portuguese Overseas Territories, 56
post-battle adjustment reaction,
    106
post-traumatic growth, 153, 158,
    160, 167, 172
Post-Traumatic Stress Disorder
    (PTSD), 16, 153-54, 156-57, 159,
    161, 167
poverty, 161, 174, 178
Pozo de Zorro, 201
prisoners, 206, 234
Process of National Reorganisation,
    204, 223, 265, 268
Project Alpha, 145
propaganda, 9, 65, 67, 75, 214, 216,
    247
protectionism, 45, 47, 57
public services, 56
Puerto Argentino, 54, 174
Puerto Argentino Military Hospital,
    156, 171
Puerto Belgrano Naval Base, 69, 79,
    81, 83, 85, 89
Puerto Belgrano Naval Hospital,
    156
Puerto Deseado, 32
Puerto Soledad, 30, 35
Punta Arenas, 186
Pym, Francis, 19

Q

Queen Elizabeth II, 57
Quiroga, Diego F. García, 11, 13, 15,
    65-103, 186, 189

R

racism, 184
rape, 176
rapprochement, 44
Rattenbach Report, 58-60, 175-76
Reactivation Proposal, 59
Reagan, Ronald, 20-21, 147, 175
reconciliation, 103, 172, 199
Red Cross, 166-67, 210
Reid, Anne, 191
Retiro, 235
Reuters (press agency), 122, 125,
    127-28, 131-33
Rhodesia, 44, 52, 56
Richardson, Ian, 199
Ridley, Nicholas, 57-58
Río de la Plata, 173
Río Gallegos, 20, 165, 168, 170-72,
    251
Río Grande, 19, 56, 176
River Plate, 241, 256
Royal Army Medical Corps, 107
Royal Marines, 19-20, 69, 72-73, 76,
    84-85, 87, 91-92, 95-96, 98-99,
    102-103, 156, 170, 175, 179-80,
    182, 185-88, 191, 193, 196-97,
    200
Royal Military Academy Sandhurst,
    113
Rozas, Carlos Ortiz de, 59
Ruda, José María, 12, 25, 44, 50-51
Rwanda, 47, 118

S

Saint Lawrence Convention, 31
San Carlos Water, 20-22, 101, 111
San Francisco Conference, 38, 146
Santiago, 186, 219
Sapper Hill, 89-91, 156
Sarlo, Beatriz, 219
Sassoon, Siegfried, 108
Saturno, Fulgencio, 199
Saunders Island, 26, 28-29, 34

Scotland, 133-35

Scots Guards, 21, 22, 97, 104, 107, 109, 113, 115, 184

Scott, Robert Falcon, 264

Second World War, 16, 44, 126, 129, 164

Secretaría de Políticas Integrales sobre Drogas de la Nación Argentina, 160

Seear, Mike, 10, 13, 15, 75, 164-72

self-determination, 7, 40-41, 47-50, 52, 58, 146

semiotics, 202, 212

Seventh American International Conference, 38

Shackleton Mission, 55, 56, 142

Shackleton Report, 57

Shakespeare, William, 70

sheep farming, 56

Sinatra, Frank, 265

Singapore, 179

Sir Galahad, 251, 255

Sir Tristram, 251

social security, 56

Solar, Lucio García del, 51

South Africa, 56

South Atlantic Medal Association 82, 158, 172

South Georgia, 19-21, 69, 79, 143-45, 175

South Sandwich, 39, 143-44

South Thule, 57, 144

Southampton, 19-20, 78, 165

sovereignty, 7-8, 11-16, 25-43, 44, 49, 51-60, 66, 69, 71, 77, 83, 142-46, 148-49, 171, 175-76, 220, 227, 263

Soviet Union, 44-46, 66, 129, 198

Spain, 26-32, 34, 37, 45, 65, 120

St Malo, 243

Stewart, Michael, 52, 54

"stiff upper lip", 119

Strasera, Julio, 173

Stromness, 144

submarines, 20, 81, 83-84, 120-40,

154, 262-63, 265

substance abuse, 106, 159-60

suicide, 107, 153, 158-59, 203, 206-207, 221, 275

Summers, Brian, 194, 197

Summers, Phil, 194

Sun Tzu, 78, 85, 97

Sun, The, 76, 248, 264-65

Sunday Times, The, 179

Superb (submarine), 120-40

Super-Étendard fighter aircraft, 176

survivors, 206, 211, 222, 231

T

Task Force (Argentina), 69, 78, 83-85, 90

Task Force (UK), 19, 125, 129, 137, 139, 164-65, 247, 250, 255, 263

Teal Inlet, 21

Télam (press agency), 132

television, 15, 120-21, 133, 146, 175, 179, 202, 204-206, 216

Tenth Inter-American Conference, 39

Terragno, Rodolfo, 126, 241

terrorism, 13, 46, 67-68, 209-18, 227

testimony, 205, 208, 214, 221, 224, 227

Thatcher, Margaret, 13, 16, 19, 71, 76, 77, 102, 125, 129, 134, 143, 148-49, 175, 180, 242, 244, 246, 248, 250-51, 256

theatre, 231

Thénon, Susana, 244, 248, 250, 260, 265, 267, 273

Thomas, Wynne, 250-51

Tierra del Fuego, 186, 232

Times, The, 127

torpedoes, 126, 155, 265

torture, 72, 96, 174, 176, 204, 208-209, 222-23, 254, 266-67

Total Exclusion Zone, 19-20, 22,

154, 176, 186
tourism, 56
trade, 45-46, 56-57
trade unions, 174
tragicomedy, 180
training, 67-68, 78-81, 85, 106, 110, 115, 119, 164-66, 196
transport, 54, 56
trauma, 74, 99, 105-107, 109, 119, 153-60, 166-67, 171-72, 193, 203, 206, 212-13, 216, 221, 227, 238
Treaty of Friendship, Trade and Navigation, 33
Treaty of Madrid, 27
Treaty of Tordesillas, 27
Treaty of Utrecht, 28
Treaty of Versailles, 31
trench foot, 105, 153, 155-56
Trinidad and Tobago, 47
Two Sisters, 21-22, 164, 170-72

U

UK census (2012), 9
UK Foreign and Commonwealth Office, 53, 120-21, 124, 134, 185, 186, 190
UK Ministry of Defence, 190, 198
Un cuento chino, 202
unemployment, 107, 153, 160, 167, 168, 171, 174, 178, 267
United Nations, 7, 12, 19-22, 25-44, 47-55, 59, 109, 127, 131, 142, 144, 146-47, 246
    Charter, 38, 40-43, 49-50
    General Assembly, 12, 39, 43-44, 48-52, 54-55, 142, 146
    Resolution 31/49, 55
    Resolution 505, 21, 147
    Resolution 1514 (XV), 12, 25, 39-40, 43, 49-51, 142, 146
    Resolution 2065, 44, 47-49, 51-52, 54, 56
    Resolution 3160, 55

Security Council, 19, 21, 44, 146-147
Special Committee on Decolonization, 7, 50
United States, 31-32, 34-35, 44-46, 56, 127, 129, 145, 147-49, 173, 175
Universal Declaration of Human Rights, 41
University of Nottingham colloquium (2006), 9-11, 75, 77, 157
UPI (press agency), 125, 132
Upland Goose Hotel, 184
Urbieta, Nicolás, 164-171
Uruguay, 46

V

Valéry, Paul, 238
Vamos ganando, 201
Venezuela, 45, 126, 179, 184
Vernet, Luis, 32-34
Versailles Summit, 21
veterans, 74, 77, 107, 118-19, 153-63, 167-72, 203, 205-206, 221-22, 224, 229-230, 233, 275
Veterans Welfare Organisation, 109
Videla, Jorge Rafael, 46, 68, 173-74
Vietnam War, 56, 106, 147, 153-54, 157-59, 258
Vignes, Alberto, 56
Vindica, 202
violence, 203, 212
Vitullo, Julieta, 227-29, 235, 236

W

Wall Mountain, 20, 165
Walsh, Rodolfo, 174
Watts, Patrick, 191, 193
Wearing, Michael, 189
Weisæth, Lars, 166, 171
Welsh Guards, 21-22, 251
West Falkland, 105, 117

Western Malvina, 28, 32
Wether Ground, 22, 169
Williams, Anthony, 59
Wilson, Harold, 13, 44
Wireless Ridge, 22, 146

X

Xenophon, 248

Y

Yacimientos Petrolíferos Fiscales, 55
Yentob, Alan, 189
Yorke Bay, 84, 94

Z

Zambia, 47, 190
Zavala Ortiz, Miguel Ángel, 51-52